# FABULOUS FAKES

*By the same author*

Antique and 20th-Century Jewellery
Art Nouveau Jewelry
The Jewellery of René Lalique

Vivienne Becker

# Fabulous Fakes

## THE HISTORY OF FANTASY AND FASHION JEWELLERY

**GRAFTON BOOKS**

A Division of the Collins Publishing Group

LONDON GLASGOW
TORONTO SYDNEY AUCKLAND

*For Ruth*

'A moment ago I stopped to take part in one smart woman's decision
regarding a new necklace. She is wearing periwinkle blue – the colour
the Lelong opening in Paris this week featured – and she didn't want a
necklace to match but one which showed a little contrast. She asked my
advice about a choker of lapis-coloured Prystal. It was exactly the right
length for her frock and when we found some earrings to match there
remained no doubt in her mind. Women are just beginning to realize
that a new piece of jewellery for each frock is worth the sweet pain of
choosing and paying for it.'

Lucy Park
*Palm Beach News Bulletin, c.* 1930

Grafton Books
A Division of the Collins Publishing Group
8 Grafton Street, London W1X 3LA

Published by Grafton Books 1988

*British Library Cataloguing in Publication Data*

Becker, Vivienne
    Fabulous fakes: the history of
    fantasy and fashion jewellery.
    1. Costume jewellery, to 1987
    I. Title
    739.27
ISBN 0-246-13100-4

Photoset in Linotron Electra by
Rowland Phototypesetting Ltd
Bury St Edmunds, Suffolk
Printed in England by
Butler and Tanner Ltd
Frome, Somerset

# CONTENTS

# ACKNOWLEDGEMENTS

This book could not have been produced without the generous help and enthusiasm of all my colleagues and friends, collectors, manufacturers and passionate devotees of costume jewellery around the world.

My special gratitude to Tania Hunter and Veronica Manussis of Cobra & Bellamy, Sir Kenneth and Lady MacMillan, Lawrence Feldman of Fior, Ray Martin of Attwood & Sawyer, Billy Boy, Michael Grosse of Henkel and Grosse, Nicky Butler of Butler & Wilson, Kenneth J. Lane, Brian Norman of Harvey & Gore, John Jesse and Irina Laski.

My grateful thanks also to David Callaghan of Hancocks & Co., Diana Foley, Lynn and Brian Holmes, Jack Ogden, all of London for photographs and information; to Don McDonnell of Walter Scaife, London; to Carlton Fishel, James Northrop and Tricia Lee of Trifari, New York; to Cynthia Shulga of Napier, New York, Diane McCloone of Monet, New York; Rita Sacks and Angela Kramer of New York who all opened archives and collections for me; to H. Terzka of Swarovski, Austria; Horace Attwood; to Joel Degen for his superb photographs.

Special thanks to Toby Eady, to Katherine Purcell for unflagging assistance, to Suzy Menkes, Dan Klein, Clive Kandel, Maria Mendrinos, Marianne Taylor, Vivien James, Samuel Beizer, to Vicci Turner and Oliver Cox, JoAnne Davidson, Claire Guest and Kevin and Nel Coates for all their support, friendship and encouragement, and to Tim Rice for inspiration. And to everyone at Grafton Books who made my work so enjoyable, Anne Charvet, Katherine Everett, Rosamund Saunders, Steve Abis.

# REFACE

Today, more than ever, costume jewels have become the dream
merchants of fashion: fabulous fineries conjured out of humble materials
peddle fantasies of impossible or unattainable extravagance, of luxury,
beauty and child-like joy. This dream-selling is just one of the many
roles jewellery has had to take on to supplement its basic purpose of pure
adornment. Through the centuries jewels have been worn to attract good
fortune to the wearer, ward off evil spirits, commemorate love or death,
to signify power and wealth and status. As jewels of sentiment, the real
and precious will surely never be replaced. But as sheer ornaments to
fashion and beauty, as intimate social comments, costume jewels must
be unrivalled.

   The word 'fake' in the title is perhaps misleading and in many cases
does an injustice to the wealth of original design, wit and imagination
that has been lavished on non-precious jewels through the ages.
Certainly, paste, plastic and base metal often masquerade as the real
thing; but just as often costume jewels have blazed a new and
independent trail of design and decoration, evolving into imaginative,
thrilling creations that make the very most of the fantasy and freedom
offered by their genre.

   Since they are not intended to last beyond the latest craze, jewels of
little or no intrinsic value can be more evocative of their age and wearer
than expensive gem-set heirlooms. They pander to the most fleeting
whims of fashion, and so capture the changing moods of each era. For
these reasons I have tried to recreate to some extent the atmosphere of
each age, to show the prevailing influences and crazes, the frivolities or
insanities of fashion, the changing roles of women and their attitudes to

their own femininity, expressed through their clothes and jewellery.

The definition of costume jewellery has been a tricky one, and everyone seems to have a slightly different view of the parameters of the subject. There are few hard and fast rules, and the definition within this book is of necessity a subjective one. From the viewpoint of today's massive mania for self decoration, I have tried to trace the lineage of non-precious jewels intended primarily for fashion and adornment. I have looked at non-precious jewels in the context of their particular age, avoiding rigid rules governing materials or manufacture. Jewels set in silver or even in gold have been included wherever these were the most appropriate available metals for the purpose, as in the case of stunning 18th-century paste, while modern jewellery, with the benefits of sophisticated alloys, had to be totally non-precious to qualify.

With the 19th century, the definition of costume jewellery becomes especially difficult; every conceivable material from volcanic lava to humming-bird heads was turned into fashionable trinkets, set in silver or more usually gold, embellished with gems and flaunted as the latest novelty in an age excited and satiated by the most bizarre baubles. The division between real and fashion jewellery is not altogether clear. It is hard to know for certain if materials such as coral, mother of pearl, tortoiseshell inlaid with gold would have been regarded at the time as fashion jewellery; they seem to fall into the in-between realm of less expensive, real jewels.

Costume jewellery is truly a 20th-century term bred during the era of couture or dressmakers' jewels (considered by some as the only true costume jewellery) which in turn led into the years of huge commercial production and the growth of the major mass manufacturers. Again throughout the book I have largely concentrated on commercial, popular jewels, steering away from 'art' jewels. Obvious exceptions include Schiaparelli's zany creations which were certainly not for mainstream taste, and many of the jewels of the 1980s selected for their sheer fantasy and innovative use of weird and wonderful materials. My excuse for flouting my own rules must be that I was swept along with the freedom, fun and amazing variety of the subject and the realization that, after all, costume jewellery has always been about breaking rules, traditions and boundaries of reality.

# $\mathcal{S}$YMBOLS OF POWER

La Goutte d'Eau, René Magritte, 1948. Painted at the height of the 1940s vogue for costume jewellery, Magritte's surreal imagery depicts a torso covered with drops of water crystallized into gem-like body ornaments.

From the earliest times, jewellery has played a vital role in the struggle for survival. The triumphant hunter wore animals' teeth, claws, bones or feathers as proof of his prowess and superiority. The by-products of food-finding, leather, animal hairs, berries, olive leaves, flowers were all worn as personal adornments. Their value lay in the conquests they represented, in their rarity or mystical affinity to nature. In the highly sophisticated civilizations of the ancient world, rare metals and gemstones were wrought into amulets and talismans, worn as enhancers of female attractions, status symbols and often as funerary adornments to smooth the wearer's path into the next world. These precious materials showed dazzling properties of hardness and durability, and so were imbued with magic and mystery and with healing or supernatural powers. As such, gems and jewels became widely sought-after, and expensive. Demand exceeded supply and skilled craftsmen were naturally tempted by the possibility of a large market for fake and imitation gemstones.

Amongst the skilled and talented craftsmen of the ancient world, the glassmakers were particularly brilliant. Perhaps the earliest forms of imitative costume jewellery were ancient Egyptian coated glass beads that were made to look like semi-precious stones such as lapis lazuli or cornelian. For purely decorative jewels or 'costume jewellery', glass, faience and enamels were popular along with a wide variety of organic materials such as wood, amber and coral, ivory, bone and jet. For special festive or ritualistic occasions, Egyptians wore totally natural floral ornaments such as wide collars composed of cornflowers, olive leaves and berries.

*Ancient Etruscan necklace of glass and gilt metal beads, mostly ribbed or melon-shaped, with two grotesque masks of coloured glass.*

Shells provided perfect, ready-to-wear beads and ornaments and were very popular with the ancient Egyptians, who prized the cowry shell in particular as a fertility symbol. With the growing popularity of jewels and trinkets, clever tricks were devised to adapt other materials, such as natural quartz or rock crystal, which was decorated with a beautiful coloured coating, usually blue, as an alternative to the enormously popular faience or glazed earthenware beads. Faience had been used for jewellery since the very earliest times. The earthenware beads were made in huge quantities in many different shapes and forms, from simple narrow cylinders, usually blue or green, to complex moulded and pierced shapes. The simplest beads were produced by shaping the material around a straw or a twig, even a thread which would then be burnt away on firing. The beads were then threaded into wide collars of regular geometric design, often representing lotus petals, dates or cornflowers and very similar to the huge natural floral collars. Red faience earrings or hair rings often imitated cornelian, while finger rings of this material frequently bore inscriptions or motifs such as the scarab, falcon or Udjat-eye – the eye of the sky god Horus.

It was glass, however, that the ancient Egyptians found to be the most suitable and versatile medium for popular, decorative jewels, as well as for fakes. In factories employing sophisticated techniques, huge quantities of glass beads were produced in a wide choice of brilliant colours and interesting shapes, the most popular of which was the 'eye' bead, again representing to the Egyptians the magical eye of Horus. Attractive multi-coloured beads were made from mosaic or 'millefiori' glass or of swirly random patterns; others cleverly simulated banded agates. Occasionally, whole pieces of jewellery were made from glass: rings, earrings and bangles, in designs that either imitated precious jewels or explored the exciting possibilities of the glass itself, using rich colours and moulded motifs.

The art of gem engraving reached a magnificent high point in classical antiquity, and glass was ideal for faking or imitating the much-treasured engraved gemstones or intaglios (in which the design is incised into the stone). Ingenious glass intaglios were intended either to deceive or to be sold as decorative objects in their own right. Sometimes a piece of glass was engraved or carved in the same way as a gem; at other times the glass was pressed or cast in moulds.

Apart from these engraved gems, there was a thriving trade in all kinds of fake gemstones, many of them extremely convincing. Pottery beads glazed red could look just like cornelian or, given a bright blue coating, could masquerade as turquoise. Pliny, the Roman official and writer on natural history, who provides us with the best contemporary descriptions of gems and materials available to the ancient world, also advises on detecting glass imitations by methods still valid today (air bubbles, softness, warmth to the touch), all of which suggests that the faking of gems was widespread. The cleverest glassworkers copied coloured precious gems such as emeralds, which were often passed off as the real thing by unscrupulous dealers.

Pearls were beautifully imitated by these inventive Roman and Egyptian glassworkers. The earliest form of fake pearl was achieved by lining a glass bead with a thin layer of gold or silver foil to produce an iridescent sheen. The term 'Roman' pearl was used for artificial pearls for centuries afterwards.

Glass was a precious, expensive commodity during the Middle Ages, and royal jewel caskets often included fake or imitation gemstones. The Renaissance and the rediscovery of classical art marked the end of the Middle Ages and the beginning of a new and spectacular age of jewellery. Literally a rebirth, the Renaissance of the 15th and 16th centuries brought about a dramatic revitalization and enrichment of all aspects of the arts and sciences. The art of the goldsmith, enameller and jeweller was raised to a status equal to that of painting and sculpture, and jewels became noble and glorious works of art, created by artists such as Holbein and Cellini. Jewellery was largely sculptural and figurative at this time, influenced not by classical jewels (which had not yet been rediscovered) but by classical architecture and sculpture. Brooches, hat badges, pendants were all elaborately modelled in gold, richly jewelled and enamelled, their intense colouring echoing the rich brocades and embroidery of Renaissance costume. For the most part, jewels were still valued as symbols of position and power and of artistic and cultural appreciation, especially since sumptuary laws in England and all over Europe had restricted the wearing of precious gems and jewels to the upper echelons of society and the Church.

In the early Renaissance, men were far more richly bejewelled than their female partners, and wore hat badges, the most popular Renaissance jewels, as signs of rank, as well as figurative pendants, massive chains and collars. The emphasis was very firmly on gems, especially on coloured stones such as rubies, emeralds, sapphires, their colours intensified by deep enamels. It was only in the later 16th century that women began to wear more jewels than men. At this time European sovereignty was dominated by women, and under the glistening

influence of Elizabeth I, Elisabeth of Austria and Catherine de Medici, ladies began to cover their bodices with trellises of pearls; their coiffures were entwined with chains and jewels; they wore short necklaces, huge pendants and long chains. It was inevitable in such an age of profusion and richness in personal adornment, that costume or imitation jewellery would thrive again.

Throughout the 16th century, Venice was an important centre for trading in gems and pearls. The city was also famed for its fabulous glassmaking, which led to a flourishing trade in imitation pearls and finely made costume jewellery of gilt metal and foil-backed gems. Fine paste gems were also made in Milan, and progress was made at this time in the foiling of stones and mounting them in airtight settings. These gilt jewels answered the needs of fashionable ladies unable to keep up with the trend towards increasingly lavish costume. Imitation jewels were also very often worn for portraits since it was vital that the sitters were painted in as much finery as they could muster to proclaim their wealth and social rank. Costume jewels, identified from existing examples, can be spotted in paintings by Titian and Tintoretto. They were always direct copies of real jewels. The gilt base metal was usually cast and chased, just like gold, in the usual sculptural manner, with lions, sea horses, scrolls, leaves, often carefully enamelled, with the back also chased in detail, as it would be on a real jewel. The glass gems were set into deep square collets or metal mounts and were sometimes mixed with real gems or with faceted quartz.

Pearls were highly important accessories to the great ladies of the late Renaissance. Elizabeth I and Catherine de Medici both lusted after the finest gems and jewels and covered their clothes and hair with glinting treasures, embroideries and ropes of pearls. The jewellery market was busy with clever imitations bought mostly by ladies of fashion with lesser budgets, although many of the pearls that glimmered on the gowns of Elizabeth of England had never known an oyster. In 1569, a bill recorded that 520 pearls were ordered by the Queen at a penny each. The Italians excelled at fake pearls during the Renaissance, and an Italian book of 1440, *Segretti per Colori*, lists recipes for false pearls involving small shells and fish scales to achieve a lustre. By the 17th century, however, the French specialized in imitation pearls. A rosary maker called Jacquin, who had set up his business in 1686 on the outskirts of Paris, was known to produce the best and most lustrous examples for which he received a warrant from Louis XIV. Just like the ancient versions, glass beads were lined with an inner coating of a nacreous essence made from fish scales, and the beads were often filled with wax to give extra weight and substance. Jacquin's descendants, notably his great-grandson Truchy, continued to be the finest imitation pearl manufacturers during the 19th century.

From the late 16th century, women took an ever larger share of the jewellery market, and as gentlemen's jewels became less conspicuous, ladies' finery became more lavish, sparkling and flirtatious. In many ways the 17th century can be viewed as a transitional phase for jewellery, as the emphasis shifted slowly from the setting onto the gemstone itself and, more important, as jewels came gradually to be regarded much more as ornaments to fashion rather than as symbols of rank, religion or

A DÑI, 1619

Portrait of a Lady, *Marc Gheeraerts (Junior)*, inscribed and dated 1619. She wears an elaborate necklace, chain bracelets of pearls and semi-precious stones, and long lacy chains probably made of black glass, used also for dramatic draped earrings pinned to the ruff, one hung with a single gemstone, the other with a pearl and a finger ring. Glass chains and jewels to encrust clothes were popular in the 16th and 17th centuries.

power. Slowly, jewels became lighter in both colour and design, and throughout the 17th century the most significant change in the history of jewellery was fermenting: diamond cutting was developing and improving, revealing the visual delights of the gemstone. Diamonds were becoming more plentiful as the Golconda mines in India were opened, and attempts were now made at simulating the gem with the ravishing new image. But although the Venetians had found a way of producing colourless glass in the 14th century, there was still no suitable hard clear glass to mimic the diamond, and rock crystal tended to be used as a rather dull substitute. The 18th century arrived in a blaze of sparkling diamonds, and the Age of Reason, of unrivalled elegance, wit and taste, also brought with it an explosion of riotous glamour, of scintillating ornament and the first truly great era of fabulous costume jewellery.

# One

# GEORGIAN SPLENDOUR

The 18th century was the supreme age of glamour, light and artificiality: the perfect ingredients for an atmosphere that bred the first great era of paste and costume jewellery. The brilliance of the spirit and intellect of the age was echoed in the decorative arts and especially in jewellery design; this century was also the great age of the diamond and its lustrous sparkle tyrannized fashion, creating a desire for everything that glittered, caught the light and drew attention to the wearer. There were several vital factors of social, economic and jewel history that all together set the mood of scintillating reflections and exquisite artifice in which the very finest paste jewels first sparkled seductively.

Outward appearances in the 18th century were everything; a certain fashionable falseness was everywhere. Both men and women worked seriously towards an unrivalled magnificence in their dress, their ornaments and movements. Ladies wore false hair piled wondrously high, powdered and laden with feathers, bows, jewels, the occasional stuffed bird or ship in full sail or flowers (kept fresh in vases of water hidden in the depths of the coiffure). In the 1740s and 1750s, the fashionable *pompon* was a prominent central hair ornament, consisting of a complicated arrangement of velvet, feathers, ribbons and usually

'Toilette de la Duchesse des Plumes, ou le triomphe de la folie du siècle.' A French 18th-century caricature showing the preparation of an outrageous, fashionable coiffure. Feathers from a peacock and a turkey represent in turn the pride and stupidity of the lady of fashion.

studded with imitation jewels and gems, sometimes arranged as butterflies, feathers or flowers.

The false hair was fixed with lard and whiting and the towering constructions involved so many hours of work that they had to remain in place for a month or two, during which time just about anything could crawl inside and nestle there. Nightcaps had to be made of silver wire to keep the rats out, although the truly fashionable wore nightcaps of gilt wire costing from 6 to 10 guineas.

Not only were fashionable ladies stretched upwards, their dresses pulled them widthways too, further distorting their shapes. They could barely move inside the enormously wide *panniers* over their hips. They took up a whole carriage, and when they sat, the hoops ended up around their ears on either side. These statuesque ladies of fashion, slow moving indeed, wide and high, with huge plumes nodding graciously in the air, were once petite creatures some five feet tall; now they could be seven to ten feet high, towering over the gentlemen as they drifted into the ballroom. Beneath the hair sculptures their faces were thickly painted with a pallid white that distorted their features, and were covered with many patches and beauty spots of all shapes. They had carmine mouths and their eyebrows were plucked or replaced with strips of mouse skin that occasionally slipped down the face during a hot *soirée*.

The bosom became a focus of attention. Décolletages were daringly low, with rounded breasts pushed tantalizingly upwards and decorated with bows, lace or ribbons, jewels or nosegays of real or artificial 'made' flowers that protruded eccentrically. Eventually this fashion was interpreted in jewels, and sprays of twinkling gem-set blossoms were pinned to the neckline. There was nothing like diamonds, or brilliant paste, worn at the ears, breast or throat to light up the face and bosom, to add vital glistening glamour.

The gentlemen shared this love of pretence and finery. Jewels, real or paste, sparkled in their cravats, gleamed on their shoes and buttoned their jackets. Their clothes were costly and elaborate; sometimes one of their two pocket watches was false; they wore rouge to improve their complexions and false calves of parchment and bandages to improve the shape of their legs.

Clearly jewels played an important part in this era of extravagant luxury and personal adornment that reached a high point around 1760–80. But in the first half of the 18th century certain events took place that drastically changed the appearance of jewels, and the circumstances of wearing them. Domestic lighting had greatly improved

*Maria, Grand Duchess of Tuscany (1772–1807), painted around 1800, wearing a protruding stomacher brooch in the form of a flower spray; long pendant earrings fall over her curls and she wears more real and jewelled flowers in her hair.*

*A plate from* The Gallery of Fashion, 1790–1822, *shows a Court dress, the body and train of lilac and silver, the petticoat of festooned silver tissue, worn with a turban headdress.*

owing to new and better wax candles which burnt more brightly, and this new soft flickering candlelight was an important and characteristic feature of the age. It added a shimmering brightness to every aspect of life after dark, and it also meant that parties and entertainments of all kinds, balls, masques, operas, could all take place at night and that ladies could dress up much more than was customary during the day. A new distinction grew up between day and evening jewels. Night-time revels and candlelight brought romance, glamour and intrigue to social life.

Light was also the vital clue to the new craze for diamonds that was to inspire paste jewels. Around 1700 great progress was made in techniques of cutting diamonds, a problem that had exasperated lapidaries for centuries. The hardest of all natural substances, diamonds can only be cut with diamonds. A rough diamond in its natural state is not very beautiful; it is only when diamonds are cut correctly that their life and fire are released, producing that legendary desirable and secretive gleam. Diamonds had long been prized for their rarity, their hardness, myth and magic, but not for their beauty or ornamental worth. Gradually, experiments in the 15th and 16th centuries led to the first facets and with them the huge potential of the diamond as a decorative ornament began to emerge. At first there was the table cut, in which the natural octahedron was cut with one square facet at the top. This was popular throughout the 16th and 17th centuries; and then eventually the rose cut was developed in France, which had become a centre for the art of the lapidary largely owing to the splendour of Louis XIV's court. The stone was given a flat round base and a domed top faceted in triangles to look like an opening rosebud. The rose cut, with its soft, greyish gleam and gracious charm, is particularly evocative of 18th-century jewellery.

In about 1700 the early brilliant cut was devised, it is generally believed, by an Italian, Vincento Peruzzi, who is credited with changing the course of jewellery history in unleashing the much coveted fire and glory of the stone by creating 58 facets. Improved polishing and setting followed, and there was a significant change in jewellery design: a shift of emphasis from the Renaissance style of decorative metalwork and enamels to the actual stone itself. Gem setting became the principal art of the jeweller. Settings were devised to flatter the gems; the idea was to see as little metal as possible and it did not take long to realize that diamonds looked far better set in silver to complement their whiteness. The combination of the faceted, polished stones with the improved lighting and finery and evening festivities of the age brought supremacy to the diamond.

To help matters further, diamonds were discovered in Brazil around 1725, making them more available although still rare. They were *de rigueur* at Court and whatever was worn at Court led the way for all fashions. It was also during the 18th century that jewellery became more closely linked to clothes, as important accessories and highlights to an outfit, and it therefore followed that jewels became subject to the whims and changes of fashion, a vital characteristic of costume jewellery. For instance, at one moment, fashion decreed that earrings hung to the shoulder, and the next no earrings were to be worn at all. The preoccupation with lightness extended to the fabrics of clothes. In place of the rich and darkly glowing brocades came lace, muslins, light silks and silver ribbons. Silver fabric and trimmings such as tassels and fringes and foiled embroideries and spangles were very popular in the late 18th century and all lent themselves well to light, sparkling jewels. From the first decades of the century, the search was on for a substitute for or supplement to the dazzling diamond.

At this point, as costume jewellery is about to enter the scene on a large scale, jewellery becomes intimately linked with social history and with shifts in class structure. In the first half of the 18th century the social scene was changing, and by the mid-century class distinctions were fading. Out of the growing industrial age came a thriving new middle or business class: the self-made businessmen and their families for whom wealth and disposable income was a novelty. They naturally developed a taste for finery, for self-improvement, and with this following of high fashion came a craving for the sort of sparkling ornaments worn by the aristocracy at Court. Once signs of power and rank, jewels and gemstones now became the symbols of financial success. It would seem that by the mid-century class competition was rife. In *The World*, 1755, one critic observed, 'We are a nation of gentry; we have no such thing as common people among us; between vanity and gin the species is utterly destroyed . . . Every tradesman is a merchant, every merchant a gentleman, every gentleman one of the nobless.' And the nobility, it seems, were forced into debt to maintain their finery and thus their position in society.

Diamonds remained relatively rare and certainly costly, yet fashion demanded a lot of them: ladies wore wobbling *aigrettes* and butterflies in the hair, feather jewels and flowers at the bust, sets of flowers, looping bows and bouquets and flower sprigs, and long girandole or chandelier earrings.

In Paris in 1724, Georges Frédéric Stras, a young jeweller from Strasbourg, came to join Mme Prévost in her small jewellery business on the Quai des Orfèvres. Stras was quick to spot the huge gap in the market and the need for a reverent rival to the divine diamond. He created jewels made of paste, a special glass that could be cut and polished to sparkle convincingly in the candlelight. The new twinkling glass jewels took Paris completely by storm in the 1730s; they were irresistible, and ladies of fashion, rank and wealth wore little else in the way of jewellery, much to the chagrin of 'real' jewellers. In 1757, when a certain Mlle

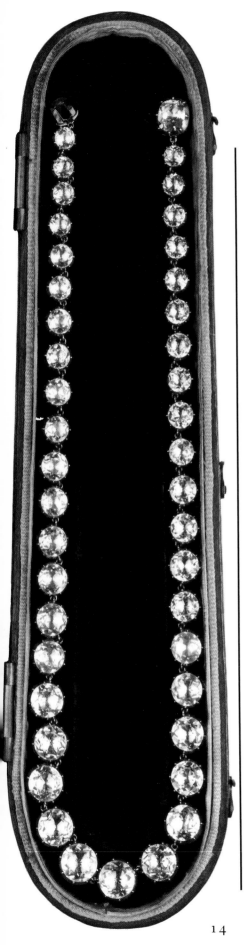

A rivière *of white pastes, set in silver collets, backed with gold. English, c.1780.*

Barbuty finally persuaded her young man, a painter, to accept her marriage proposal, it was to Stras's shop that she rushed to buy a pair of earrings with false diamonds. At just the right moment paste jewels satisfied the growing desire for the luxurious and flattering effect of diamonds. Stras became the most famous jeweller in Paris, the most famous jeweller of his age, and gave his name to paste which is still often called 'Strass'.

There had been a profitable trade in fake gems in Paris for about a century. Fake stones made of a kind of *pâte de verre*, a reconstituted glass, were worn in Paris in the 17th century, but no details are known of the nature of other counterfeit diamonds. According to M. de Villers in his account of a visit to Paris in about 1657–8, imitation gemstones were the speciality of a Sr d'Arce, or Georges d'Arc. M. d'Arce was well known for his invention of fake diamonds, emeralds, topazes and rubies, which had brought him so much financial success that he could afford his own carriage and two houses. It appears that he was just producing the loose stones without making them up into jewels. In 1722 a crown was made for Louis XV by Ballin, Rondé and Duflos. After the Coronation, the most famous stones, the Régent, Sancy and Mazarin, were replaced by paste.

The famous Stras or paste jewels, the ancestors of today's chic accessories, were made of a special glass that had been pioneered in England by English glassmakers, and it is unlikely that Stras actually formulated the glass. But as he was more of a fine jeweller than a chemist, he was able to turn the glass into ravishing ornaments. He understood diamonds, jewellery design and manufacture, and presumably also marketing, promotion and above all what made women look and feel good. He also discovered a way of tinting or foiling diamonds to give them colour, an invention which he advertised with a great flourish on his trade card. He sold fine paste jewels alongside real jewellery, a custom which continued through the 19th and early 20th centuries.

The glass paste used for simulated gems was a high-quality transparent lead glass developed by George Ravenscroft (1618–81), a technician employed by the Glass Sellers Company in London under the direction of the Duke of Buckingham. There had been a glassmaking industry in England since medieval times, when it was very much under the influence of the great Venetian glassworkers. In the 17th century it was still largely dependent on imported (or escaped) Italian labour and expertise. Venetian glassmaking was such an admired and closely kept secret that workers were forbidden to leave Venice on pain of death. Still, many managed to escape and spread their knowledge and their art. In 1615 wood was prohibited from use as fuel for glass furnaces in England, as there was a fear of shortage of timber for ships. Coal had to be used instead and this brought its own technical problems; coal fumes meant that the glass melt had to be covered and higher temperatures were needed, so that a lead oxide had to be added to reduce the melting point. When Ravenscroft was called in around 1660 to advise and experiment, he sought a way of breaking the ties with the Italian workers and creating an English glass. He changed the composition of the glass, adding English flints instead of the Venetian pebbles and changing the alkali from soda to potash. The result, in about 1675–6, was the particularly fine English lead glass, which was hard, brilliant and lustrous and had gem-like properties. It could be cut and polished and set like diamonds, and this is just what Stras did.

Georges Frédéric Stras (1701–73) was born and brought up in the village of Wolfisheim near Strasbourg where his father Jean Frédéric Stras was a pastor. Stras was apprenticed to Abraham Spach, a Strasbourg goldsmith, from 1714 to 1719. Spach's workshop had been in business for four generations so that Stras was able to obtain a solid grounding in goldsmiths' skills. In 1724 he moved to Paris to join Mme Prévost in her small but fashionable jewellery business, and it did not take long for the young jeweller to make his mark. Since France did not excel in glassmaking at this particular era, it seems likely that Stras may have imported his special glass from England or Bohemia, whose thriving glass industry, fast rivalling that of Venice, took the lead in the 18th century. French glass improved greatly from about 1780 when the French managed to imitate English lead crystal. With great foresight, Stras explored the possibility of having the glass cut like gems and then set, probably in his workshops in Paris, into glorious jewels of his conception.

Stras's *poinçon* or goldsmith's hallmark was GFS (his initials) and a crowned sword. Between 1730 and 1734 he became famous for his paste jewels, and on 15 May 1734 he was appointed jeweller to the King of France. In 1735 the artist Charles Nicolas Cochin engraved for him an elaborate trade card showing Venus at the sea edge, holding coral and jewels and accompanied by Triton. In 1740, Stras was honoured with a mention in the *Dictionnaire de l'Académie*: 'In 10 years, Strass [sic] had made his way, everyone knew him, women benefited from his brilliance, and his name passed into the language.'

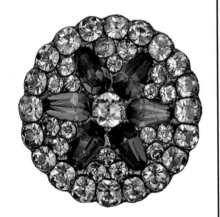

Two paste cluster brooches, with richly coloured blue and green pastes, set in silver. Both show the immaculate setting of specially cut and shaped stones. Late 18th century.

Stras eventually moved more and more into the realm of real diamonds, gradually abandoning paste. He also sold jewellers' accessories, loose stones and his famous 'tinted' diamonds. Around 1750 Stras took on a colleague, a German goldsmith called Georges Michel Bapst. It is possible that Bapst may have known Stras from Strasbourg although this is not certain. In 1752 Stras handed over the business to Bapst, who married Stras's niece in 1755. This is significant since the name of Bapst continues through jewel history as the most famous of French Crown Jewellers, eventually merging into the successful 19th-century firm of Bapst et Falize, the last successors to Stras. Stras died a wealthy man in 1773. Clearly he had competitors and imitators in Paris, especially in the 1750s and 1760s, but none has been celebrated or remembered in the same way. Chéron was another Paris jeweller who also produced pastes of a similar but harder substance imitating diamonds and coloured gems, and after 1779, a Paris jeweller called Lançon was making excellent paste at 53 rue Fontaine au Roi. By 1767 a corporation of false workers or *bijoutiers-faussetiers* had over three hundred members. This trade was very highly thought of, the workers exceptionally skilful, the designers talented.

Like diamonds, pastes were set in closed mounts until roughly 1800, when it was discovered that by leaving the back of the setting open more light and brilliance was captured and reflected in the stones. Until then, stones were enclosed in little cups of very thin metal, almost always silver in the case of colourless paste, gold usually for coloured pastes. The edges of the metal were cut down and pinched tightly around the stones to form an airtight case. A mark of the finest 18th-century paste is the use of very fine, very tightly fitting settings that cover the edges of the pastes and form smooth, well-rounded backs to the stones. This setting of pastes required even more skill than that of diamonds, since the tools for setting were harder than the pastes and likely to damage them. The reason for the absolute tightness of the settings was to protect the foil that invariably backed the stones.

In the 18th century, foils were used to line the settings of almost all stones, real or paste, and these foils would corrode if air seeped inside. The foil, a paper-thin piece of very bright metal such as copper or silver, which was then coloured, lined the little cups into which the stones were set. This improved and evened out the colour and brilliance of all stones, although the foil is of course not obvious. Poor-quality diamonds and semi-precious stones could be made to look like the most brilliant and deeply coloured lustrous examples. In good-quality 18th-century paste there should be no sign of the foil at all; if it is crumpled and visible, it could possibly be a later reproduction. It seems astonishing that these foils have survived so perfectly and that there is no loss of brilliance in the best 18th-century paste – evidence of the high degree of skill and care that went into the making of these fashionable jewels. Sometimes a black spot is visible at the very base of a stone: the facet at the lowest point of the stone called the culet was frequently covered with black paint in an attempt to improve its brilliance.

If the idea at first was to find a substitute for the expensive diamond jewellery worn at Court, it was certainly not long before workers found that paste could in many ways outdo the genuine article, in exciting cutting, setting and design which all produced a look quite distinct from that of diamonds.

The emphasis in 18th-century jewellery design was very firmly on the stones themselves, and on jewels completely covered or paved with gems. This was a problem with diamonds as they could only be cut into conventional shapes, which did not fill all the spaces in a particular design and which could not fit snugly side by side.

Paste was not subject to the same natural limitations of high cost and intransigence, and its principal advantage was that it could be cut to fit any space completely, whatever the shape. It was in this particular aspect of stone cutting that paste came into its own and developed its own

*Pair of white and aquamarine paste drop earrings, with bow motifs, silver set. French, c.1760.*

17

techniques, characteristics and personality. Since cost was not a problem, experiments in cutting techniques could be taken much further and errors that would have been catastrophes with diamonds proved to be instructive stepping-stones for paste cutters. The most important characteristic of the finest 18th-century paste is the use of shaped stones: hexagons, octagons, trapeze shapes and triangles which fitted immaculately next to each other, entirely filling the design, and with only the thinnest sliver of a metal wall between each stone. The setting of these shaped pastes needed special skills, often of a higher technical standard than those required for diamond setting. The glass stones had to be set with such a degree of accuracy that the facets of the varying shapes of the stones reflected off the metal settings, adding to the special soft but lively brilliance of this type of paste. It was the first sign of the exciting freedom that paste offers the designer and jeweller, to create jewels that suggest a fantastic indulgence and wild extravagance.

It was in the 18th century that the splendid partnership of flowers and jewels was truly established. Flower emblems were widely used in the decoration of jewels in the 17th century when a manic wave of botanical fervour swept Europe. Flowers, especially new species, became the most favoured of decorative devices, used for textiles, wallpapers, botanical prints as well as for suitable adornment to female beauty. In the 18th century this passion for flower ornament fell under the spell of the diamond and the ever-popular gem-set or paste flower spray was born.

Nosegays as they were called, or bouquets of real or artificial flowers – presumably of silk – were important adornments for the hair or the breast and were widely worn at Court. They were large and very noticeable and in the 1750s the latest idea from France was the 'bosom bottle', a flat pear-shaped glass bottle to hold water and keep the flowers fresh. A jewelled or paste bouquet, however, remained fresh and sparkling without this contraption. As jewellery became so much a part of high fashion during the century, vital trimmings of clothes, such as flowers, ribbons, bows or frogging or 'Brandebourgs' were all effectively interpreted in jewels. To add to the dazzling effect, flower jewels were sometimes mounted on little springs or tremblers, so that the blossom quivered with every breath or movement of the wearer.

As a sign of human supremacy over nature, the 18th-century jewels depicted nature in a highly artificial manner. Flowers obeyed the will of fashion and the skill of craftsmen. There was no attempt at authenticity, jewel flowers were not supposed to look like any recognized species of

*Group of late 18th- and early 19th-century paste jewels, showing the move from the strong stylization of 18th-century flower and feather jewels towards the colour and realism of 19th-century design.*

real flowers. Paste flower jewels show this stylization and naïveté of design to perfection; flower heads were always simplistic, two-dimensional like a child's portrayal of a blossom. Large diamond-paste flower brooches shone with a wide-open innocence that contrasted with their ingenious artifice. Around a centre deeply embedded with a single stone spread the evenly proportioned arched petals that end with little pointed stones and are sometimes outlined with a graduated trail of stones to emphasize line and movement. The specially shaped stones fitted perfectly into flower motifs. Other floral brooches looked like sprigs or sprays of little flat flowers, with stems that were wide and stiff, and stiff curved leaves arranged in shapes to suit the symmetry of the brooch or to show off the cut of the paste stones. This stylization of flowers is a particularly endearing and evocative characteristic of 18th-century paste jewellery.

Other themes from nature were given a similar non-naturalistic treatment and these can often provide stunning examples of the use of shaped stones. Butterflies, simplistically portrayed and encrusted in paste-gems, are amongst the most beautiful of 18th-century jewels, along with little brooches shaped as a stylized twisted leaf motif, a slim slightly curved slither in which the stones have been set to create an impression of fluidity, as if they have drifted naturally into the outline.

Just as flower bouquets were turned into opulent costume jewellery, the silky and extravagant ribbon bows that were liberally scattered over ladies' gowns were also immortalized in famous Stras. Usually French, the bow motif was a legacy from 17th-century jewellery design when the fashion for silk ribbon-work decoration began to be interpreted in gold and gems. Eighteenth-century bows were often known as Sévignés, after the famous letter writer, Mme de Sévigné, who wore them in sets of varying sizes. They were luxurious and feminine with huge rounded loops shimmering with paste gems. The largest would be worn at the centre of the scooped neckline to highlight the bosom, and smaller brooches were pinned underneath in a tapering 'V' shape. The motifs were sometimes tied in a rippling double bow, from which might hang a tassel or long slender drop-shaped motif. Smaller bows often featured as part of the designs for pendants and earrings in matching sets of jewels or combined with floral designs to produce the most characteristically 18th-century, pre-Revolutionary jewels.

Ribbon bows often tied simple sprouting bouquets or flower sprays on paste brooches or they decorated jewels shaped eloquently like feathers, another favourite 18th-century design that was beautifully executed in

*Two white paste jewels, a brooch and a pendant, both based on a stylized shell motif, set in silver-gilt. West European, late 18th century.*

shaped pastes and frequently worn in the hair, glittering echoes of the soft plumes that waved in the immense coiffures. The feathers were simple and sleek with evenly spaced, slightly arched fringes in fine proportions on either side of a gently curved spine.

While simple flowers or butterflies could have been made in either France or England, more elaborate designs, like the luscious girandole or chandelier shape which worked particularly well for earrings (and still looks as glamorous today as ever) were most typical of French paste. In a girandole design there is usually at the top a motif which might be a bow, a complicated knot device or spray of flowers, even a single stone, from which hangs a horizontal branch and three pear-shaped drops. Brooches like this were worn at the centre of the neckline, but the form was most often used for earrings.

Very often it is difficult to distinguish between English and French paste of this period, but generally the English repertoire of designs was smaller and designs were more streamlined, with simple outlines and stunning proportions. The quality of the stones and setting are usually superb.

In both England and in France buckles of varying shapes and sizes decorated hats and breeches; they were worn on ribbons around the neck or wrist and particularly on shoes to light up the flourish of a deep and elaborate bow. Paste shoe buckles were made in large quantities in England once the huge craze began in the mid-17th century. Samuel Pepys put on his first pair on 4 January 1659. After initial distrust and disapproval, the fashion had gathered much confidence and flamboyance by the great paste era of the 1740s and 1750s. It was said

*Two pairs of exceptionally fine chandelier or girandole earrings, (left) white pastes set in gold, (right) white and foiled deep pink pastes set in silver. Probably French, both c.1760–80.*

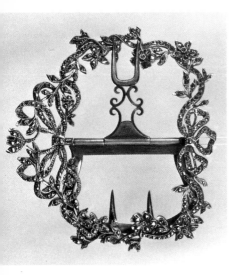

Silver and marcasite belt buckle, incorporating a bow motif. French late 18th century.

that in those days of social change you could tell a man's standing by his shoe buckles. Paste and cut steel were worn for evenings and always by fops or dandies whose buckles reached ridiculous extremes, curling down over the sides of their shoes and glittering outrageously with pastes. Buckles were ideal vehicles for the setting of shaped stones which fitted beautifully into the curved outlines to cover the whole front of the shoe with sparkle. Silver-set paste was often combined with gold settings which would be intricately engraved or 'bright-cut' with little facets to make the soft pinkish gold glint alongside the pastes. Shoe buckles disappeared from fashion at the end of the century with the invention of the shoelace and even a bucklemakers' petition to the Prince of Wales failed to revive the fashion except for Court wear.

*Rivière* necklaces were also essentially English: literally streams of individual stones in their snug, pinched settings, elegantly proportioned and very gently graduated so that each stone is slightly different in size from the next, with no sudden jump in size, producing an overall smooth and fluid line of gems. Individual collet-set stones were sometimes sold in boxed sets, each stone with a slide fitting on the back

A set of silver-mounted red paste and cut-steel buttons, with a buckle, to be worn alternatively strung on silk to form a choker necklace, in their original heart-shaped box. English, c.1790–1800.

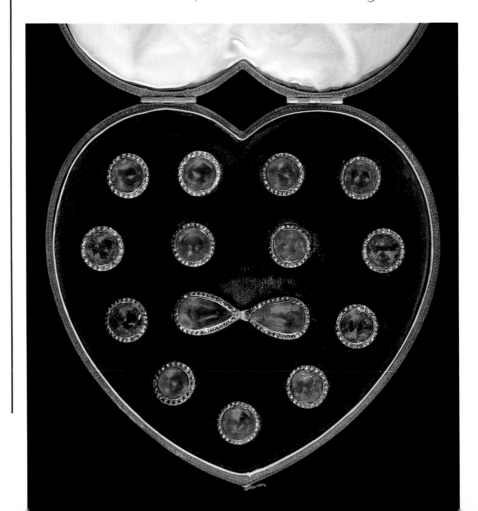

*A rare coloured paste ring designed as a stylized tightly closed bud, set in silver. Probably English, c.1785.*

*A white paste hair ornament, in the form of a crescent with a tuft of stylized feathers; c.1780.*

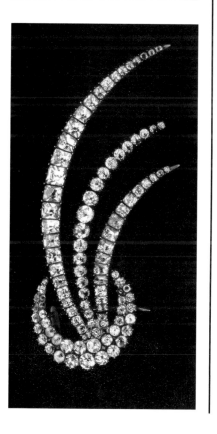

to be worn threaded on a piece of silk or velvet ribbon. Other popular necklaces were formed by linked trefoils or flowerheads. The very pleasing shape of the Maltese cross was a favourite form for English brooches and pendants towards the end of the 18th century and continuing into the early years of the 19th. Maltese crosses, looking exactly like diamond equivalents but executed in coloured pastes, were popular in the early 19th century, before 1830, and set in gold.

There is another style of 18th-century jewel, probably English in origin, often mistakenly known as 'Queen Anne' paste but made much later in the second half of the 18th century. Usually found as earrings or brooches, the design looks like two oval pastes set side by side, sometimes at a slant, and then filled in at the gaps at top and bottom with smaller pastes or a trefoil.

Surprisingly perhaps, rings were relatively little worn during this period, probably because hands were not much admired or considered important; they were overshadowed by the bosom as the most exciting part of the body. But when they were worn, rings were large enough to attract attention. They curved around the finger in long, oval, marquise or oblong shapes, their surfaces paved with pastes or covered with a foil-backed slice of blue glass in imitation of the fashionable royal blue enamel, and trimmed with pastes, perhaps with a central classical urn.

A profusion of paste buttons, however, made up for the lack of rings. Gentlemen wore lots of ornamental buttons, most of them just for show with no buttonholes or real function, and like buckles these were ideal vehicles for grandeur and glitter.

Since so much trouble was taken with hairstyles and since so much hair was worn, hair ornaments were vital accessories to the lady of fashion and paste could sparkle most convincingly from such towering heights. Aigrettes were jewels shaped like a little tuft of plumes and often held real feathers in place. Sometimes they were mounted on tremblers, with perhaps a crescent moon from which sprouted movable sprays of pastes. In the late 1790s the all-pervading classicism, combined with Napoleon's Egyptian campaign, inspired exotic headdresses based on the swathes of a North African turban or a Mameluke cap and pinned at the front with a crescent or drop-shaped jewel. The fashion for things Egyptian caught on in England after the Battle of the Nile in 1798, and the fashion leaders, labelled by the magazine *La Belle Assemblée* as the 'first-rates', all wore green morocco slippers laced with crocodile-coloured ribbon, Mameluke capes and turbans or Mameluke caps pinned with jewels. Flower jewels were worn in the hair, as were

arrows, and often they were worn together with tiaras or little truncated diadems, looking aristocratically like sumptuous real gems and combining favourite decorative features, feathers or slim scrolls, flowers or simple collet-set stones to match a parure or set of jewellery.

In the last quarter of the 18th century women's magazines began to be illustrated with engraved and hand-coloured fashion plates which did much to communicate and spread the latest ideas in clothes, hats and accessories. Probably the earliest fashion magazine was the *Galerie des Modes et des Costumes Français*, 1778–87, followed by several other French publications and then in England by the excellent journal, *The Gallery of Fashion*, first published in 1794 with plates by van Heideloff.

As jewellery became more and more a part of fashion, its design was influenced by ideas and styles from all over Europe. In southern Europe in the 18th century, the grandeur of the Courts of Spain and Portugal meant lavish gem-set jewels and an equivalent search for substitutes. Inexpensive semi-precious gems like the pale lemon chrysoberyls or colourless crystals tended to be used instead of pastes in Portugal, but Spanish jewels were very often set lavishly with pastes in designs that sometimes had a strong religious tendency in the use of crosses and large religious Orders. Spanish paste in a strong colour combination of green and white reflected the wide use of emeralds from Spanish South America. Generally Spanish and Portuguese jewels have a large and robust look, with stones and pastes of sunny hot-blooded colours, acid or bronzed yellows, but they lack the refinement of French or English examples.

A white and topaz-coloured paste watch key, set in silver gilt. Probably Portuguese, c.1760–70.

The sentiment that was to shape the destiny of 19th-century jewellery began in the late 18th century and was strongly influenced by the classicism of those years. Great archaeological discoveries at Pompeii and Herculaneum combined with a reaction against rococo styles to create a strong feeling for classical ornament. This neo-classicism was reserved, linear, haughty and based on architectural designs and objects of classical antiquity. The Adam style, set by Robert Adam, architect and decorator, swept England in the 1780s and then moved to France and to America. As the 19th century approached, slightly more elaborate designs with a classical flavour were added to the range of paste jewels: the cornucopia, horn of plenty, overflowing with flowers, the classical torch or trophy, the quiver with bow and arrow, the wheatsheaf and the harp or lyre, an especially popular motif that continued to be successfully set with pastes until about 1830. In France, bloody Revolution brought a

Parure of aquamarine paste jewellery, set in gold. English, c.1810.

*Pair of brooches formed as pansies,
the pale amethyst and citrine pastes
set in Pinchbeck. English, c.1810.*

*Harlequin paste necklace, set in gold,
French c.1820; and paste and
silver-gilt lyre brooch. English, c.1810.*

*A rare white paste flower brooch, with unusual jagged edges to the petals, the flower centre set en tremblant and the reverse showing the open-backed unfoiled stones, a very early example of open-back setting; c.1780.*

gruesome end to the trades in frivolous and exquisite luxuries and to the leaders of society who patronized them. However, the skills amongst the craftsmen did not die and trade was resumed in the early 19th century when the *nouveaux riches* and pleasure-loving citizens, long deprived of adornments, went in for jewel-wearing with a vengeance.

Little lovable paste-set birds, carrying sprigs of flowers or a forget-me-not in their beaks, winged their way towards the heady romanticism of the 19th century. The bird motif was also derived from Normandy peasant jewels and the Saint Esprit motifs, a dove and cross. Flowers lost some of their strict stylization, and nature crept back into favour in the form of paste bug jewels, especially large stag beetles, their crunchy bodies created with rounded pastes, foil backed to glow rose pink or purple and yellow, a curious costume jewellery craze in about 1800. Butterflies and flowers perked up, and more life, movement and colour fluttered into their shapes. The pansy, symbol of remembrance and sentiment, is one of the most memorable and desirable of early 19th-century paste jewels. Brooches and pins in the form of pansies looked quite realistic in soft purple and yellow pastes, the stones beautifully shaped and set. More insects were bred to hover on young ladies' costumes amongst the folds of lace or silk, with coloured bodies and diamond-paste wings. In complete contrast to the white paste fashion of the 18th century, the first decades of the 19th century saw a fashion for harlequin pastes, multi-coloured pieces with rainbows of soft foiled colours, all mixed together in one jewel, little rectangular cluster brooches, necklaces, lyres. Until the 1830s or 1840s, the Georgian-style pinched-collet closed-back setting was still employed for pastes, but around 1800 jewellers discovered that diamonds were vastly improved if the backs of their settings were left open to the light, and after some years paste jewellery began to follow suit. This can be a useful guideline for collectors, bearing in mind there was usually a time lag as paste followed diamonds, and in some transitional pieces you can see that some stones have been left open-backed while others are still closed in, which added more movement and variety to the stones in the jewel.

In the world of real jewellery colour also came back into vogue, in the form of semi-precious stones such as citrines, amethysts and aquamarines worn in the 1820s, and these were brilliantly mimicked in English and French paste. There were signs, too, that the paths of costume jewellery and real jewellery were about to converge, as paste workers gradually concentrated more and more on imitating the real thing. Along with the harlequin jewels, aquamarine and amethyst pastes

*Diadem front in a gold setting of scrolled design, with white and amethyst pastes. French, c.1820–30.*

are amongst some of the most stunning examples of the early 19th century, set in gold in fine 18th-century style mounts and often created in matching suites, with necklace and pendant, brooch, earrings and hair ornament.

Different countries excelled in different kinds of pastes; the Venice glassworks were renowned for their turquoise pastes, and the English for their lustrous colourless lead glass, although the French were fast catching up in quality at the turn of the century. Worried by English supremacy in the field of glassmaking, and the popularity of English novelty jewels and trinkets such as looking glasses in the best Paris shops, the Académie Royale des Sciences set up a commission in 1782 to look into the matter, and French crystal improved dramatically after this time, so much so that they became leaders in the field, taking healthy export orders at the trade exhibitions in the Louvre in Paris in 1806 and 1819. It seems that the top manufacturer of glass paste was a chemist and manufacturing jeweller called Douhault-Wieland who won a prize in 1819 and who supplied France, Portugal, Spain, Germany, Poland and Russia. Lançon continued to produce fine paste in the 19th century, and other notable manufacturers included firms or individuals called Mention and Bourguignon.

It is important to add here however that paste jewellery was much appreciated for its own merits and individual qualities, for its fashion and novelty value, and not just as imitation diamonds. From the start of the vogue in the 1730s and 1740s, the exciting new Parisian accessories were regarded as flattering and glamorous, and as they were composed of man-made materials – glass often set in newly invented metal alloys – they became the most appropriate ornaments to a self-made industrial society. The jewels carried the cachet of the finest craftsmanship which until then had been the prerogative of the upper classes. They were plentiful, varied, could be changed to suit new outfits and yet were expensive enough still to be regarded as exclusive luxuries. Stras jewels were worn in the highest echelons of society (as they are today); it is said that Mme du Barry owned a pair of blue earrings, and this must have set the seal of approval on costume jewels. However, the accessibility of paste jewels and the redistribution of wealth in the wake of the industrial revolution meant that ladies of all ranks, and even those of dubious morals, could now dress as finely as the best-bred (to all but the most discerning eye): a sign of a fast-changing society.

There was another important factor in the growing popularity of paste. Highway robbery was rife during the mid-18th century, and footpads

*Graduated collet necklace of aquamarine pastes, set in Pinchbeck, showing the elegant proportions of fine Georgian jewellery design. English, c. 1795.*

plagued London's streets, so that paste was extremely useful for duping the robbers when travelling. European travel was becoming gradually more widespread at the end of the 18th century with the popularity of the Grand Tour and visits to the excavations of Pompeii and other classical sites. Craftsmen were commissioned to create fine and impressive-looking jewels for travelling socialites or aristocrats who had to keep up appearances but did not dare risk losing a fortune in real jewels. Some of this kind of costume jewellery may have been made of semi-precious stones; foiled garnets for example may well have been used to imitate rubies and perhaps mixed with colourless pastes to stand in for diamonds.

To choose their treasured costume jewels, and to catch all the latest gossip, ladies of elegance and high society gathered in the chic Parisian jewellery boutiques of the Palais Royal (the jewellery quarter). Stras's shop on the Quai des Orfèvres was patronized by Mme de Pompadour and her associates, who may well also have visited other luxury novelty shops such as that owned by Defernex, situated later, from 1805 to 1828, at 243 Place du Palais Royal. The most famous shop of all for trinkets and novelties was Au Petit Dunkerque at first situated on the Quai de Conti at the corner of the rue Dauphine, moving in 1808 to the rue de Richelieu. At the end of the 18th century, in pre-Revolutionary Paris, Au Petit Dunkerque became the daytime meeting place for any member of Society who aspired to elegance. Patronized by Marie Antoinette, the exclusive shop was owned by M. Granchez (sometimes referred to as Grandcher) who was extremely successful in selling fancy goods, the latest novelties, gifts and what were called *articles de fantaisie* made in

*Group of white paste jewels: a Maltese cross, a simple stylized butterfly and a flower spray. English, c.1790–1810.*

France and other countries. From England he imported the best of craftsmen's jewellery, fine paste and expensive cut steel (see chapter 2) as well as other English-made glass goods. Au Petit Dunkerque sold fine diamonds alongside its elegant paste, and in 1819 at the height of the early 19th-century pasteworkers' skill, it was very hard to tell the difference between a 'comb for 30 francs and a comb for 10,000 écus' (*L'Opaline Française*). Au Petit Dunkerque closed in 1835.

One of the novelties to be found at Au Petit Dunkerque would surely have been the distinctive opaline paste, a speciality in France and England, at its best in the early 19th century. Opal glass was produced by

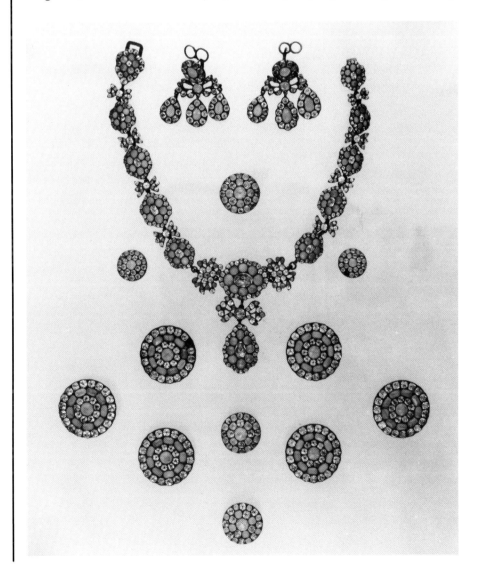

*Group of opaline paste jewels, set in silver. Probably French, c.1760.*

a special technique known in England in the 16th and 17th centuries and later in France. The *bijoutiers-faussetiers*, always on the look-out for new ideas, soon found that this semi-opaque glass in soft pastel colours could be set over pink foil to achieve an opalescent effect that was supposed to give the impression of the milky moody glints of opal. In fact it does not closely resemble the opal, because of the overall consistency of the different colours, but it does have a charming and feminine look of its own. In England, the centre of the trade in opaline glass jewellery was at Uttoxeter. Bows, butterflies, girandoles, flower jewels were all made in opal-paste.

In London, too, the best of jewellery shops sold fine paste alongside their precious stones. As early as the 1750s, Wickes & Netherton, set up in 1721 by George Wickes and later to become Garrards, advertised a 'Variety of False stone work in aigrettes, earrings, buckles' to follow the success of Stras's jewellery.

Before we leave the story of 18th-century paste it is important to mention its rival, rock crystal, which was widely used in England and Europe as another diamond substitute. The term crystal can be confusing in the context of costume jewellery, when crystal often refers to fine-quality glass. In jewellery terms, however, it means rock crystal, a natural mineral, a colourless quartz. Rock crystal was faceted, foil-backed and set in the same way as paste although it could not rival the extraordinary shapes and tight settings of the glass gems, and it does not have the same scintillating brilliance as paste. It has a more transparent, more diluted shine. Crystal was far more popular in Spain and Portugal, where it was used like pastes, than it ever became in England or France. The rock crystal was found in deposits near Bristol and in England crystals became known as 'Bristows' or Bristol stones while in France they were nicknamed Rhine or Alençon stones. Bristows were much worn by fops and dandies, set in buttons and buckles in much the same way as diamonds to glimmer in the complicated folds of a cravat or to enhance a brilliant appearance. Ideal for travelling jewels, crystals were often set in gold in huge suites of impressive jewels.

Gold has always been the traditional symbol of wealth and power and it was unlikely to be totally eclipsed even by the 18th-century diamond. Gold, or at least a gilt surface, was still necessary for a number of trinkets required by fashion, especially watches, watch chains and the seals and gewgaws that hung on them. Gold watches were indispensable accessories for both ladies and gentlemen in the second half of the 18th

*Glamorous suite of gold and rock crystal jewellery. English, c.1760.*

century, and particularly in the 1770s and 1780s when the fashion reached extremes. Fops often wore two watches, one being a mock watch or *fausse montre* as it was known. Ladies, too, wore huge and elaborate watches, which could be as 'big as a warming pan'.* They were engraved, enamelled or gemset and hung from the waist on a large hook, along with seals and charms and assorted knicknacks or 'toys'. Fashion plates show 18th-century ladies with large watches that hung down on the folds of the skirt, on one side, just on the hip.

Appropriately, it was a watchmaker called Christopher Pinchbeck (1671–1732) who, in the 17th century, invented a metal alloy that brilliantly simulated gold. Created in much the same spirit as Stras, to satisfy a growing demand from a new, wealthy and fashion-conscious but discerning market, Pinchbeck was implemented much more as a direct imitation of gold. It was an alloy of copper and zinc, although the exact recipe was never disclosed and the invention was a closely guarded secret. So successful was the alloy that it was widely imitated itself. It was expensive-looking, tactile, with better wearing properties than gold and a surface that was probably finished with a gold wash to prevent tarnishing and to create a soft, warm 'bloom'.

Pinchbeck began to be most widely and creatively used during the 18th century as it was ideally suited to the great age of costume jewellery and made a perfect partner for paste. Christopher Pinchbeck's son continued the business after his father's death, maintaining the secret and high quality of the metal in the face of fierce competition. In 1733, he was forced to place an advertisement in the *Daily Post* warning the public about cheap imitations. Like Stras, Pinchbeck benefited from the prevailing high regard for artificial substances and also from this unrivalled era of fine craftsmanship. Enormous pride of production was lavished on personal ornaments irrespective of intrinsic value.

'Real' Pinchbeck, worked and decorated in the same way as gold, was the perfect solution for the huge watches and chatelaines worn by ladies of fashion. The chatelaine was a favourite 18th-century accessory, used rather like a lady's handbag for keeping together all her vital everyday objects; a basic hook plate was hung with chains on which were kept keys, seals, watch and watch key, pencil and an *étui*, a little cylindrical case containing thimble, button hook, scissors, toothpick and other necessities. In the early 1770s a kind of hookless chatelaine came into

*T. Baker, *Tunbridge Walks*, 1714. Quoted in *English Costume in the 18th Century* by Cunnington and Cunnington.

*Intricately worked chatelaine of coloured Pinchbeck. French or English, c.1760.*

fashion; it was called a Macaroni and was worn with two dangling ends hanging from a belt. A vital feature of 18th-century dress and the most important daytime accessory, the chatelaine offered endless opportunities for high-fashion decoration. Pinchbeck chatelaines could look cunningly like gold, and were beautifully and intricately ornamented. During the 18th century, casting techniques for gold, silver or metal were used for less expensive trinkets, and certainly for the manufacture of silver mounts for paste jewels. Separate sections of the chatelaines were cast and then finished and assembled by hand. The cast metal shapes were then chased, engraved, decorated with repoussé work (hammered in relief from the back) or ornamented with enamels or coloured Pinchbeck in perfect imitation of exquisite three-coloured gold. Gold, and Pinchbeck, could be coloured by altering the composition of the alloy to create unusual effects of pink, yellow, green and, less often, blue gold. This delicate decoration that provided a perfect and charming vehicle for the craftsman's skills was applied to intricate chased metalwork of flowers, shells, scrolls in the late 18th and early 19th centuries.

To achieve another subtle colouring effect, very much in tune with the fashion for metallic and spangled fabrics, Pinchbeck chatelaines were decorated with silver, set with pastes or with glinting faceted steel studs. Rather than rococo curvaceous chasing, designs were based on 'chipped' or faceted engraving to catch reflections of light. Like buckles, however, chatelaines went out of fashion in the early years of the 19th century; the new classical craze meant that women's gowns were narrow and clinging like the dress of a Greek goddess and there was nowhere to hang a heavy chatelaine.

The 'real' rich Pinchbeck, as opposed to its imitations, intricately worked and coloured, was often mixed with fine pastes to make jewels that must be considered the noblest ancestors of today's costume jewellery. When Pinchbeck and paste, both at their best, are found together the results are always exciting, with the expensive look of high-fashion jewels that were much treasured. The colours are burnished and rich, the textures are silky, the stones are lively and the overall shape and design proud and feminine. The best of these objects are often tiaras in which Pinchbeck settings of pierced openwork danced with flowers set *en tremblant* or were laced with feather or scroll designs. In the opening years of the 19th century, classical-looking Hellenistic arched tiaras were made with tooled or bright-cut – faceted – metalwork often set with coral or coral-paste beads, scored all over in a pineapple

An early 19th-century gold-mounted
Harlequin necklace, set with
graduated coloured pastes and
natural, oriental pearls. The pastes
represent pink topaz, yellow topaz,
amethyst, aquamarine, topaz,
emerald, peridot. English, c.1815–20.

Three openwork Pinchbeck tiaras set
with glass imitation cameos and coral
beads. English or French, c.1820.

motif and mixed with little faceted glass beads. The most classical of all
head ornaments were decorated with a Greek key pattern or set with glass
imitation cameos. Examples of paste and Pinchbeck pieces that have
survived are evidence of the amazing dedication and skill that were
applied to jewels of humble materials.

Original Pinchbeck is in fact quite rare today, and not always easy to
distinguish from its many competitors; fine tiaras set with 18th-century
paste or three-coloured metalwork and jewels that clearly demonstrate
the best craftsmanship are usually the safest guidelines to identification.
Needless to say, the French luxury trades were quick to create an equally
successful simulant which could be marketed as a French product and
sold in the busy Paris shops selling novelties and *articles de fantaisie*. In
1729, a firm called Renty of Lille came up with a very good copy, and at
the same time Leblanc of Paris invented his own version, named 'métal
Leblanc' after him. There were other Pinchbeck copies called 'l'or de
Mannheim', 'Tombac' and 'Pomponne', invented in 1785 at the Hôtel

Pomponne in Paris. Pomponne was a copper alloy finished with a very thin layer of gold. 'Similor' was used in Germany, as well as France.

The flickering and romantic candlelight and ingenious workmanship of the 18th-century age of splendour were also responsible for the start of other fashions that must be regarded as ancestors of modern costume jewellery. To create beautiful jewels from cheap and unexpected materials presented an irresistible challenge to the many craftsmen in England and France and all over Europe.

The steel industry was the next to be mesmerized by the effect of the faceted diamond and the desire for glimmering beauty. A small but specialized steelworking industry based at Woodstock in Oxfordshire turned its attention in the late 18th century to producing handsome jewels and expensive accessories made of shiny, faceted blue-grey steel that glimmered intriguingly in flickering candlelight. The uneven light coming from so many sources in one room heightened the full impact of jewels made of steel studs, faceted, riveted and clustered like diamonds. This unusual glinting beauty, combined with the mechanical associations of riveted steel, have made cut steel jewels the most evocative ornaments of the great Industrial age. The fashion had its roots in the 18th century, in the diamond era but, as high-fashion costume jewellery, cut steel reached its height of popularity in the early 19th century and its story is fully traced in chapter 2.

The flash of steely brilliance, the metallic hues of embroidered spangles, foil fabrics, silver ribbons, created yet another effective jewel fashion of the late 18th century. Marcasite made an unusual diamond substitute, colourless yet polished and glittering. Often confused with steel, marcasite is in fact a natural substance, iron pyrites, which has a very shiny, metallic lustre and can be cut, faceted and set just like gemstones. Following the same route as paste, marcasite began to be very popular in the 1770s and 1780s, initially as a diamond lookalike and especially in Switzerland where sumptuary laws strictly limited the wearing of diamonds. Gradually, as the centuries changed, marcasite developed a style of its own and its cognac-coloured gleam combined with light, bright plaques of glass in red, royal blue or powder blue in an interpretation of an earlier fashion for diamonds and enamel on rings, watches and chatelaines. Such enamel and marcasite jewels were very expensive, recherché ornaments, on sale no doubt at shops like Au Petit Dunkerque, where they were often chosen in preference to diamonds (which could cost less than high-fashion marcasite jewels) by Europe's nobility and high society. So the century that had begun with fashions totally dominated by the diamond ended with a wild surge of enthusiasm for expensive diamond substitutes which became more chic, more admired and more exciting than the real thing, expressing all the skills, the fantasy and fashion of this great age of costume jewels.

# Two

# NEO-CLASSIC TO ROMANTIC

After the horrors of the French Revolution, the new regime in France aimed to sweep away the painted and powdered pomp and artificiality of the previous age. Gone was the distended and distorted vision of the 18th-century lady with her towering white coiffure that could house a model ship in full sail; the new era and its fashions hurtled towards an opposite extreme. Paris launched itself into an absolute fever of neo-classicism that had been brewing on both sides of the Channel since the 1760s.

Neo-classicism was the style, characterized by a formal icy elegance, based on ancient culture, art and artefacts, that decorated the lives, homes, buildings, costumes and ornaments of fashionable society in England and France from about 1760 to 1820, reaching a height of popularity around 1800.

Astonishing archaeological discoveries at Herculaneum, Pompeii and Paestum had been made during the years 1738–56, sparking off a passion for objects of classical antiquity, with pure sleek lines that made a welcome change from effusive rococo. In England serious studies of antiquity were undertaken by antiquaries, artists, architects and designers. Several volumes of designs were published spreading the images of ancient art, sculpture and architecture. This intense interest in classical traditions was reflected in European art and design, in architecture and interiors, in silver, in Wedgwood's ceramics and, later, in somewhat diluted form, in jewellery design.

The move towards classical decoration began simultaneously but independently in England and France. In France, the return to classical simplicity and purity had a spiritual link with Roman democratic virtues, coinciding with the Napoleonic era of high-minded severe grandeur, and fuelled by Napoleon's own personal interest in archaeology and particularly by his Egyptian campaign in 1798.

The neo-Greek taste was a more specific, light-hearted fashion that developed from the original, intellectual branch of classicism. Not particularly authentic, it was a more approachable and amusing way for ladies to be in the swim of fashion, without having to take it all too seriously. The idea was to look as much as possible like a Greek statue, or rather how they imagined a Greek statue to be, with a proud, chiselled beauty and a tragic air. From the 1780s and 1790s hair was dressed *à la grecque*, either short in springy curls like a Roman emperor, or piled high at the back into a chignon with a fringe or border of curls or long wisps, *à l'antique*. In complete contrast to the huge, stiff 18th-century gowns, dresses were narrow and simple, fluid and softly draped, usually white, flimsy and transparent for the most daring and most fashionable. The waist was very high under the bust. The most extreme classical costumes were worn in the mid 1790s, in Paris, by a group of *avant-garde* trend setters known as *Merveilleuses*. Their dress consisted of a simple shift of diaphanous muslin, cut very low at the bosom and split up the sides to the knee or thigh, showing bare legs or flesh-coloured tights. A well-known *Merveilleuse*, Mme Tallien, walked down the Champs Élysées in an outfit like this, with gold rings on her thighs, her calves, and diamond rings on her feet. As if this wasn't chilly enough, ladies sometimes resorted to dampening their gowns so that they clung to their statuesque bodies. Paris doctors publicly warned of the dangers of the fashion, the possibility of severe, even fatal, chills. Fashion always triumphs over common sense.

Accessories and jewels had to be suitably classical, of course. As no pockets could be concealed, handbags were first introduced at this time, swung from a long handle wound like a thong around the hand or arm, and in further homage to ancient Greece these 'ridicules' (as they were known for obvious reasons) were sometimes shaped and decorated like amphorae. Jewellery, which reached such a height of perfection in the classical world, completed the striking image. During the most intense years of the craze, around 1800, under the Directorate, gold jewels were

A Merveilleuse *in Greek-style costume, portrayed in a French caricature entitled 'Les Héroïnes d'aujourd'hui'; c.1798.*

*A dancing* Merveilleuse *and partner, portrayed in a late 18th-century engraving.*

worn in profusion: three bracelets on each arm, one high, one near the elbow and the third on the wrist, rings on every finger including the thumb, large hoop earrings or drop earrings known as '*poissardes*' (fishwives), long gold chains of knitted gold mesh in the form of serpents or of geometrically shaped gold- or metal-mounted plaques of agate or cornelian, worn slung diagonally across the body, short gold necklaces of fine chain draped in a style that became known as '*en esclavage*'. Deep belt buckles were worn under the bust, and diadems shaped like arched Hellenistic crowns placed low on the forehead, sometimes worn with a hair comb at the back. All these fashions were interpreted, a little later, in costume jewels of Pinchbeck or similar metals, in steel or in semi-precious stones.

English ladies were not quite so extreme in their neo-classic fervour: they maintained a respectable amount of clothing, including ample underwear, but wore narrower gowns of softly draped fabrics, in pale colours, white, apricot, lavender, with a very high waist and a low neck into which was discreetly tucked a fichu or shawl. Swept along by the general interest in faraway civilizations, they were fond of the fashion for turbans or the fez-like Mameluke caps (see chapter 1) in which they fixed an aigrette of paste or cut steel, like stars in a Persian night sky. They wore cashmere shawls and Indian cottons, and necklaces of classical fringe design perhaps or rows of chains wound round the neck. Despite a wave of pre-revolutionary Anglomania in France, English ladies still took their lead from Paris and from French illustrated fashion journals, although there was a gap in communications during the Napoleonic wars. Owing to this mutual admiration, French and English fashionable jewellery share many motifs, such as laurel wreaths, quiver and arrows, hymeneal torches, pairs of Roman doves, Greek key patterns and formalized geometric designs.

Napoleon's marriage in 1796 to the beautiful and exotic Josephine Beauharnais gave Europe a dazzling, dominating fashion leader. Her passion for jewels and gems, very real and very precious, verged on a mania, and with her encouragement fashionable jewels became an indispensable part of classical attire. For the jewel trade, Josephine was heaven-sent; the Revolution had been bad for business, as the most innocuous jewels could lead the way to the guillotine. During the Reign of Terror gruesome ornaments were worn: a thin red ribbon round the neck, little silver gilt brooches shaped like guillotines, rings stamped with Revolutionary characters and jewellery set with chunks of stone from the Bastille.

In Paris in 1791, the system of masterships or *maîtrises*, the long and rigorous apprenticeships for French goldsmiths, was abolished. This resulted in a lowering of standards, but also in a wider scope for less expensive jewels. Many goldsmiths and jewellers drifted into other trades, very probably the fancy goods or trinkets trade, and used their skills to produce the popular costume jewellery that could so well express the more fleeting absurdities of fashion and the classical and sentimental frivolities of the day.

Neo-classic designs were very well adapted to the fashion for cut steel which was thriving in the early years of the 19th century and continued to be enormously popular until the end of the Victorian era. Steel jewellery had begun to be worn in England in the second half of the 18th century (see chapter 1) and had spread to Paris, courtesy of Anglomania, to become an entrancing high-fashion accessory immaculately produced by the skilled craftsmen of the French trinket trade.

The industry of decorative steelwork, particularly for sword hilts, had developed in England certainly in the 17th century and possibly much earlier in Elizabethan times. The original centre was the little Oxfordshire town of Woodstock, although little is known of its origins. It was flourishing by 1720, apparently thanks to a certain Mr Metcalfe who had organized the cottage industry into a much larger and more

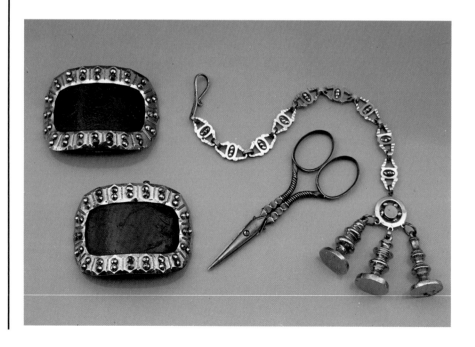

*Pair of scissors, shoe buckles and a fob chain and seals, all in cut steel. English, late 18th century.*

prosperous venture. By the mid-18th century Woodstock products were well known as the most refined, exquisitely made and expensive accessories. The type of objects produced included scissors of detailed pierced openwork which cost as much as 15 guineas in 1778, watch chains, sword hilts and Stars or Orders for the nobility. The items were always intricately designed and worked with facets, fancy openwork and a very high polish that greatly appealed to a society obsessed by the glitter of the faceted diamond. The material may have come from the horseshoe nails that littered the streets, as these were made of a very soft steel, although this seems an unreliable source for the large-scale industry that Woodstock was fast becoming. Perhaps the horseshoe nails were used for some of the hand-cut and pierced or woven mesh chains. There were small industries in Salisbury and Wolverhampton but the most serious rivals to Woodstock came from the growing industrial centre of Birmingham.

Shoe buckles were an important aspect of the production of 'toys' or trinkets at both Woodstock and Birmingham, and when these went out of fashion at the end of the 18th century, leaving the industry somewhat idle, workers were drawn to other forms of jewellery, especially the fast-changing fashion accessories glinting with the prospect of large financial rewards.

In the early steel work of the late 18th and early 19th centuries, the soft bluish grey steel was cut and faceted into tiny individual studs which were then densely packed together and fixed individually to a base plate by tiny rivets at the back of each stud. The base plates were cut into special shapes from thin sheets of metal, often brass or low-grade silver alloy. Several base plates of different shapes and sizes, fixed together by little steel girders, might be needed to achieve the right result for a complicated necklace or bracelet. It is possible to tell an early example by turning it over and seeing the little black rivet heads driven through the base plate. This usually indicates the finest work, which continued until around 1820–30. After that time, production became highly mechanized, standards were lowered and groups of studs, usually of uniform size, were stamped out in strips rather than being individually cut. A feature of the earlier work is the high number of facets on each stud, as many as 15, while the later cut steel jewels show only perhaps five facets on each stud. It was the high number of facets that created the dazzling sparkle of the finest cut steel jewels, along with the technique of densely packing the studs together and inclining them at slightly varying angles to the light for maximum brilliance. Another feature of the earlier work is the variation in sizes and shapes of individual studs resulting in a greater range of intricate patterns. Often fairly large studs were surrounded by rings of smaller studs. On some of the 18th-century jewels, a formal pattern of flowerheads and sliver-like leaves would be arranged geometrically with space in between, creating a very different effect from that of the densely covered early 19th-century examples.

Birmingham presented the greatest competition to the élitist industry in Woodstock, and it was at this time that the city, which had long been a centre for gold- and silversmiths and also for light steel engineering, was turning into a flourishing centre for the mass manufacture of jewellery and trinkets, or 'toys' as they were called. The trade had thrived on massive orders for shoe buckles over the previous century.

*Group of 19th-century cut steel jewels showing the variety of whimsical, sentimental or natural motifs and the use of steel studs of various shapes and sizes. French and English, c.1860.*

Unfortunately Birmingham was already acquiring a reputation for rather shoddy work, a situation that the enterprising Matthew Boulton hoped to set right.

Matthew Boulton (1728–1809), the great industrialist, had been brought up in the Birmingham industry and in 1759 he inherited his father's toy-making business producing small metal objects such as buttons and buckles. It was not long before he expanded his business considerably, and one of his most important and popular lines was the cut steel jewellery so fashionable at the time. With all his family's experience in steel-working and trinket-making Boulton's work was extremely fine, intricate and glittering and was made at his new factory at Soho, near Birmingham, in conjunction with John Fothergill. So successful was he that in 1770 Boulton employed 700 or 800 people, using every machine available for working all materials.

It is not usually possible to identify positively either Boulton's cut steel or that of Woodstock. Nor is it known how long Woodstock continued its steelwork. In the last decades of the 18th century, Woodstock was probably unable to compete as a 'cottage' industry making superior goods at very high prices.

In France, steel jewellery was considered the height of fashion from 1819 to 1830, although workers in Paris had been refining steel ornaments since the late 18th century. A Yorkshireman called Sykes had moved to Paris in 1780 and began making, or perhaps only retailing, cut steel. Although nothing more is known of him it seems that he was responsible for the beginnings of cut steel in Paris. If he had a factory, he certainly had a shop as well, for he was succeeded in this venture by M. Defernex (or Deferney) who took over the boutique at 243 Place du Palais Royal, selling jewels and fancy goods including cut steel and fine paste to high society.

A manufacturer called Dauffe was one of the first Frenchmen to make cut steel, around 1780, but it was Frichot who devised a mechanical process for producing steel jewels that were fine, very effective and chic and not too expensive. Frichot displayed his achievements at the 1819 exhibition and they were an immediate success. The fashion caught on, so much so that Frichot employed some 1,975 workers and had a prodigious output of steel jewels and small objects. Frichot was famed for huge and impressive parures; brooches like flowers; buckles of all forms to be worn on a hat, on a ribbon, around the neck or wrist; handbags and purses known as *gibecières*, long and supple mesh money bags. At this time the firms of Henriet and Schey were also well known for cut steel

NEO-CLASSIC TO ROMANTIC

and the final seal of approval was set on this fashion when a magnificent set of cut steel comprising comb, chains and bracelet, was made by Deferney for the Empress Marie-Louise.

In the very early years of the 19th century Parisian cut steel enjoyed an élite popularity, when it was still very expensive and an acceptable alternative to diamond jewels. The famous Paris boutique Au Petit Dunkerque (see chapter 1) sold steel goods that were more expensive than gold. Steel was often combined with the favourite semi-precious stones of the time, such as moss agate or cornelian, while classical motifs included Napoleon's eagle, the Greek key pattern and laurel wreaths.

Just about every kind of jewel was made in cut steel, which in England had become a fashionable and expensive novelty by the 1770s and 1780s. In 1785 steel embroidery was introduced to ladies' costume; flat steel sequins, or 'paillettes' of the kind that made up long chains, were sewn in rows down the satin skirts of dresses to draw attention and the glimmer of candlelight to the wearer. Chatelaines were superbly interpreted in cut steel, very often in classical designs, using the effect of contrasts between smooth polished steel and faceted beads and baubles. Hook plates might be of geometric octagonal or oval shapes; seals were simply proportioned or perhaps in the form of a lyre, and watchkeys glimmered with facets. The chains on which the implements were hung were made of beautifully wrought slim shapes, sometimes with rings or beads between the links. All this intricate work was a magnificent display of the craftsman's mastery over materials. In a sense it was this superb and expensive workmanship that compensated for the scarcity of other status symbols such as diamonds.

Decorative buttons were worn by men as pure ornament and were produced in enormous quantities in Birmingham, where factories had the necessary tools for repeating the basic shapes. In the late 18th century Matthew Boulton specialized in high-quality buttons which were exported all over Europe, and which were the most popular items in a wide range including chatelaines, buckles and fine chains. In 1767 Boulton supplied Queen Charlotte with two of his best steel chains. Such chains could take many months to make; composed of very thin slices of steel, hand-cut and pierced into round or floret shapes, and very highly polished to look like sequins, they are some of the most beautiful of all cut steel items. Even more technically brilliant were the chains or bracelets made of woven steel mesh, the hard metal transformed into a silky supple ribbon, occasionally produced in four colours to echo the coloured goldwork of the 18th century. Wide bracelets, sometimes worn

*Group of cut steel chains of polished discs and links, the example in the centre ornamented with Wedgwood jasper-ware rosettes. English, c.1800.*

in pairs, were made of wire mesh and decorated with riveted sequins or polished steel butterflies or flowerheads. Dating probably from the early years of the 19th century, these are now extremely rare.

In the early 1800s the strong classical formality relented and designs moved towards the century's romantic mood. Early 19th-century cut steel jewels offer the most charming motifs: brooches formed as birds, lizards, bees, flowers, ears of wheat, stars, crescents, keys, hatchets, comets, butterflies, the elegant fleur-de-lis, which was particularly French, and the padlock, particularly English and sentimental and found only rarely on superb substantial chains or bracelets of plump cable-link design. Flexible bracelets are generally earlier in date than the stiff bangles, which are also usually simpler in composition. Bracelets could be formed of linked sequins, of mesh, as mentioned above, or of elaborately encrusted designs, usually formal rather than figurative, composed of rosettes, a strip of Greek key pattern or linked circles. Bangles showed greater variety, as very often the band was made of stamped rows of steel studs, with endless different central motifs: a buckle, butterfly, flower or perhaps a solid band of steel would be edged with a lacy scalloped design. Earrings can look surprisingly modern and achieved a similar effect to paste in lighting up the features. They were long and drop or chandelier shaped, sometimes with slender abstract designs or with fringes of steel. The most elegant necklaces were made in the classical spirit, and took the form of fringe necklets with formal abstract motifs. The precision of material and workmanship produced jewels that were wonderfully fluid and refined; true to classical design they were beautifully proportioned, some with drapes or little icicle-like pendants. In later years, these were succeeded by the heavier, more glittering romantic necklaces of graduated flowerheads, stars or rosettes heavily encrusted with densely packed steel, and flowers that were often

*Two romantic cut steel necklaces composed of elaborate flowerhead motifs of densely clustered steel studs; c. 1840–60.*

49

deep and three-dimensional with layers of petals riveted through the flower centre.

Hair ornaments of many kinds were widely worn during this period: combs, coronets, diadems, aigrettes. The simplest and most flirtatious hair ornaments were small combs on two or three prongs surmounted with a sparkling flower, butterfly, insect or crescent. These would be slipped into a chignon or mass of curls or ringlets. Larger combs looked very much like other popular hair combs of the period, and can show some of the finest 19th-century steelwork, heavily studded to create complex patterns, including a crownlike motif with five spheres standing on little curved points, a theme often found in gold or Pinchbeck mid-19th century jewellery. Steel tiaras were of the simpler bandeau type, and covered the gamut of designs from neo-classic to romantic, from perhaps a straight band of Greek key pattern, a graduated series of fleurs-de-lis or entwined laurel wreaths, to flowers and butterflies.

With the reappearance of the waist in the 1830s, belt buckles were very much in vogue, and were made in every shape and form in steel as well as every other material possible. Tight-waisted costumes of the 1830s and 1840s drew attention to buckles which were usually deep and oblong-shaped, or tinged with the Gothic taste for pointed sculptural outlines, always highly ornamental, chased, engraved and gem-set, or made of elaborate Pinchbeck decorated with steel sequins.

The cut steel jewels that have the strongest flavour of popular neo-classicism and of the Great Industrial age are those that are combined with Wedgwood's jasper imitation cameos. They are the most beautiful and technically fascinating examples of costume jewellery of this age and mark a partnership between two formidable forces of the Industrial Revolution, Matthew Boulton and Josiah Wedgwood.

Classicism, and particularly Napoleon's brand, brought with it a massive craze for cameos and engraved gems. Like neo-classicism itself, the mania for cameos began in the 18th century as a very serious, intellectual and intense study of antique engraved gems. As always, the craze, somewhat diluted, filtered through to the mainstream of popular fashion. From about 1804, ladies in Paris wore cameos just about everywhere they possibly could; a lady with any pretension to fashion might conceivably wear a necklace or a long chain of linked cameos, a cameo for a belt buckle, one at least on each bracelet, a pair of drop earrings set above and below with cameos, several on a hair comb and diadem and one or more on a band wound round the forehead. In the home, cameos or large classical plaques became an integral part of interior decoration, and they were even used to decorate the smartest carriages. Clearly there were not enough of the genuine ancient articles to go around, and there was a flourishing market in fakes as well as in good honest reproductions in hardstone, shell or even glass – such as those perfected by the Scotsman James Tassie – and, in ceramics, by Wedgwood. Sometimes a 'doublet' made an ideal and effective compromise for fashion jewellery: it was a piece of moulded glass fixed to a hardstone background. Cameos were incorporated into the most lavishly expensive or the most modest jewels, and the examples came from the very highest echelons of society: Napoleon himself took an avid personal interest in the glyptic arts – the art of gem engraving – while Josephine and the ladies of the Court took an equally avid interest in wearing the most sensational antique or reproduction cameos with their classical gowns.

In England the craze for cameo jewellery began around 1800 and continued until about 1880, during which time the grand art was interpreted in every material conceivable. By the 1770s Josiah Wedgwood's pottery production at Burslem was extensive and constantly expanding, and in 1774, at the height of the enthusiasm for ancient gems, he introduced his famous unglazed jasperware which could be used to make decorative imitation cameos. The white relief stood out from a coloured background of soft blue, lavender, rust, olive green or black and usually depicted scenes from classical history or mythology, as well as a range of modern 'heroes' such as Milton, Isaac Newton or a character from popular contemporary literature, usually the sentimental type, given a classical treatment. In the mid-1770s Matthew Boulton wrote to Wedgwood asking for cameos that might be suitable for ornamenting boxes and jewellery and the two entrepreneurs began a close and successful collaboration. Cameos and plaques in sleek classic shapes, octagonal, oval, rectangular, were set into cut steel jewels so that the hard metallic glints contrasted with the soft, matt, powdery finish of the jasperware. Every kind of cut steel jewel was adapted to incorporate cameos or little circular plaques with flowerhead or swirl motifs or, perhaps most pleasing of all, Wedgwood beads perfectly round or elliptical, with little spiralling trails of white, mixed with long slender links of cut steel to make a stunning long chain. Occasionally artificial pearls were added to complement the mixture. The best of these jewels were created in the late 18th and early 19th centuries, the epitome of both classicism and the Industrial age.

Other materials were mixed with cut steel during the 19th century, among them enamels or painted porcelain plaques of classical or peasant figures, usually of Swiss origin and in rather lurid colours. Later, in the mid-19th century, jet was found to make a successful partner to steel, which could add some life and sparkle to solid, grim mourning ornaments.

James Tassie (1735–99) was undoubtedly the most skilful maker of moulded glass imitation cameos, a talent bred from the academic study of ancient gems and one which Tassie turned to commercial use after he moved from Glasgow to London in 1766. His glass intaglios and cameos were copied, not very well, by Birmingham manufacturers and used in inexpensive jewels and trinkets. The London glassmaker Apsley Pellatt also made some small jewel-like glass cameos using his special method for encrusted cameos. Generally speaking, these have not survived very well and jewels with Tassies are extremely rare.

Another phenomenon of early 19th-century costume jewellery that transformed a dour, industrial material into delicate and feminine jewels was Berlin Iron work. One of the strongest and most appealing characteristics of this jewellery that looks like very fine black lace is its successful interpretation of themes that range from a noble classicism to the naturalistic and romantic images of 19th-century historicism. Berlin Iron came to the forefront of attention during the Napoleonic War of 1813–15, and so apart from its extraordinarily decorative qualities it tells the social, political and art historical tale of its era.

It was originally conceived not in Berlin but at Gleiwitz in Silesia as a sideline for armourers and iron founders whose products were diminishing in demand. The history of the jewellery begins at the end of the 18th century, when two foresighted characters, Friedrich Anton Freiherr and Friedrich Wilhelm von Reden, set about developing and modernizing Prussia's iron industry. Their technical experiments resulted in their being able to use a thinner liquid iron to obtain finer ironwork. Plans for a new foundry at Gleiwitz were made in conjunction with Wilkinson, the British iron engineer, in 1794–6, and the first artistic cast ironwares were made in 1798. They were cameos and medals, cast after patterns brought by Reden from England. Some 1,254 medals and cameos (as well as other wares) were produced in that first year. So successful were they that in 1805 the figure for cameos had increased to 6,503. In 1804 the Gleiwitz Foundry exhibited in Berlin at the Royal Academy of Arts and Mechanical Sciences, and in that year the

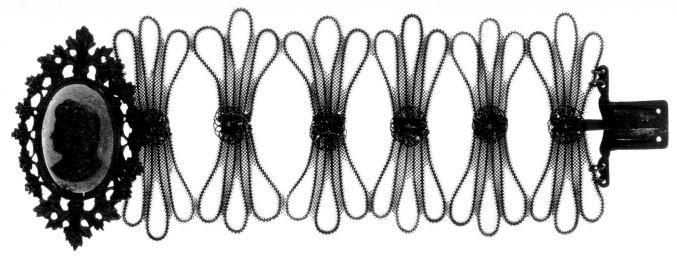

*One of a pair of Berlin Iron bracelets composed of delicate gauze-like bows, each tied with a central rosette, the polished leafy clasp decorated with a cast iron profile cameo of Bacchus; c.1810.*

Royal Berlin Factory also began to make small and decorative ironwares, cameos, plaques and jewellery. Very soon the Royal Berlin Foundry overtook Gleiwitz as the most prolific maker of trinkets and jewels. When the iron mines at Sayn became German property after territorial gains of 1815 a third Royal Foundry was established there, and there were other private factories, notably at Ilsenburg-am-Harz. However, the Royal Berlin Foundry was the best known manufacturer of iron jewels and the one from which the method took its name. Unfortunately the factory had only two years to refine techniques before Napoleon marched on the city. With his usual acquisitive approach to the art and culture of his victims, Napoleon seized the moulds from the Berlin Foundry and took them back to Paris. These casts were not used, but work on small decorative ironware progressed and a trade had grown up in Paris by 1828, continuing until the mid-19th century.

The heyday of Berlin Iron jewels came when the Germans fought their War of Liberation against Napoleon. Wealthy patriots were asked to donate their gold jewellery to finance the war effort, and in return were given a piece of iron jewellery, inscribed '*Gold gab ich für Eisen 1813*', '*Eingetauscht zum Wohl des Vaterlands*' or, less often, '*Unvergesslich 1813*'. Some were dated to commemorate specific battles. Small iron crosses proudly displaying a head of Frederick of Prussia were especially popular.

The fashion, once started in this way, did not end with the War. Berlin Iron's novel and highly individual beauty appealed to European fashionable tastes; its severe restrained matt black appearance conformed to the aesthetic ideals of classicism, and it was also suitable for mourning wear. Iron jewels were first worn for mourning in 1810 on the death of Queen Luisa, wife of Frederick William III of Prussia. She was greatly mourned by the people and an iron cross became a way of demonstrating this remembrance. The material itself symbolized constancy, and the work was regarded as much as a technical curiosity as a decorative accessory and exported all over the world. Like cut steel, Berlin Iron was appreciated for its own attributes and skills and not seen as a substitute for more expensive jewels.

Classical iron jewels are particularly successful for their symbolism, in both material and concept, of the strength of classical heroism. From the

Two Berlin Iron necklaces, (left) a festoon style set with cast cameos of heroic heads, on polished discs, within frilled and corded borders; (right) the fine tracery in complex Gothic design; c.1810–30.

Berlin Iron bracelet composed of plaques with floral motifs and cameos, showing the overlap of neo-classic and romantic themes; c.1830.

start of production in Berlin in 1804 to about 1820 many jewels incorporated 'fake' cameos with proud profiles set against a gleaming polished steel background, mounted in brooches, bracelets, earrings and necklaces in which the cameos were linked by draped chains of finely woven iron. In other jewels the cameos were set on a flexible ribbon of woven iron mesh, which conjured an extraordinary softness from a tough, masculine material. Meshwork, thought traditionally to have been made in Silesia but now believed to be English workmanship of the early 19th century, was a popular offshoot of Berlin Iron work. It looks like supple, dark blue-grey gauze which was often plaited, pleated or woven into fancy designs for whole sets of jewels, and occasionally ornamented with pierced steel sequins. In other jewels cameos would be framed by milled wire or by cast ornamental frames, the solid-looking cameos contrasting with the lacy openwork of the border. The iron itself is not naturally black, and the even, dark matt effect was achieved by coating the metal with black lacquer. The best pieces were sometimes ornamented with gold.

Historic interest is added when Berlin Iron jewels are signed with the names of private foundries or factories, the most famous being August Ferdinand Lehmann, Hossauer, Geiss, Devaranne of Berlin, Edward Schott of Ilsenburg.

Simeon Pierre Devaranne (1789–1859), presumably of French origin, was trained as a goldsmith and was recorded as a manufacturer of cast iron in 1828; by 1850 he owned his own foundry. In 1825 he had been asked to send cast iron wares to a Parisian firm of goldsmiths and exhibited at several European exhibitions, including London's Great Exhibition of 1851, where his work was much noticed. He used cameos and figures in his work, including busts of Byron, Walter Scott and Wellington, which seems to show that he exported much of his work to England.

The firm of Geiss made equally sensational jewellery, but is best remembered for lacy openwork designs, especially a vine leaf pattern that was both classical and naturalistic, and very effective. Johann Conrad Philipp Geiss (1772–1846) had also trained as a goldsmith, which accounts for the success of his iron jewels. Having spent some time at the iron foundries of Malapane and Gleiwitz he began his own production of small wares in 1804.

All these factories employed the talents of individual designers, the most important being Karl Friedrich Schinkel (1781–1841) who worked for the Berlin foundries. Schinkel was celebrated for a charming neo-Gothic style which lent itself particularly well to Berlin Iron jewellery when the neo-classic influence dwindled. As an interlude before the onset of neo-Gothicism, naturalistic themes such as fruit, butterflies and flowers were substituted for busts and formal trelliswork designs. Schinkel realized that the architectural nature of iron was perfectly suited to the Gothic style, and in the 1830s, under his influence, iron jewels began to look more and more like exquisite miniature wrought iron work – little Gothic follies outlined with scaled-down pointed arches, filled with medieval traceries and trefoils. This was the first of a long line of regurgitated styles taken from history.

In Paris, the classical elegance of the matt black jewels was welcomed when society was plunged into mourning after the assassination of the Duc de Berry in February 1820. The widowed duchess was a

*Berlin Iron bracelet, mixing elaborate Gothic openwork with foliate motifs, signed Geiss à Berlin; c.1830.*

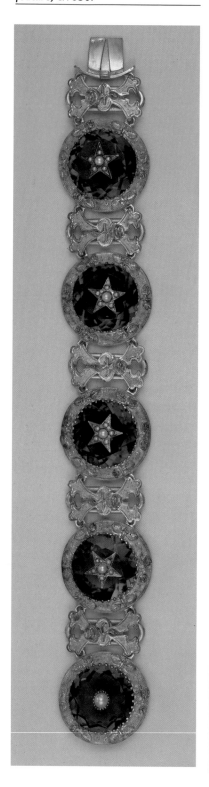

spectacularly fashionable lady who was able to turn steel and jet into
scintillating complements to her beauty. By 1827, iron jewellery was all
the rage and Paris had several manufacturers, among them a M. Dumas,
and Caqué, an engraver at the Paris Mint famed for classical designs.
The plain simplicity of the strong black material suited the aesthetic
ideals of classicism. The French could turn out iron jewellery at such a
competitive price that foreigners were forced to lower their prices.

As with cut steel the quality of Berlin Iron varies and the most
attractive pieces usually incorporate the finest of lacy filigree work. The
skill in Berlin Iron jewellery lay in designing and making the moulds and
in obtaining a high degree of precision in the outlines. Earrings can be
extremely decorative, long and drop-shaped with hollow spherical or
torpedo-shaped openwork; bracelets, often worn in pairs, were wide with
decorative clasps; necklaces if classical were draped and studded with
cameos, if romantic they consisted of linked openwork sections; brooches
were much simpler, taking the form of individual plaques.

By the middle of the century Berlin Iron was discarded in favour of
personal ornaments that were richer, more colourful and flamboyant,
and more in tune with the full blossoming of a true 19th-century
atmosphere in both France and England. Ladies of fashion turned their
pretty backs on the severity of classical design and industrial materials to
welcome instead new and important influences of romance, sentiment
and naturalism.

In France Napoleonic classicism had come to an end in 1820 (rather
than in 1815 after Waterloo). At this time fashions and jewels underwent
a major change, and a more ornamented look of coy frilliness took over.
With the restoration of the monarchy and the return of aristocrats from
exile, there was an inevitable reaction against all that had gone before,
particularly against the haughtiness and formality of classical decoration
as well as the outrageously abandoned women's fashions. Dresses now
reached right to the throat; the waist returned to its normal place; skirts
were more voluminous; sleeves too became wider and wider and in the
1830s developed into a focus of attention. Women's hairstyles became
more elaborate, involving lots of curls, rolls and ringlets. At first ringlets
were piled quite high and fixed with feathers, ribbons and jewels; then
they moved down towards the cheeks where they hung in great shiny
clusters from a smooth crown parted neatly in the centre. Large hats also
with plumes and ribbons became wide to balance the shorter, wider skirts
and enormous balloon-like sleeves.

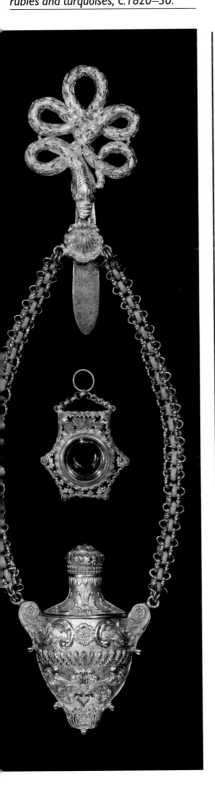

With the newly restored Bourbon monarchy in France came a new gilt grandeur which was sadly subject to economies necessitated by the effects of war. Semi-precious stones were worn, large and plentiful, amethysts, topazes, aquamarines, providing an extravagant show for much less cash than precious stones would have required. The large softly coloured gems were set in a new kind of goldwork that economically made the most of a small amount of gold. It was called *cannetille* after a particular type of Napoleonic embroidery. Stones were set in nests of tightly curled and twirled fine gold wires, interspersed with small motifs of gold flowers and shells or scrolls, all ornamented with trails of tiny gold granules in the classical manner. Huge suites of impressive jewels were made in this way, and the chains of necklaces or bracelets were formed by intricate knitted gold mesh, supple and silky. This goldwork was faithfully copied and often improved in Pinchbeck and other gold imitations of the 1830s and 1840s, by which time very long chains, earrings and pairs of bracelets were also the height of fashion. Pinchbeck enjoyed a great heyday in this pre-Victorian era and once again came to the rescue of the increasing numbers of fashion followers. Exquisitely worked Pinchbeck created the required effect of bosomfuls and wristfuls of jewels without crippling expense. At the same time, the work on Pinchbeck jewels was as fine as the real thing, and still expensive and recherché enough to be exclusive.

At the end of the 18th century the scantiness of dresses had made the wearing of large fur muffs essential, and the muff would usually be hung on a long and decorative chain round the neck. Although wearing an eyeglass without good reason was considered an impertinent affectation, quizzing glasses along with watches and huge crosses were also hung on these chains, which were sometimes caught at the waist or pinned to the bosom. Gradually, as the chains became bigger and bigger and more elaborate, Pinchbeck examples became the most fashionable since they were often the largest and most extravagantly decorated of all. Huge, plumply rounded links of Pinchbeck or other gold-coloured metals were patterned or textured with tiny raised dots, stars, spots or chevrons on a matt, rich golden surface. The links gave the impression of massive weight when in fact they were exceptionally light. Sometimes chains composed of smaller links were worn looped twice around the neck. Variations in patterns of chains included magnificently complicated rectangular links, ornamented with a stippled surface in which the metalwork was scattered with tiny granules or raised pin-head bumps to produce the effect of a delicate frost or gauze-like surface. Clasps were

always highly decorative, often barrel-shaped and covered with filigree and turquoises or pastes, or in the curious form of a delicate little disembodied hand – the sentimental hand of friendship. This was usually a gloved hand with a tiny ring on one finger and a filigree and paste-set cuff.

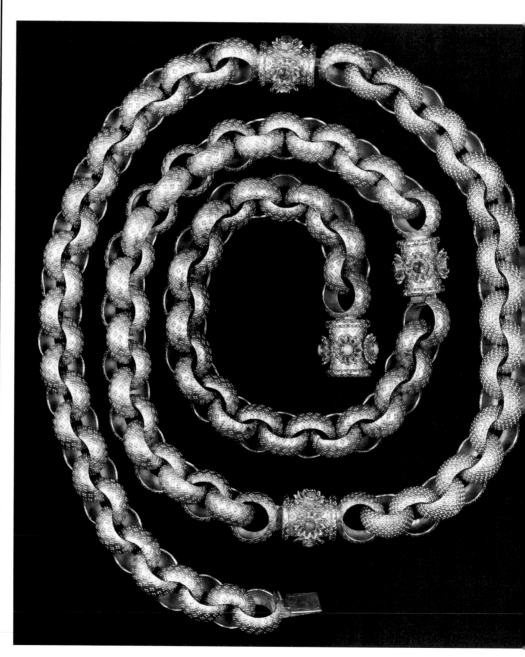

*Pinchbeck chain of textured links with barrel shaped clasps ornamented with filigree and paste-set flowers. The chain separates to form a pair of bracelets and a short chain; c.1825.*

*Classically inspired serpent earrings in a Pinchbeck version of mesh-like* cannetille *work; c.1830.*

Chains were also made of pearls or coral or jet, and were sometimes enamelled or set with gems. In England, in the late 1830s, pearls were still very much in vogue as they suited the lingering fashion for muslin dresses and were also ideal for holding a muff. In 1838, the journal, *World of Fashion*, decreed that it was of very little importance whether the pearls were real or false, suggesting that 'Roman' pearls might serve just as well as the real thing. Roman pearls were made by filling spheres of very thin glass with an iridescent paste, called *essence d'orient*, made from fish scales. These were fragile, but 'Venice' pearls were longer-lasting, being made from a different kind of glass bead. Venice pearls were on sale in London at the time of the International Exhibition of 1862.

Bracelets added the finishing touch to any careful toilette of the 1830s, and they became the most essential fashion accessories of the period, worn in pairs, sometimes two or three pairs at a time. Popular bracelets were made of chains of the same kind of links as those of long chains, rounded and textured or oblong and stippled, often fastened with a hand motif or with a pretty heart padlock covered with filigree work. Another very effective kind of Pinchbeck bracelet was composed of a wide mesh of thin wires of metal woven like neatly slanting stitches. The mesh band fastened tightly around each wrist with a huge and decorative clasp, either in a formal pattern or encrusted with *cannetille* work of flowers, shells, curls and coils, embedded perhaps with small pastes or turquoise forget-me-nots and set off with a flourish of three-coloured Pinchbeck. The fashion for recherché coloured and highly chased metalwork extended to many other fashionable accessories, too: seals, watches, watch fobs and quizzing glasses were all just as carefully fashioned in Pinchbeck as in real gold, with richly engraved flowers, leaves, scrolls, shells.

Decorative clasps began to show the all-pervasive sentiment of the 19th century and one particularly charming vogue from this period was for jewels that flirtatiously spelt out messages of love. A conundrum of coloured pastes (or real gems) could be contrived by arranging the stones in rows, clusters or flowerheads so that the initials of the gems spelled out words like REGARD or DEAREST. (Ruby, emerald, garnet, amethyst, ruby, diamond; diamond, emerald, amethyst, ruby, emerald, sapphire, turquoise.)

*Cannetille* work was replaced during the 1840s by the first machine-made jewels, produced to imitate *repoussé* or hammered goldwork. This style can be recognized by goldwork that looks more

solid, more voluptuous with larger rounded scrolls and swirls, their outlines reminiscent of medieval architecture. These jewels had a more substantial look that hinted at the bold forthright optimism of the Victorians. The components were stamped out by machine from thin sheets of metal, gold or imitation, and then hand-finished and assembled. The mounts were set usually at this period with pale semi-precious stones, such as pink topaz, mixed with the favourite small turquoises, or with pastes in imitation of these stones. Pinchbeck was very widely used for this style of machine-made jewel, particularly for pairs of bracelets or for brooches and earrings with polished gold wavy edges. Sometimes bracelet clasps or front sections of bracelets were made to be threaded on ribbon to produce a similar effect.

Queen Victoria came to the throne in 1837, at the height of the burgeoning romantic age. This fresh young girl of 18, plucked from a very simple life to be queen of a great world power, personified the fairy-tale romance of popular novels. The early years of Victoria's reign were submerged in a mania for the Middle Ages, a manifestation of the longing for romance. Everything vaguely Gothic was considered glorious: art, architecture, costume, characters. Historical Gothic spine-chilling novels were all the rage and ladies swooned at Sir Walter Scott's swashbuckling historical romances. Perhaps as an antidote to increasing industrialization, public imagination idealized and glamorized the Middle Ages, redolent of chivalrous romance, righteous love and valour, rich and dramatic beauty of heraldry and history. Young ladies imagined themselves as heroines, dressed in medieval garb, enclosed in castles surrounded by swirling mists, delving dangerously

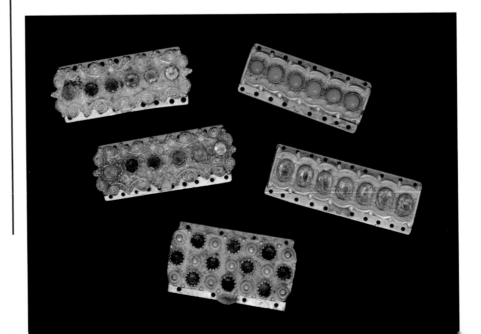

60

Jewels made of richly gilt metal or 'Abyssinian' gold; a bracelet typical of the 1840s and 1850s, and earrings in the archaeological revival style of the 1870s.

into dark and secret underground passages or gazing out from a high window for a glimpse of a hero or a knight in armour. This neo-Gothic taste of the 1830s and 1840s served as an introduction not only to the 19th-century obsession with past styles but also to the equally passionate obsession with romance and sentiment.

Dresses began to take on the look of medieval costumes; collars had castle-like crenellations; huge sleeves were slashed to show puffed sleeves beneath and long beaded girdles were wound round waists and often hung with chatelaines in the style of the lady of the manor. Hair was dressed elaborately *à l'Agnès Sorel* (the beautiful diamond-adoring mistress of Charles VII of France) and stuck with jewelled daggers and arrows. Another tribute to the Renaissance was paid by the brief fashion for a jewelled head ornament known as a *ferronière*, so called after a

Portrait of Claire de Bearn, Duchess of Vallombrosa, by Francis Xavier Winterhalter, signed and dated Paris, 1840.

*Gilt metal naturalistic hair comb, with vine leaves and bobbling grapes on spiralling tendrils. English, c.1850.*

painting by Leonardo da Vinci in the Louvre. It was a chain or cord which went around the head with a single jewel or ornament hanging down on the forehead. For a while there was a specific craze for the Mary Stuart look, and dresses had Elizabethan-style ruffs and huge slashed sleeves. The Mary Stuart fad had in fact begun in France, in 1829, when the great fashion leader the Duchesse de Berry organized the '*quadrille Marie Stuart*', a huge fancy dress party at the Tuileries designed to recreate a medieval atmosphere. This set off a spate of medieval costume balls and tournaments.

Clothes and accessories provided the quickest and most effective route to fashionable medievalism, and it seems there was much rivalry amongst society leaders over the degree of Renaissance splendour they could conjure up. It was an atmosphere of escapism and dressing up in which costume jewellery could flourish; overall effect took precedence over intrinsic value.

In general the medieval-style accessories were merely based on romantic fancy; no attempt was made at authenticity, and the result was resolutely Victorian. However in France, by the middle of the century, a serious style of jewellery design was practised by the finest goldsmiths of the day, a style that became known as the '*style cathédrale*', a sculptural figurative fashion which was then copied by manufacturers of cheaper jewels. The firm of Schlichtergroll of Vienna, amongst others, turned out costume jewels in silver gilt and paste so that the fashion-conscious ladies of the middle classes could join the historic frolics, and Berlin Iron in architectural Gothic styles was still being worn at this time. This passion for the past was to continue in different ways throughout the century and was a prelude to the full flowering of the great romantic age which was to have such a widespread effect on costume jewellery trends.

Alongside neo-Gothic styles, jewellery design at the start of Victoria's reign fell under the spell of naturalism. This deep interest in the natural world, especially plants and flowers which were linked to love and sentiment by a tradition of symbolism, was perhaps a nostalgic attempt to set right the dehumanizing effects of the Industrial age.

As the cult of naturalism blossomed, jewels came alive with endless curling tendrils of classical vines, tiny bobbled bunches of grapes and flowers that spoke an eloquent language of love; pansies meant remembrance, forget-me-nots spoke of true love, the ubiquitous ivy leaf stood for wedded bliss. Young ladies occupied themselves with studying the language of flowers, drawn from an eastern tradition and prettily set out in tiny illustrated books. Jewels dripping with symbols of nature and

*Smooth gilt metal locket, with a rich 'bloomed' gilt surface, decorated with a pale pink paste pansy, the symbol of remembrance; c.1860.*

*Gilt metal and paste-set 'REGARD' brooch, the lovers' knot motif formed by entwined twigs; c.1860.*

love made perfect expressions for excessive Victorian sentimentality. Popular daytime jewels were inexpensive, made of all sorts of cheap materials, so that metal alloys were set with enamels and pastes in order to accommodate the passing whims of fashion and love. In the mid-1840s the new electro-gilding techniques took the place of Pinchbeck, and in 1854 lower carat golds were introduced: 15, 12 or 9 carat which was often suitable for fashion jewels, although cheaper metal substitutes continued to be used throughout the century. There were endless hearts, love birds, love knots, jewels with compartments for a lock of hair or a portrait as well as the jewels that spelled out affectionate messages. One of the most popular trends in costume jewellery around the mid-century was for jewels that looked like twisted knotty boughs of trees, made from every kind of material imaginable, to suit all pockets. The knot or twist was a bold, fluid emblem that adapted to various Victorian themes: the love knot became a knot of twisted branches, the Algerian or Moorish turban-like device popular in the 1840s was later converted into the coiled and entwined serpent motif. Ivory, jet and coral were carved to look like thorny nests of branches, while there was an enormous range of gilt metal brooches of plump and bulbous knots, glossy and plain or engraved and fancy, bare or leafy with little sliced ends shaped like truncated boughs. Many of these were set with pastes, garnets, amethysts and they continued to be worn until the end of the century. A bangle might also be shaped like a branch, of metal or silver gilt textured like bark, the severed ends engraved with the ring markings of a tree.

As the relentless march of the wealthy Victorian industrial society wore on, jewellery was worn by a much broader cross-section of society: successful businessmen and industrialists moved to grand houses with porticoes and pillars, and dressed and bejewelled their wives accordingly. Etiquette was a vital aspect of 19th-century existence; it was important to wear the right clothes at the right time of day. Of course accessories had to match each outfit and different jewels were needed for different occasions, increasing the amount and variety of jewellery manufactured. The middle classes were also increasingly prosperous, and even some members of the working classes, the milliners, dressmakers and florists, could afford a few indulgences in the way of fashionable attire. Mass manufacture also meant that attractive-looking jewels could be produced at a price low enough to tempt the parlour-maid and the housekeeper or the butler trying to woo his beloved. By the mid-century, enormous quantities of jewellery were being made and worn. Keeping pace with radical social changes, fashions changed rapidly and the fickle Victorians developed an insatiable appetite for novelties; for amusing witty 'toys' and accessories, each style quickly discarded in favour of the newest whim. Manufacturers vied with one another to come up with the latest ideas for trinkets and constantly sought new materials, new techniques, new themes. Just about every conceivable material was explored and exploited and there was a much less clearly defined line between real and costume jewels, which in the 19th century were not necessarily made of totally valueless materials: the concepts behind jewellery made of, say, coral, tortoiseshell and ivory were those of the costume jewellery industry.

One of the great wonders of the Victorian era was the growth of travel. Well-to-do businessmen began to take their families on holidays abroad; the Grand Tour was no longer as rigorous and uncomfortable as previously, and young ladies finished their education by a chaperoned visit to Italy to see the classical sites. In 1855 Thomas Cook organized the first package tour from Leicester to Calais, so that people could visit the Paris Exposition. It cost 31 shillings. Jewellery, which may well have been classed as costume jewellery, made the perfect souvenir. Intricately carved ivory brooches, from Dieppe in France and from Switzerland, were carved with little hunting or country scenes showing stags with extravagant antlers in woodland clearings with feathery trees. Others were carved with hands holding flowers or baskets of fruit. Shimmering mother of pearl could be similarly worked. Cameos and mosaics of glass came from Rome, and coral, plump and polished or minutely carved (although not strictly speaking a costume jewellery material), was turned into pretty and fashionable ornaments that enjoyed enormous popularity in the 1850s and 1860s. British manufacturers were quick to adapt these ideas for their own inexpensive trinkets, and cheap imported cameos and mosaics were often set in gilt metal borders. At the height of the fashion for ivory jewels, around 1850, British manufacturers tried to create a rival fashion for ivory-coloured Parian or porcelain jewels moulded into similar intricate flower bouquets. Mrs Mary Brougham was the leading maker of Parian jewellery. Belleek, the creamy, lustrous porcelain, was also used for brooches but the fragility of both materials made them impractical and few examples survive.

Costume jewellery was able to capture the essence of fleeting, fast-moving fashions so that some of the strongest, most evocative of Victorian jewellery motifs are to be found on costume jewellery of the period: the hand, carved in ivory or jet, or modelled in silver or gilt metal, was an ancient device that took on peculiarly Victorian characteristics: elegantly tailored fingers, fancy gloves and jewelled cuffs, holding flowers or a visiting card. Its precise significance is unclear; it is a romantic emblem suggesting love, friendship, peace; or perhaps it echoes Queen Victoria's own idea of casting her children's hands as miniature sculptures. The recurrence of the hand in the decorative arts also suggests the contemporary interest in biology and natural life.

The serpent, another ancient motif from nature, wound its slithering way through the entire repertoire of 19th-century jewellery design from the early romantics to the High Victorian years of the 1880s and in all materials from the most precious to the most humble. Associated both with nature and with classical antiquity, the serpent with its tail in its mouth was the symbol of eternity, and was tamed into meek submissiveness in 19th-century jewellery so that benign round snakes' faces peered out from earrings, necklets and bracelets, made of jet, ivory, Pinchbeck, gilt metal, even human hair.

Jewellery made entirely out of hair marked the apogee of Victorian sentimentality. Jewellery of sentiment rather than fashion, hairwork followed the fate of most Victorian whims – it enjoyed a brief, intense

*Jet snake bracelets, smooth or faceted; c. 1880.*

popularity in the 1840s and 1850s, during which time it was contorted into every shape, size or possible permutation of pattern, and then it was utterly rejected and added to the pile of *passé* passions. The idea evolved from an 18th-century fashion for mourning jewels incorporating locks of human hair, often arranged as weeping willows. It was a short step for the actual jewel itself to be constructed from woven hair and turned into a love token. In 1838, hairwork was considered in the worst possible taste, but then suddenly, in the 1840s, became totally chic. Hair was miraculously woven, plaited and glued into place, and as with so many Victorian ideas, served as a showcase for the great skills of the craftsmen who produced watch chains, necklaces, bracelets, brooches, earrings. Thick plaited bracelets were fastened with ornate gold clasps; bow brooches were hung with tiny gold tassels and a heart; coiled serpent brooches were finished with a heart dangling from the serpent's mouth; earrings were wound with trails of gold filigree. The most intriguing pieces are those made in a kind of hollow openwork, like a springy net, which was suitable for long earrings, for brooches and for pendant crosses consisting of little round bubbles of woven hair.

Surprisingly perhaps, the French took eagerly to the idea of hair jewellery. At the end of the 18th century, when absurd hairstyles went

*Plaited and twisted hair bracelet with a barrel-shaped gold clasp textured, coloured, chased, encircled with pearls and bearing a Gothic-style inscription dated 1829.*

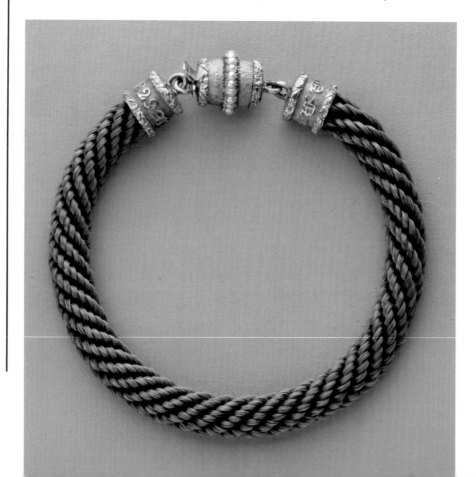

out of fashion, many Parisian barbers, hairdressers and perruquiers turned to the art of working hair. In the late 18th century, Sieur Delion of the Mouton d'Or, in the rue Saint Denis, specialized in hairwork, and even the Imperial jeweller, Nitot, is known to have created an extravagant hair bracelet set with gold, gems and pearls. Spectacular hairwork was shown at the Great Exhibition in 1851 by many reputable jewellers, and in particular by Lemonnier, a Paris jeweller whose achievements in '*fantaisies diverses en cheveux*' caused a great stir. Later in the 1850s, Charleux had the finest reputation in Paris, challenged in England by a firm called Forrer.

At the height of the fashion, magazines issued serious warnings against unscrupulous hairworkers, who carelessly mixed up the hair they had received or, worse still, substituted horsehair, which was easier to work. To avoid such disasters ladies were encouraged to arrange the hair themselves into little pictures, and complete kits were sold with glue, tools, background plaques. There was an associated short-lived fashion for jewels of horsehair, white, black or dyed red, tightly coiled and wound into discs, and, following current Victorian fashions, long chains, bracelets, earrings and brooches were all made of horsehair.

The Romantic Revival received a huge boost from Victoria's own tendency towards sentiment and especially from her great love for Prince Albert. A fairy-tale romance and a magnificently splendid royal wedding in 1840 fuelled the flames of sentimentality. Queen Victoria enjoyed giving jewels as gifts; she loved inscriptions; she loved compartments for portraits or locks of hair. A stickler for manners and etiquette, the Queen had always insisted on observing the strict Court rules for mourning, and when her own beloved Albert died in 1861 and her love turned to equal depths of morbid misery, she plunged into widowhood and a mourning from which she never fully emerged. It was bad news for many young widows and for manufacturers of frivolous jewels; but the Queen's sad loss was the great gain of the little Yorkshire seaside town of Whitby, home of the jet industry.

Jet was the favourite material for mourning jewels and the only material permitted for jewels worn during full mourning. The fashion for jet jewellery had gradually been growing since the 1850s, when Queen Victoria, mourning the death of a cousin, wore jet to an official banquet. Jet is basically fossilized driftwood, a kind of coal or anthracite, and the best quality is found near Whitby. Jet was used in prehistoric times, for Bronze Age ornaments, and there are several references to the material

by Roman writers. It seems that medieval monks at Whitby Abbey worked jet for crosses and rosaries, but then the trade declined during the reign of Elizabeth I to revive only in the 19th century. In 1832 there were two shops employing 25 people; in 1850 there were some 50 workshops in the town. Wellington's death in 1852 boosted business, and by 1872 under Victoria's lugubrious influence and an influx of holiday-makers Whitby boasted more than 200 prosperous shops, employing 1,500 men, women and children.

It was the Great Exhibition yet again that had done much to promote the jet industry, and in 1854 Isaac Greenbury of Baxtergate in Whitby, a leading manufacturer, received an order from the Queen of Bavaria for

*Elaborate Whitby jet necklace with floral motifs carved in high relief, hung on cable links and fringed with tapering polished drops; c.1870.*

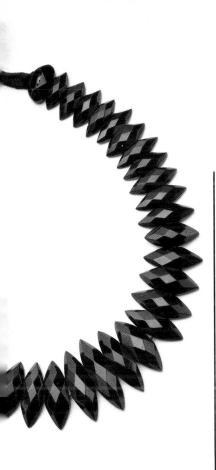

an immense chain, over four feet long. The Empress of France ordered two bracelets. As business prospered the town was a hive of jet-carving activity: people worked long hours, in appalling conditions, in attics, in sheds, to turn out jewels of smooth and shining blackness. At the height of the fashion, every shop window in the town was filled with the awesome black jewels, large and bulky or intricately carved, matt or gleaming. Young boys were trained in carving and polishing skills and also in drawing. There were specialists in each aspect: cameo engraving, flower carving, chain making. Tools for hand carving were precious and were handed down from father to son. Jet was drilled on a lathe, polished on a succession of wheels, the last of which was covered in hide to obtain the highest possible shine. Women were employed to thread and fasten and finish the pieces.

The range of jet jewels was enormous, encompassing every Victorian ornament: simple bar brooches, cameos, lockets, earrings, bracelets. There were wondrous chains with cable, rectangular or oval links, endless varieties of long beads, smooth, faceted or carefully carved with flowers. There were complicated necklaces draped with ornate fringes of motifs faceted and polished, and scalloped-edged. Huge brooches were shaped like entwined oak branches, like twists, spirals, knots, ribbons; heart-shaped pendants were carved with elaborate bouquets of flowers; lockets were plump and oval with carved monograms, cameos or crosses. The long earrings that were so popular in the 1870s could be immensely complicated, polished, faceted, carved and often set with cameos. Bracelets came in every shape and size, usually threaded on elastic, with shiny lozenges of various shapes, faceted, carved or textured with a criss-cross pattern like a pineapple, perhaps with a large central oval motif. Slinky snake bracelets were worn coiled around the wrist.

Jet could be combined with other materials: carved ivory hunting scenes or pale pink shell cameos were set into twisted jet frames; little ammonite fossils coiled tightly inside smooth jet borders, while jet also surrounded painted porcelain scenes or Derby marble mosaics composed of little coloured stone flowers set into black marble. The opera singer Adelina Patti proved that, worn in the right way, jet jewellery could look dramatic rather than mournful. Patti was famous for her magnificent jet beads worn row upon row, and at a time when glamorous females were beginning to exert great influence on fashions, she turned a social necessity into an exciting accessory.

Eventually jet substitutes enabled manufacturers to cope with the ever-growing demand which could not be satisfied by Whitby alone.

Whitby jet's main competitor was known as French jet, a black glass which shows reddish-purple tinges, especially at the edges when held to the light. In the best traditions of pure costume jewellery, French jet could outshine the shiniest and crispest of jet carvings. The glass took an extremely high polish and was cut into many facets to make the most of its reflective qualities. It was always backed with a black-coated steel. The ultra-feminine delicacy of French jet was perfect for earrings, necklaces and hair ornaments composed of flowerheads with lots of finely tapered and pointed overlapping petals. Necklaces of faceted discs were hung with gleaming clusters or with graduated flowers; shimmering long chains took the place of beads; buttons and jet sequins were sewn to dresses and long arrows were worn on the shoulder or in the hair.

Irish bog oak, another alternative to jet, was especially popular between 1850 and 1855. A dark brown fossilized wood with a dull finish, it came from the peat bogs of Ireland and was carved in fancy designs such as the hand holding a wreath, a favourite motif for mourning jewels. Many crosses were made in bog oak, and jewels with Irish motifs like shamrocks or harps, set perhaps with little Irish pearls, were amongst the curiosities admired at the Great Exhibition. The 19th-century obsession with the past ensured that Celtic medieval jewels unearthed in Britain were greeted with delight and reproduced in all materials to suit all pockets. Bog oak lent itself to effective, inexpensive but extremely well-made copies of penannular brooches like the 18th-century Hunterston brooch. The wood was carefully carved with Celtic motifs and fixed with a silver or silver gilt metal pin across its centre.

Many imitation jet jewels, especially cameos, were made from a composition material of ground wood powder, coloured and compressed into a mould. By the middle of the century the first plastics were being developed (see chapter 4), and in 1836 Charles Goodyear invented a method of hardening or vulcanizing rubber by heating it with sulphur. His rubber products were displayed at the Great Exhibition and it was not long before the process was adapted to create a very hard rubber called vulcanite or ebonite. Vulcanite jewellery was mass-produced in huge quantities, following the style of real jet, and was one of the most convincing and successful imitations. Intricate designs and cameos could be moulded with good definition and detail.

Overuse and inevitable boredom led Whitby jet into a decline and by the 1880s the frantic activity of the Yorkshire town was dwindling. Whitby could not compete with cheap substitutes and, added to this, in 1887, the year of her Golden Jubilee, Queen Victoria agreed to relax her

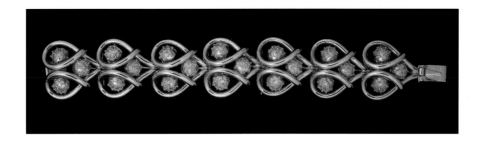

Rich gilt metal bracelet, the
heart-shaped scrolls enclosing spheres
decorated with filigree and
granulation; c.1860–70.

Three High Victorian gilt metal
bangles cleverly following the style
of real gold jewels, with 'bloomed'
gilt surfaces, enamel, pastes and onyx
beads enclosed in enamelled borders
of Greek key fret design. English,
c.1880.

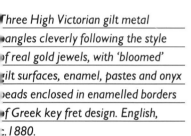

mourning rules so that ladies could return to lighter and brighter clothes and jewels.

Jewellery of the High Victorian period of the 1860s to 1880s was marked by an unrivalled variety of materials, influences, inventions. It was a time of great self-confidence and prosperity for the nation; there was little or nothing craftsmen or entrepreneurs could not conquer, and novelty after novelty emerged from the factories of London and Birmingham to thrill an ever-eager clientèle. Apart from jet, jewels on the whole were extremely bright and colourful. Gold, the traditional material of wealth, made to look rich, massive and creamy, became the most important element in jewellery design. So much so that during the 1850s, ladies sprinkled gold-dust in their hair. Real gold was given a rich colour known as a 'bloom', achieved by an acid bath (which dissolved the outer alloy leaving a film of pure gold) and gilt or gold-coloured metal successfully imitated this effect, with a similar patina. In contrast to the leafy flirtatious engraving of the early Victorian jewels, plain expanses of gold surfaces were admired, and adapted very successfully to hugely confident gilt metal bangles and lockets, rich, heavy and gently rounded, decorated with the very latest kind of ornamentation. Enamels or star-shaped settings embedded with turquoises and pearls were added for extra colour; mounds of metal covered with pavé-set turquoises or pearls, or decorated with enamels, appeared on the centres of lockets, bangles, pendants and brooches. Articulated fringes and flexible chains added movement, while granulation, wirework, filigree and Greek key patterns satisfied the new appetite for archaeological-style revivalism.

In Italy a serious study of newly discovered ancient gold jewels and metalwork had sparked off a far-reaching craze for jewels made in the ancient or archaeological manner, although on the whole the Victorians cared little about authenticity so long as their jewels had a whiff of ancient culture about them. This craze of the 1860s to 1880s encouraged the use of gold and inspired a range of costume jewellery made of a brightly coloured base metal appropriately called Abyssinian gold. A typical gilt metal bangle would be set with banded black onyx cabochon stones, surrounded by a black enamel key fret design. Another might be set with paste diamonds within black enamel borders and hung with a small oval pendant locket similarly decorated. Other gilt metal bangles were effectively left quite plain but bloomed, with an engraved buckle pattern or 'gipsy' set with large single paste-diamonds. The gipsy setting was a favourite Victorian technique in which the stone is deeply

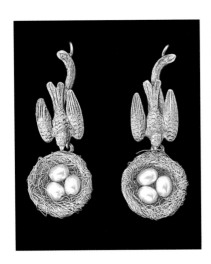

White and gilt metal novelty earrings designed as birds hovering over nests containing fake pearl eggs. English, c.1870.

embedded so that its surface is level with the surrounding metal. Another model was decorated with smooth rounded bosses all the way round, a design that demonstrates a brief and rarefied French craze of around 1860 for jewels that looked like manacles, shackles, handcuffs with screws or bolts. Metal lockets might also be found set with rivet heads or with pastes or decorated with enamels in the prevailing styles. Hair ornaments were particularly successful made in 'bloomed' metal or in Abyssinian gold and often incorporated crown-like, plain rounded spheres or the ever-popular knot motif, even a lingering simple ivy leaf with spiralling tendrils.

Earrings grabbed the limelight as the favourite items of jewellery during the 1870s. Made in convincing gilt metal as well as the popular 15-carat gold, they became the focus of attention and idiosyncratic design. Extraordinary novelties such as gilt metal birds' nests filled with fake pearl eggs were considered quite delightful, while classic earrings caught the archaeological revival mood, the rich gilt metal modelled in the shape of an amphora or torpedo and enriched with filigree and granulation.

The 1860s and 1870s were years of caprice and whimsy in costume jewellery. The Birmingham 'toy' industry was booming and there was a huge increase in the amount of jewellery worn, especially the less expensive decorative novelties of mass-produced gold, silver or base metal. The search for novel designs became more and more frenetic, and jewels ever more eccentric and amusing. During the 1860s insects, repulsively fascinating, crawled all over the very smartest ladies. Veils and hats were dotted with beetles, flies, moths, bluebottles, ticks, earwigs, lice. Insects were usually made of gilt metal, intricately engraved and enamelled or set with pastes, but they could also be made entirely from glass. Vauxhall glass was especially appropriate to this vogue and enjoyed a revival of popularity around the 1860s and 1870s.

Made in much the same way as French jet, Vauxhall glass was a particular type of mirrored or foiled glass or paste, faceted and backed with metal. It was not intended as imitation jewellery but as a decorative idea in its own right. It had been used for jewellery since the 18th century and its name derived from the early mirror glass manufactured at the Duke of Buckingham's glassworks at Vauxhall in London since the late 17th century. The term is almost certainly a misnomer, since there is no evidence to suggest that the glass jewels were made at Vauxhall. Little is known of the manufacture of Vauxhall glass, but in the mid-19th century it was produced as an exciting novelty by Birmingham

*Vauxhall glass brooch and earrings in the form of moths, their metal bodies realistically modelled. They bear the registration mark for 1869, the design patented by Elijah Atkins of Birmingham.*

*Group of Vauxhall glass jewels in a favourite Burgundy red colour, a flowerhead necklace, a diadem, and an insect brooch. English, c. 1860–70.*

makers such as Elijah Atkins of 48 Great Hampton Street. Atkins registered a design for a matching set of purple Vauxhall glass brooch and earrings in the shape of moths, with faceted wings and bodies of gilt metal engraved like the insect's body. Some years earlier Vauxhall glass had been worked into hair ornaments, earrings and brooches, usually made from little pointed petal-shaped sections, all faceted and glimmering, and assembled as clusters or flowerheads. Insects and flowers were the most usual designs, while favourite colours included a deep garnet red and a particularly magical grey-white shade, the colour of silvery mist.

Jewellery fads now came thick and fast; along with their hordes of bugs, ladies delighted in wearing jewels representing watering cans, flies on ladders, coal scuttles, birds' nests, boaters, buckets, trains, trowels, and for a while there was a rage for earrings shaped as blue and white willow pattern dinner plates, part of a widespread Japanese craze.

Around the 1880s and 1890s, sporting jewels were in vogue, jewels with horseshoes, riding crops, caps, bits and bridles, often incorporating an incongruously effusive ribbon bow or flower. These jewels, sometimes found in base metal, hinted at a provocative female perversity and the raciness of the naughty nineties.

Before the overwhelming Victorian clutter gave way to a pre-Edwardian elegance in the 1890s, just about every material was converted into a decorative fashionable ornament, and many areas of Victorian jewellery during this period might be regarded as decorative costume jewellery. From the 1860s to 1880s, there was a passion for *piqué* jewellery, tortoiseshell inlaid with gold and silver, worn as 'fun' jewellery at the time. At first it was hand-made, but by the 1880s, the height of its popularity, it was machine-made, the gold and silver inlay stamped out in sheets and pressed into the tortoiseshell when it was heated. A similar combination of colours and textures was achieved by Toledo work, the Spanish process of inlaying metal with gold and silver, a technique adopted by jewellery makers in the 1880s. Shakudo was the Japanese technique of mixed metal decoration, used originally for samurai swords and now applied to trinkets and jewels for the West. Bohemian garnets were tiny blood-red pyrope garnets, rose cut and pavé-set in base metal or pink-tinged low-carat gold, and piled up into huge clusters of stars, crescents or flowers, assembled into brooches, necklaces, earrings, lugubriously dark and dramatic against a pale Victorian skin. Venetian glass beads were highly prized during this period for their superb colour and technical perfection, along with jewels made from unusual minerals like Bluejohn or fluorspar found in Derbyshire.

One of the most interesting phenomena of Victorian costume jewellery is the appearance of aluminium. Aluminium jewellery is rare today but when it is found it is always immaculately made in stunning High Victorian style. In the 1860s aluminium was still a rare metal which aroused interest and curiosity and was wrought into jewellery shown at the Paris Exhibition in 1867. The metal had been discovered in 1827 but it was not until the mid-century that a way of processing it was developed. It was used principally by French jewellers very much as a curiosity to attract attention at international exhibitions. It was light and bright, could be engraved or stamped to produce the desired effect of bulbous and boasting knots, swirls, entwined branches, often completed by a quatrefoil leaf motif. It combined very well with the fashionable overlay of pink gold, widely used in silver jewellery in the 1880s.

*Group of* piqué *jewellery showing both classical and romantic motifs.* Piqué *was possibly regarded as costume or secondary jewellery at the time; c.1860–80.*

Portrait photograph of the Hon. Elaine Guest by Bassano, 1898. Her elegant toilette includes large paste buttons, a chatelaine, a sequinned belt and long muff chain.

Aluminium perfectly suited the change of mood that took place in the 1880s and 1890s, when colourless jewels came back into fashion. There were several reasons for this change, including Victoria's relaxation of mourning regulations and the introduction of a new and beautiful Princess of Wales who took over as fashion leader. But most significant of all, lighting once again took a hand in the evolution of costume jewellery. Electric light was introduced for theatres and other social events in the 1880s with the result that the richness of Victorian jewellery began to look rather brash and tawdry. Diamonds, on the other hand, looked much better and, luckily, new deposits had been found in South Africa in 1867 so that they were now more plentiful. Women's silhouettes changed drastically, too, and clothes became narrower, shapelier, and fabrics lighter, more feminine and delicate, crying out for new jewellery. Princess Alexandra enjoyed wearing white and chose diamonds for her brooches shaped as stars or crescents and for her hair ornaments and chokers, inspiring a new era of paste costume jewellery.

Group of jewels in mixed non-precious metals: the bracelet (top) and brooch of architectural Gothic inspiration, made of aluminium and gilt metal by Charles Henry Villemon of Paris, c.1860; the central bracelet in the Renaissance revival manner, in cast iron with gold decoration and a Limoges enamel plaque showing a girl in 17th-century costume, possibly made by Tissot for Boucheron. French, c.1870.

*Silver-set floral spray brooch, in the French naturalistic manner, set with pastes brilliant-cut like diamonds, and hung with articulated drops à pampilles to look like trickling dew drops. French, c.1850.*

Imitative diamond paste had not been entirely neglected in the 19th century. In France, the pleasure-loving Second Empire, dominated by the beauty and luxury of Empress Eugénie, adored diamond jewellery, especially the kind of wondrous botanical creations that aimed at copying nature as exactly as possible. Diamond jewels, massive sprays of realistic flowers, with branches or stems mounted on springs or 'tremblers', became wobbling wonders of intrinsic wealth and encouraged a species of paste copies, sadly of uninspired design. The most common type of 19th-century paste brooch in the naturalistic mood was designed as a spray of flowers and leaves, with the paste gems set in deep 18th-century-style silver mounts and hung with dripping ripples of pastes, intended to look like dew drops in a style copied from the real jewels that became known as *'en pampilles'*.

The Empress Eugénie also loved precious pearls and it was during the 19th century that the French refined and perfected the art of making artificial pearls. The manufacture of fake pearls had been initiated in France by a man called Jacquin (see Symbols of Power, above), who set up his business just outside Paris in 1686. The art was evidently passed down from generation to generation, for a descendant of Jacquin called Truchy was mentioned in the reports of the 1844 and 1849 Exhibitions. From 1834, the firm of Constant-Valès and later that of Topart were responsible for bringing the art of imitation pearls to the current height of perfection. They were considered the best in the world. At first, these French imitation pearls were made by injecting pearl essence inside glass beads, adding a further coating of wax to the outside to improve the colour and lustre. After 1834, when the luminous, translucent opaline glass was developed, manufacturers were able to dispense with the wax coating. The use of opaline glass beads introduced a clever way of imitating pink pearls: a coral bead was enclosed in the glass, producing a lustrous soft pink 'pearl'.

So convincing were these French fake pearls in the mid-19th century, that when the Empress Eugénie proudly wore a magnificent deep collar, recreated by Bapst, the Crown Jewellers, using the diamonds from the Crown Jewels, no one could have guessed that the spectacular 73 drop-shaped pearls that hung in the diamond trellis-work were in fact all fabulous fakes.

# *Three*

# &DWARDIAN ELEGANCE TO THE SHOCK OF CHANEL

The new century opened with passion and optimism in the arts, and the world of fashion rustled into the modern age with a new and intense femininity. The lady of fashion now had a slender and sinuous outline, swathed in hazy gauze, drifts of whitest lace, whispering silks of oyster, olive, lavender or grey, hand-sewn, hand-embroidered or shimmering with beads, sequins or jet to catch and reflect the new 20th-century light of hope and prosperity.

The new 'S' shape accentuated the natural curves of the woman, her bust thrown forwards, hips tilted backwards. Hats were huge, voluptuous and feathered so that heads could turn only very slowly and gracefully. Skirts were still long, shoes were tight, waists boned and corseted, with the overall result that the lady of fashion was quite helpless; she could not dress without her lady's maid nor move easily without some assistance from a gentleman. Since the 1890s important steps had been taken towards the emancipation of women, but this Edwardian womanhood still exuded an untouchable, submissive femininity.

Conventional jewels had changed significantly from the heavy gold and coloured showiness of the High Victorian years to a new lacy delicacy echoing the image of fragility that still hovered around the most fashionable ladies. Diamonds dominated design but they were arranged in very light, intricate settings of a new fineness made possible by the use of platinum during the first decade of the century. The finest platinum and diamond jewels were created after 1910. A great change had come over diamond jewels, reviving their popularity and so increasing the demand for copies.

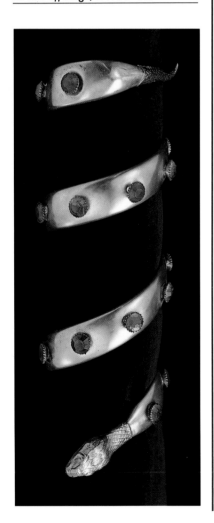

The look of diamonds had benefited from new cutting and setting techniques, from increased supplies in South Africa, and from experiments with platinum. Freed at last from their rather heavy second-hand 18th-century image, diamonds began to look pretty, classical, feminine and easy to wear. As a profusion of diamonds came back into fashion with a vengeance, so interest in charming, well-made paste substitutes stirred again.

There were jewel-laden leaders of the new femininity all around: from the *demi-monde* of Paris, the famous ladies known as the '*Grandes Horizontales*'; the impulsive and eccentric Sarah Bernhardt, whose artistic jewels on or off stage constantly made the headlines; to the regal English beauty of Princess Alexandra, whose bodice was encrusted with diamond stars and crescents and draped with ropes of pearls, sheer delight for jewellery manufacturers and fashion followers alike.

Another very important element affected the popularity of costume and imitation jewellery around the turn of the century; this was the cult of the famous *femme fatale*, the actresses and music hall artists, the celebrities and *demi-mondaines* for whom valuable and lavish jewels were essential barometers of success and security. These famous courtesans occupied an important position in society at that time, and to prove this they always piled on their jewels for public appearances and for the photographs eagerly seized on by their fans. The gems were much talked about and the subject of fierce battles based on jealousy. One story tells of a battle between La Belle Otero and Liane de Pougy who heard that Otero was intending to dine at Maxim's that evening wearing every jewel she owned to impress and annoy her rival. At Maxim's, Liane de Pougy waited patiently as Caroline Otero achieved her sparkling effect, then she made her own entrance, dressed very simply in white with no embellishment, not a jewel in sight; behind her came her maid staggering under the weight of the overflowing jewel casket she was carrying.

If real jewels were out of reach for ordinary mortals, the influence of these fashion leaders and notorious celebrities was enormous. They cast a spell over fashions in clothes, hairstyles, jewellery, perhaps more than is generally realized. Their influence was particularly strong at this time when increased communication, photography, travel, the accessibility of theatre and music hall and the famous art of the advertising poster could spread these images of womanhood. Jewels became part of the personalities of the fashion leaders and also a means through which their admirers could imitate their glory; but they also began to be regarded as

decorative ornaments, regardless of intrinsic value. It was the overall impression that counted, and as jewels became a way of selling dreams, Edwardian elegance also introduced the start of the great 20th-century phenomenon of costume jewellery.

Sarah Bernhardt exerted great power over her audiences and devoted fans around the world. Her obsessional preoccupation with detail extended to her stage costume and in particular her lavish stage jewellery. Her adornments were elaborate, bizarre, exotic, often covering her from head to toe, so that she glistened with Byzantine or Egyptian glory that sent her fans into raptures. Her jewels, on or off stage, were endlessly talked or written about. Sarah was besotted with jewels as expressions of her forceful individuality. She even turned a pet chameleon into a live jewel, fastening it to a gold chain and pinning it on her shoulder. At the other end of the scale, she was patroness and inspiration to the greatest artists and jewellers of the Art Nouveau period. Cheap copies of her jewels were very popular accessories of the day. These metal and paste pieces, possibly with some enamel, were probably made by the Maison Gripoix (who later made Chanel's jewels) and were sold in fashionable boutiques in Paris. The firm Bijoux Bardach, in the rue Ambroise, also made some of her stage jewellery and possibly some of the popular copies.

For her important stage jewels and some of her most extravagant personal jewellery Bernhardt searched out and commissioned the best artists of the day, notably René Lalique who designed enormous and fantastic jewels for her roles in *Iseyl*, *Gismonde* and *Théodora* in 1894. Bernhardt was an accomplished sculptress and artist herself and had adventurous taste, and her flair and extrovert personality were formative influences on Lalique's unrivalled talent. Lalique overturned traditions and transformed inexpensive materials into great works of art, introducing a new chapter to the history of jewellery design. It is significant that several important 20th-century jewellers who began by working with costume jewellery used its fantasy and freedom to unleash their imagination and break down the usual boundaries.

Mass production had both changed the manufacture of jewels and created a new, wealthy class to wear them, while at the start of the century, women were taking some important steps towards financial independence in occupations other than actress or courtesan. Several of the leading couturiers of the day, Lucile, Jeanne Lanvin, Callot Soeurs, were women. Mass-produced jewels were available to the parlour-maid, to the milliner's assistant and the florist as well as to the daughters and

*Silver and paste-set shoe buckles in the form of owls' heads, piercing eyes set with paste cabochon sapphires. The owl was a favourite late 19th- and early 20th-century motif; c.1880–1900.*

wives of tradesmen and industrialists. If the cheap jewels had originally, in the 1880s and 1890s, had an overly sentimental style of their own, in a kind of upstairs downstairs syndrome, by the turn of the century they were beginning to look like the grand jewels of aristocrats, only made in base metal or silver and paste.

As the gem-set pendants, the stars, crescents, arrows, bows began to be more and more whimsical and worn in ever greater profusion, few could afford so many real diamonds, and since it was the total look that mattered, a fine paste version would do just as well. Besides, the best were well-made jewels, still quite expensive and sold at elegant shops such as Asprey. Certainly these were luxury items, hand-finished, hand-set and beautifully made. And as designs for diamond jewels bloomed again, and fashion flowered, so the trade in good paste revived on both sides of the Channel. For the most part, however, paste costume jewellery was limited to the imitative type. 'French' paste was still considered the finest, for its immaculate settings and convincing sparkle; whether or not the actual glass paste came from France is debatable.

By this time Daniel Swarovski (1862–1956), born in Georgenthal, Bohemia, the centre of the glass industry, had left his native country and set up a company manufacturing paste stones in the Tyrol. Swarovski had trained in his father's glass-cutting factory and soon realized that the manual cutting of glass was inadequate to meet the growing demands of the market. He began devising methods of turning this handicraft into an automatic process. In 1883 he visited the 'First Electrical Exhibition' in Vienna. Not only was he fascinated by all the new ideas and inventions, but he foresaw the great potential in this new source of energy. In 1892, Daniel Swarovski applied for a patent on his first invention, a machine for cutting glass gemstones with perfect precision. This innovation gave him an immediate and important advantage over companies using traditional methods. It was at this time that Swarovski looked for a suitable new location, away from prying competitive eyes, where he could develop and expand his project. He found what he was looking for in the mountains of the Tyrol and on 1 October 1895 he and his family moved from Bohemia to the tiny village of Wattens. Swarovski leased an empty factory with a small water power plant, providing the new source of energy which was to be the most important element in his plans for mechanization.

Starting with the energy supplied by the Wattens mountain brook, and moving on later to faster flowing water, Swarovski was able to develop the

*Classical, sentimental jewel of silver gilt and paste, the love birds hovering above Cupid's quiver of arrows, complemented by sweet Edwardian flowers and ribbon bows. Probably French, c.1910.*

precision grinding and polishing of hundreds of paste stones in one process, the technique that has dominated 20th-century paste production.

By the turn of the century, the 'Tyrolean-cut stones' became known for their quality and were in great demand in the jewellery centres of France, England and America. In 1900, the factory and additional land was bought by Swarovski, whose business was thriving and who now employed 100 workers. Electric lighting was installed in the workshops to aid efficiency and productivity. Perhaps another secret of the company's enormous and enduring success has been the Swarovskis' concern with the overall welfare of their employees.

As imitation diamond jewels became increasingly fashionable in the early years of the century, the Swarovski company opened a larger, modern factory in 1906; a water power station, higher up in the valley was in operation at the end of 1907. Up to that time, the glass for the stones had been processed from Bohemian-made raw glass. In 1908, ever keen to perfect his product and to become self-sufficient, Daniel Swarovski, now assisted by his three sons, began to experiment with glass manufacturing. The success of the experiments led to the setting up of a laboratory and glass works in 1911. They were now able to refine the crystal-glass to a perfect brilliance. The Swarovskis could also produce fine coloured glass, and now had at their disposal the resources to expand into a large-scale industry, which remains today one of the most important enterprises in Austria.

*Edwardian silver shoe buckles, set with white and coloured pastes; c.1900.*

Group of favourite Edwardian silver and diamond paste jewels, imitating real jewels: a half hoop bangle (top) and ring (centre), a swallow on the wing (right) and a winged aigrette with quivering stones set on knife-wires, intended to be worn in the hair with a tuft of feathers. c.1890–1910.

There were several other glass-paste manufacturers in or around Bohemia, which also had its own jewellery industry and was known for its stone cutting. The centre was in Gablonz, where glass pearls and stones were made for use by French manufacturers of cheap jewellery known often as 'articles de Bohème'. In Bavaria, the industry in paste started in Kaufbeuren and Schwäbish Gmund, which then gave up its glass-making for costume jewellery manufacture, importing paste from Austria. England, too, produced fine lead crystal, but the best quality paste still came from Bohemia. In France, the firm of E. Dalloz, situated outside Paris, specialized in paste manufacture and cutting and in about 1885 began a process of mechanical cutting using a tool called a 'baton mécanique'. Then in about 1895 Dalloz, together with another manufacturer called Grandclément, found a way of grouping a number of these batons together to make a tool called a 'porte pierres' which improved and refined mechanical cutting. These methods, pioneered by Swarovski in the Tyrol and by Dalloz in France, were followed in Paris by firms such as Martin, Low and Taussig. This meant that pastes of all shapes and sizes were available, as they had been in the 18th century, and jewels could now be entirely covered in paste gems to produce a very expensive, sumptuous look that corresponded to the prevailing 'garland' or Edwardian style of real jewellery.

The French were still considered to have the last word in taste and specialist skills in jewellery manufacture, and since the time of Stras, Parisian paste jewellery had a special cachet. One of the leading wholesalers of paste jewellery in London was known as the Parisian Diamond Company, located at 85 New Bond Street. There was little distinction at this time between real and fashion jewels, and paste ornaments were sold alongside the real thing at fine jewellers' shops. Some advertisements for paste jewels even omitted to mention the fact that the jewels they promoted were set with fake stones. In the late 19th and early 20th centuries, Faulkner diamonds were very popular and effective and were described in the *Illustrated London News* of 11 December 1897 as 'one of the successes of a successful generation'. While advertisements simply labelled them Faulkner diamonds, the editorial feature explained, 'Effect is a powerful factor nowadays and as all incomes do not run to gems of the very first water, we must needs gratify our natural instinct for glittering gauds with that which comes within reach.' Faulkner paste diamonds were considered readily accessible and extremely attractive in a wide range of varied designs and forms from a hatpin to a tiara. The successful company competed with

the Parisian Diamond Company from its base at 98 The Quadrant, Regent Street.

In 1901, on the death of Queen Victoria, the Parisian Diamond Company advertised mourning jewels. The etiquette of mourning was a serious business, with fixed rules and regulations regarding both clothes and jewellery. At first only jet and a plain wedding band might be worn but when the time came for half-mourning all-white jewels were considered appropriate, as white is a mourning colour. The Parisian Diamond Company suggested diamonds and pearls, with love knots and iris motifs, and they carried an equivalent range of good paste jewels in the same designs for those who wished to show their respects to the late Queen but preferred not to pay the price of diamonds and pearls. The fashion-conscious Queen Alexandra was in mourning at the time of her coronation in 1902, and surely she was glad of the all-white rule which allowed her to wear copious diamonds and pearls.

The style that became known as the Edwardian or 'garland' style began to emerge during the 1890s. It was at its strongest from 1905 to 1915, and provided an ideal vehicle for the use of fine paste and fake pearls. In real diamonds and pearls, the Edwardian or garland-style jewels are amongst the finest ever produced. Designs were made up of light and lacy openwork arrangements of laurel wreaths or garlands, ribbon bows and tidy flower baskets, of drapes and swags, designs of studied casualness, jewels of genteel femininity. Pre-Revolutionary 18th-century France was a very definite inspiration with its liking for pastoral motifs. Pendants were especially popular, sometimes worn on long chains or *sautoirs* of seed pearls or pearls and diamonds. There was a fashion for shorter necklaces known as négligé pendants, which were usually composed of a central motif from which hung two drops of unequal length. Once again, bow motifs were wildly fashionable, imitating as closely as possible the silk, lace or gauze ribbons that ornamented dresses. Tassels were also transformed from dress trimmings into jewels hung with fringes of diamonds, pastes or pearls. There was a vogue for handkerchief pendants, shaped as undulating fringed triangles, like a delicate embroidered handkerchief held at its centre. Earrings were usually long, slender and elegant, incorporating bows or garlands and simple flowerheads.

The aim was to make the diamond or paste jewels as white and light as possible. The new shapes and new progress in cutting and setting of diamonds extended the range of delicate patterns, and now diamonds

Group of society ladies gathered at a race meeting, the 'Grand Prix' at Trouville, August 1910.

Sumptuous Edwardian paste earrings,
set in silver; c.1905–10.

Group of Edwardian paste jewels
showing favourite motifs: the flower
basket, hearts, bows; the central
pendant imitates pink topazes; the
pendant (right) is a suffragette jewel
incorporating the colours of the
women's movement; c. 1905–15.

were set in platinum, the hardest, most intractable of metals that perfectly
complemented and intensified the brilliance of the stone. Platinum
could be wrought into the finest, laciest and slimmest of settings and
this suited the tendency for making jewels resemble the lacy gauze and
hand-worked fabrics of the Edwardian lady. A particularly charming
type of Edwardian jewel was made to look just like *petit-point* embroidery,
the pierced platinum openwork filled in with diamond 'stitches'. The
use of platinum and the possibilities it offered for fine knife-wire designs
or hand-pierced honeycomb patterns, for example, shaped the look of
Edwardian diamonds and influenced the look of paste.

Paste was usually set in silver, or possibly silver-coloured metal, to
imitate the platinum, and while the stones could equal or outdo the
fancy cutting and patterns of diamonds, the silver could not rival the slim

precision of platinum. So Edwardian paste jewels are slightly chunkier than the real pieces, which gives them a distinct charm of their own, and often makes them more appealing today. Many of the finest examples of Edwardian paste were in fact made as 'travelling' or holiday jewels when owners of fine jewels commissioned copies to be made in good paste to take the place of the real gems in case of robbery. Even firms like Cartier were commissioned to copy their creations in paste. Expensive jewels were very often kept in the bank, in the safe deposit, or perhaps even sold and replaced by a wife or mistress to hoodwink the generous giver of the presents. There were many manufacturers in Paris who specialized in paste jewels, gems or pearls, although whether or not they actually produced the stones is not always absolutely clear. The best known included Besson, Galand and Mme Navez, whose work looked just like the real thing with pastes in the fashionably soft colours of aquamarine, pink or cinnamon topaz. Alexandre Royé specialized in paste diamonds. The report of the Jury of the 1900 Exposition Universelle recorded a noticeable 'artistic trend' in the manufacture of imitation jewellery, although the report does not include illustrations. It is no wonder that as customers realized the success and skill of the fake jewels they were more and more tempted to supplement their accessories with paste, especially as it was the fashion to wear lots of jewels for formal occasions.

Amongst the prettiest examples found today are chokers and delicate pendants, earrings and bracelets that convincingly copied the gem-set jewels of Bond Street and the rue de la Paix. Small paste plaques designed with classical swags and drapes and laurel leaves were fixed to black velvet chokers, and bracelets looked like sparkling daisy chains.

*Cloak clasp of wood carved as fierce dogs' heads. Bavarian, c.1900.*

*Paste and enamel lizard brooch, capturing the quick darting movements of the creature; a silver-coloured metal centipede brooch. Continental, c.1900–1910.*

Earrings looked long and gently curvaceous with complex openwork or floral patterns. The fashion for very long necklaces or *sautoirs* set with diamonds at intervals inspired a range of long chains of silver, base metal or even black lacquered 'gunmetal', the pastes rimmed in circles of metal in a style known as spectacle setting. A particularly popular inexpensive daytime fashion was for bright cornflower blue paste stones clustered in a simple flower arrangement around a cut steel centre, a pleasing colour combination that worked well as a motif for drop earrings or as a ring or bracelet. Flowers were especially popular for less formal or less expensive jewellery. The flowers usually appeared as simple, classical flowerheads, with slim, elegant leaves poised in a formal arrangement. The jewels are generally of very fine quality, often set in silver and sometimes even in gold and made in the same way as the original article.

The Edwardians were fond of ingenious personal accessories and also of amusing, witty novelty jewels of a more frivolous nature. Paste was highly appropriate for this kind of whimsical jewel not intended to last very long in a lady's favour. There was a wide choice of lucky charms, such as the kidney bean or little disc intended to be flicked and spun so that it spelt out a paste-set message, and lots of animals such as pigs, monkeys and dogs. Probably most characteristic of Edwardian whimsy were little brooches designed as pairs of monkeys, pavé-set with pastes, one sitting on a branch and clinging to the hand of another dangling from a chain. Dogs and pigs were also paste-set or perhaps sculpted in silver and set with marcasite.

Along with diamonds and pearls, semi-precious stones in soft, pale colours were in fashion to tone with the favourite colours of the period: lilac, grey and oyster. The favourite stones were the pale green peridots preferred by Edward VII, and pale amethysts, since purple was Queen Alexandra's favourite colour. These delicate and shy-coloured stones were prettily echoed by pastes of many colours. However, despite the current fad for pale tones, the potential of paste proved irresistible for jewellers, who added deeply coloured imitations of rubies and emeralds to lavish garland-style jewels. More pastel colour was added to jewels by enamels, which had much improved around the turn of the century. Pale cornflower blue, lemon, lilac in wavy and silken patterns of the *guilloché* technique (the underlying metal was mechanically engraved) complemented much diamond and some superior paste jewellery.

Jet remained very much in fashion and made the perfect glittering complement to the shades of purple and grey worn for evening wear. Now that the techniques for producing fine French or glass jet (see

*Silver and paste-set lizard brooch;
the green stripe along its back
convincingly imitates the bright green,
demantoid garnets so popular in real,
diamond-set lizard jewels of the
period; c.1890–1900.*

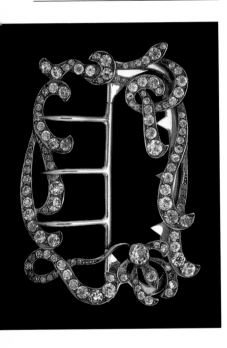

chapter 2) had been perfected, the jewels looked shinier and more delicate than ever, and much more sophisticated than Victorian equivalents. Real jet was still worn, preferably cut and polished to gleam and flatter, but jet in general was more popular for beads, for hair ornaments and combs rather than lockets and brooches. Sometimes little shiny beads of faceted jet provided an alternative to pearls for chokers, or they were threaded intricately into long strands and woven to form long ropes or *sautoirs* that looked like shimmering strands of black silk. Jet beads were sewn on dresses, on handbags, on gloves and on hair ornaments, for hair combs were essential to anchor the long wavy hair piled up into huge soft and rounded chignons. Tortoiseshell was the conventional material for haircombs, but in the early years of the 20th century it was gradually replaced by the new plastics, particularly celluloid which could look like cloudy mottled tortoiseshell or like ivory; both could be intricately carved, and perhaps the imitation ivory would be decorated with jet beads.

The Edwardian style was tinged with an aristocratic air of disciplined luxury and elegance that has often been revived, especially for costume jewels, at various times during the 20th century. The late 1950s saw a revival and more recently this style has re-emerged through the influence of Princess Diana, who shares Princess Alexandra's knack of wearing her jewels with a jaunty air of fashion that has caught the public imagination. Despite its restraint, Edwardian diamond and paste jewellery made a major step in linking jewellery and fashion and in guiding jewel design towards a graciousness and elegance and occasional dashing playfulness that set the scene for 20th-century style.

To counteract the restrained refinement of the Edwardian style, Art Nouveau introduced an emotive, melancholy and sensuous tone to jewellery design. A new decorative style which began in the 1880s and reached its pinnacle in 1900, Art Nouveau was short-lived but intense, striving self-consciously to be new and shocking, although its roots were very firmly in the past and in 19th-century attitudes. It faded from popularity largely through overuse around 1910. It was an international art movement that was at its purest in France, and aimed at unifying all the arts and uplifting objects in everyday use. Its principal characteristics include the use of a meandering, sinuous line, melancholy plant motifs and the sensual female figure, usually naked or draped in diaphanous garments, with wildly flowing hair. Weary plant and leaf motifs reflected the nostalgia and sadness of the dying century, yet the surging sense of

Below right: Gilt bronze and matt
enamel peacock feather buckle made
by Piel Frères, Paris 1900. The 'eye' is
set with a shaped blue paste stone,
the quality of the enamelling is
superb. A very famous high-fashion
jewel of its time, much praised for its
superb concept and craftsmanship
and artistry in humble, affordable
materials.

Below: Silver gilt and paste buckle
designed in fluid Art Nouveau style as
a peacock feather, the most evocative
symbol of the Art Nouveau
movement. French c. 1900–10.

movement and growth in Art Nouveau design looked forward to new ideas and new artistic freedom. The style was at its most intense when applied to jewellery loaded with visual allusions to femininity and fertility, to metamorphosis and to the earthy, ruthless beauty of nature. One of the main aspects of Art Nouveau jewellery was the inventive use of humble materials, like horn, glass, enamels, and the adaptation of 'artistic' and modern motifs, such as the female face with flowing hair or the peacock feather, the quintessential Art Nouveau emblem, to inexpensive jewels accessible to a wide audience.

In conventionally smart circles, particularly in England, Art Nouveau, with its dead flowers and naked passionate females, was considered highly decadent and in bad taste and not for the adornment of young ladies, however liberated they claimed to be. In Paris, however, around 1900, the time of the great International Exhibition, it was all the rage, but in its strongest form admired only by the *avant-garde*; in diluted and tamed versions it appealed to chic high-fashion followers, to the pert Parisienne so often referred to in fashion magazines and whose statue dominated the entrance to the Exhibition. Art Nouveau and the way it affected jewellery design did, however, reinforce attitudes to jewels as purely decorative and high-fashion ornaments to flatter beauty or express art, and stressed the idea that materials were of secondary importance, provided they were right for the theme of the jewel.

The Parisian industry in '*bijouterie imitation*' (literally fake jewellery) made the most of the craze for Art Nouveau and the new use of inexpensive materials. There were several firms in Paris who specialized in popular art or fashion jewels, and their creations were highly praised

in contemporary art journals by critics who noted the high quality of design, manufacture and artistic worth, combined with their low cost which made 'art' available to the general public. *La Maison Moderne* was an *avant-garde* boutique specializing in innovative, exciting designs in all areas of the decorative arts, especially in jewellery. A famous poster for the gallery shows a fashionable lady adorned with jewels designed in a feverishly flowing Art Nouveau style, of abstract rather than figurative design. By commissioning the best of modern designers, *La Maison Moderne* did a great deal to promote high-fashion jewels of the moment.

The best-known manufacturer of Art Nouveau costume jewels was Piel Frères, situated at 31 rue Meslay in Paris. This was a traditional family jeweller who excelled in cheap interpretations of strong Art Nouveau themes. Perhaps the most successful and best-remembered piece of jewellery is a large peacock-feather buckle of gilt metal, with the deepest, most luxuriant colours of matt blue-green enamel swept around a deep blue paste 'eye', in a shape full of movement that conveys all the silky opulence of the real feather, symbol of pride and the magnificence of nature. Alexandre Piel was at the head of the firm and worked with the sculptor Gabriel Stalin as artistic director. They took the business of creating fashion jewels very seriously, achieving the best possible effect at the lower end of the market. The quality of manufacture is superb; the enamelling in deep colours with a matt-finish acid-engraved surface was especially difficult to achieve on copper or silver.

Piel Frères was among the first to substitute the popular sculpted ivory with the new plastic called celluloid (see chapter 4), and used copper and silver, which was usually gilt, to imitate gold. Belt buckles were a speciality, and the results were stunning, as the jewels could be large and confident expressions of the latest whims of fashion. Piel Frères incorporated into jewels, brooches and belt buckles the medieval characters of popular plays and operas at the time. A silver gilt belt buckle depicting Mélisande with her wedding ring in a tangled frame of Art Nouveau flowers and plants was made while Debussy's opera *Pelléas et Mélisande* was playing in Paris in 1902.

Other firms such as Rouzé and Mascaraud, President of the Chambre Syndicale de la Bijouterie Imitation, specialized in high-fashion gilt copper or silver jewels. The jewels were partly machine-made, usually stamped out of metal, but hand-finished for fine detailing and of high quality and fanciful conception: a true beginning to the fantasy jewels of the 20th century. Buckles and buttons, closely linked to clothes, were the most usual forms of these inexpensive accessories, and one of the most

popular motifs was the female face or profile, the pert Parisian coquette, chic and smart but very slightly daring. At the great Exposition Universelle in Paris in 1900, several firms received lavish praise for their low-priced fashion jewels. Victor Prat worked in steel and filigree, and the Maison Savard created much Art Nouveau jewellery in *or doublé* (rolled gold), making fashionable 'medal' jewels, buttons, brooches, pendants, buckles. Medal jewels executed in gilt metals and mass-produced from a fine original engraving offered cheap but attractive Art Nouveau images and some of the best can still be found with the trademark FIX or FIXE.

With the Edwardian years came the great age of the pearl; never have pearls been so highly prized as during this period, from about 1900 to 1914, before the War and before the Japanese cultured pearls flooded the market in the 1920s and the price of real pearls plummeted. Pearls achieved a noble status; they increased in value far more than diamonds during the equivalent period, and became the outward signs of power, position, wealth and social standing. Gabrielle Chanel was never to forget the great pearls of the famous socialites and aristocrats who ruled over fashion in her youth.

Ladies treasured them, lied for them, sued for them. The Duchess of Sermoneta, an English noble lady married to an Italian, invested all her spare cash in pearls and very carefully bequeathed part of one necklace kept in a bank in London to her niece who was later involved in a court case with Italian executors as she tried to claim these pearls as her rightful legacy. The original necklace in question had consisted of ten rows, the total number of pearls was 583 and the value was $150,000.

Ladies wore pearls like beads, row upon row upon row of huge pearls. A typical Edwardian lady might put on one simple necklace of large pearls, over this a collar of 23 rows of pearls with a diamond centrepiece, then a long *sautoir* of alternate pearls and diamonds and of course pearl earrings to complete the toilette.

At her Coronation, Alexandra wore seven huge rows of pearls, each 24 to 30 inches long, hanging below five large diamond chokers and a great corsage ornament which covered her entire bodice, and beneath this a splendid ornament of diamonds with large pear-shaped pearls.

In his *Book of the Pearl*, published in 1908, George Kunz said that for the wearer of jewels, pearls were 'an absolute necessity; indeed they are as essential and indispensable for the wealthy as are houses, horses and automobiles'.

*Coco Chanel photographed by Man Ray, c.1935, wearing rows of fake pearls and the famous pair of enamel and paste-set bangles designed by Verdura.*

*The Duchess of Marlborough wearing her fabulous pearls, including a deep choker necklace with diamond motifs; c.1908.*

*The impact of Chanel's Verdura bangles has lasted through the 20th century; a later plastic version made by Chanel, c.1960.*

The famous and beautiful actress Gaby Deslys, showered with gifts from admirers, owned a fashionable long pearl *sautoir* given to her by the King of Portugal. There is a story, probably embroidered by time, that tells of a lovers' tiff between the actress and the King while on board ship, when she tore the pearls from round her neck and threw them impetuously into the sea. Later the King in a moment of remorse sent her another rope of pearls which Gaby accepted graciously, without telling the King that the pearls at the bottom of the ocean were in fact imitations.

At the height of the fashion for pearls, very good imitations were being made and sold particularly in France by firms such as Técla, Suclier, Richelieu, and the best imitation pearls were known as Paris pearls. Imitation pearls had been made for centuries (see Symbols of Power, above) and have taken assorted ingenious forms, from the North American Indian pearl-coated balls of clay to pupils of fish eyes. In the early 20th century, however, it was more usual for glass or plastic beads to be covered with '*essence d'Orient*', an iridescent nacreous substance taken from fish scales. Until 1939 the French specialized in manufacturing this *essence d'Orient* or pearl essence. The fish scales are crushed to give out an organic chemical compound which was strained and purified and added to other substances including a lacquer that formed a paint. Between five or ten coats were applied by dipping or spraying the outside of solid glass beads, or sometimes hollow wax-filled beads. A firm called Canvet of Paris specialized in *perles métalliques* (pearls with a metallic finish), employing some 300 workers to cope with the demand. These false versions did a very good job of imitating the rows and rows of creamy white, pink or satin grey pearls that became the height of fashion with the rise in popularity of the deep pearl choker or dog collar.

Other kinds of imitation pearls were also on the market. Sometimes a protuberance from a mother-of-pearl shell would be cut off and polished to look like an imperfectly shaped pearl and could be so cleverly done that it would pass for the real thing. In Bohemia, and sometimes in Russia, a technique was used whereby a piece of mother-of-pearl shell would be cut so that a section of natural shell was left for the part that would be most visible and then the whole polished to give an overall pearlized effect. These were used in very inexpensive beads and jewellery.

Fake pearls by the yard were ideally suited to the dramatic opulence of the new eastern-inspired style 'Schéhérazade' introduced by the fashion designer Paul Poiret after the impact of the Ballet Russe in 1910 (see chapter 4). This extravagant style, based on swathes of colourful silks draped with pearls and plumed with feathers, was the curtain raiser to Art Deco fashion, but it was anathema to the young Gabrielle Chanel. Born in 1883 of humble peasant stock, she had grown up as an orphan in an austere convent from the age of 12. The austerity of her upbringing in the midst of the luxurious age of the Belle Époque must have contributed to her practical ideas for dressing women when, after seven years there, she began to make her way in the difficult world outside, searching constantly for success and acceptance and, ultimately, for the love and respectability of marriage that escaped her. The seeming luxury of her costume jewels served only as a complement to simplicity. Her famous fakes were parodies of the fabulous and valuable pearls of the aristocrats and courtesans, and were in a sense an expression of the bitterness and sadness that eventually consumed her. She was to say to Mme Gripoix, who made her costume jewellery: 'All those aristocrats stuck up their noses at me but I'll have them at my feet.' And she did.

She began her working life as a seamstress, moving on to become an unsuccessful music hall singer, all the while developing her own particular and highly idiosyncratic style of dressing. As her social life broadened she appeared at race meetings and polo matches (an important inspiration to her designs) in unusually severe clothes, open-necked jackets, with squared shoulders and a marked absence of frills, lace and feathers. Her simple low-crowned hats, worn low in a prediction of the 1920s cloche, were considered curious next to the huge ribboned and plumed concoctions of the day, perched high on the top of piled hair.

In 1910 she opened her first shop in Paris, selling hats in the rue Cambon, but it was not until the onset of World War I that from her shop in Deauville (where she had moved with her lover) she was able to put her ideas into practice and dress women as she herself dressed with practical simplicity, making clothes from knitted 'locker room' fabrics used for men's sports shirts. In 1914 Chanel made such material into sailor tops.

Her first Maison de Couture was opened in Biarritz in 1915. In 1916 she bought left-over fabric from Rodier, a machine-knitted material in a dull beige intended for underwear. In 1916 she started dressing her clients in jersey, which had to be cut with utter simplicity, like a shirtdress, with a low waist and shorter skirts, leaving the femininity underneath to shine through. Poiret called Chanel's contribution to fashion 'Poverty de luxe'.

*Double flower spray brooch in gilt metal, glass beads and pastes, with green and white painted leaves. Chanel, c. 1920–30.*

The look was perfect for the time and was to cause a sensation, as was Chanel's short haircut of 1917. In fact, although Chanel always claimed this innovation as her own, it was the dancer Caryathis, who had appeared at the ballet in 1913, her hair shorn in a Joan of Arc style, who influenced her friend and dance pupil Chanel. The new haircut that made headlines around the world seemed to signal the new era. As women were liberated from corsets and from hair pins, as they were encouraged to move naturally in loose easy fabrics, to dress with simplicity, so another great age of opulent extravagant and ultra-feminine costume jewellery was born.

Chanel had many love affairs and was courted amongst others by the famous and talented Art Deco designer Paul Iribe, her true love, and by the Duke of Westminster. She had the jewels she was given copied, and was herself a customer at Cartier where she always chose the richest of colours and most unusual combinations of gems. But she was not blinded by the cost of jewels, it was their ornamental value that mattered; and as she mixed more and more with high society, with famous actresses and socialites, she may have regarded expensive diamonds and pearls as the traditional currency of love affairs, another sign of women's dependency on men and an obstacle to their ultimate freedom. There were bitter memories of unattainable wealth and happiness. Also she was bored by the seriousness of real jewels and by the restrictions imposed on how and when they should be worn.

At about this time other couturiers had begun to introduce specially commissioned non-precious jewels to accompany their clothes. It is doubtful that Chanel was the first, but as with the cropped haircut she accepted the credit for 'inventing' costume jewellery and she was indeed a great popularist, the first to attract publicity and public attention both for her short hair and her fake jewels. Poiret had certainly commissioned costume jewellery and Madeleine Vionnet had made necklaces of green feathers and crystal around the same time; Lucien Lelong designed wooden bead necklaces and stylish Art Deco metal and plastic jewels; Jean Patou commissioned fashion jewels from Piel Frères, and Schiaparelli and several other couturiers sold famous glass jewels made by René Lalique.

What Chanel did instigate was an entirely new and brazen way of wearing fake jewels which were very obviously and proudly false. These couture jewels, fairly conventional in themselves, were to be worn during the day, with casual clothes. It was a shocking idea. In the late 1920s, Chanel added an incongruous note to her cardigans and casual

*Gilt metal and paste jewel by Chanel, showing a barbaric African influence; c.1920–30.*

*Group of chains of gilt metal and imitation pearls, by Chanel; the gilding is especially rich and satin-like; c.1920.*

sweaters: yards of fake pearls. She mixed the glamour of an evening toilette with the basic bold simplicity of her daywear. She advocated wearing jewellery on all occasions, at all times of day, even for the beach. In 1928 she launched a range of paste-diamond jewellery by Étienne de Beaumont, head of her jewellery design. Remembering the huge and enormously valuable pearls of the early 1900s, she created unashamedly and frankly fake pearls, worn row upon row in impossibly large sizes and colours.

Apart from the fabulous pearls of the Edwardian beauties, Chanel's jewellery was inspired by her early memories of military uniforms, with their gold brocades, chains and epaulettes, bandolier-style decorations. Later she was also greatly influenced by the sporty *style anglais* and by the uniforms of English footmen and servants of the Duke of Westminster. From 1926 to 1931 Chanel immersed herself in the English style: she loved English riding clothes and men's tailoring and introduced masculine-cut jackets for women, along with waistcoats and suits to wear to the races. She adopted the English love of sweaters and of casual understatement but she added to it masses of fake jewels that might have seemed more suitable with a ball gown at Court.

This note of jewelled luxury that gradually crept into Chanel's designs only served to accentuate the plain lines and colours of the clothes: she added gilt chains, jewels made with a baroque blend of coloured fake gems, gilt buttons like those of English footmen, jewels with a barbaric or Slavic look or a strong Byzantine flavour with festooned chains and huge medallions.

In 1932, just when everyone around the world had taken to Chanel's tongue-in-cheek style of *bijoux fantaisie*, when fake pearls were especially chic, even for those who had the real thing, Chanel surprised everyone by designing a range of real diamond jewels. The huge popularity of costume jewellery plus increased wealth taxes had adversely affected the jewellery trade, and the International Diamond Guild turned to Chanel to boost interest in real gems. She worked on the collection with Paul Iribe, who also designed jewels for Cartier. The jewels looked unconventional; they were presented on wax models and there were bracelets like very broad cuffs that could be taken apart and made into different pieces, necklaces that spread over the shoulder in a shower of stars, an exciting challenge to the jewellers of the rue de la Paix. There were no tiaras, instead slim crescents pinned invisibly in the hair. There was also an Egyptian-looking fringe of diamonds that reached to the eyebrows and ornaments of sunbursts and comets hanging

*Massive pearl and paste festooned necklace, heavy and baroque, with a huge deeply coloured paste gem, like a Maharajah's ruby; the pearls have a distinctive creamy lustre suggesting the early jewels of Chanel; c.1920.*

from long chains. Iribe had clearly drawn on the experience he had gained working in the movies in Hollywood. Chanel loved to shock, and at this time of financial crisis, just when her fake jewels had gained respectability, Chanel created a clever and temporary change in tempo by working in diamonds.

Now a celebrated personality, Chanel moved in élite echelons of Paris society, and made a point of employing some of her aristocratic friends as designers. The Russian Grand Duchess Marie did embroideries, while the Comte Étienne de Beaumont and the Italian Duc Fulco di Verdura were in charge of costume jewellery. There was another aspect to this plan: Chanel had the opportunity to see rare and exquisite jewels which she was able to translate into couture accessories. In the mid-1930s she concentrated on a rich combination of paste gems, usually *en cabochon*, with a Renaissance or Byzantine look. She used hand-made glass beads, produced in France, and the jewels continued to be put together at the workshop of Maison Gripoix. The jewels designed by the young Duc Verdura were particularly successful, full of the hot-blooded colours of his native Sicily.

Fulco Santostefano della Cerda, Duke of Verdura, was born in 1895. After his father died in 1926 he left Sicily, intending to make a career as a painter, and arrived in Paris in 1927 and found a job as a textile designer with Chanel. Chanel spotted Verdura's talent and made him her head jewellery designer. The most famous of all the Chanel-Verdura jewels was the pair of wide bracelets in black and white enamel with a Maltese cross of multi-coloured stones that Chanel wore all the time, one on each wrist. Versions of these bangles were recreated at various stages by Chanel, and copied by other manufacturers, notably Kenneth Jay Lane in the 1960s.

The mid-1930s were the height of Chanel's achievements and many influences were at work on her jewel design. Apart from the unusual mixtures of richly coloured pastes and glass beads, the 'antique' gilt look was popular and used to great effect in chains made in imitation of the classical 'loop in loop' technique, a kind of closely knitted herringbone mesh chain sometimes mixed with glass like ancient fragments.

Verdura worked with Chanel until 1937, when he went to live in the United States and turned to making real jewellery which was enormously successful. It had the liberated look of fantasy jewels but was made of precious materials.

Sadly there are no records of Chanel's original couture jewels, no designs and no extensive museum collections. Probably the finest private

A later Schiaparelli necklace,
following her preoccupation with
vegetal themes, designed as a lush
fringe of pea pods, in gilt metal with
green glass beads and imitation
pearls. c. 1940–50.

collection belongs to the designer and collector Billy Boy who has made an extensive study of couture clothes, accessories and jewellery. Chanel closed her couture house in 1939 at the onset of war; she re-opened in 1954 but the great era of exciting couture jewellery had passed. She died in 1971.

While Verdura was designing for Chanel, another great combination of talents in Paris was at work on the world of costume jewellery: the partnership of Elsa Schiaparelli and Jean Schlumberger. If Chanel confirmed the respectability of *bijoux de couture*, it was Schiaparelli who instigated the true *bijoux fantaisie*.

A brilliant innovator, Schiaparelli is associated with zany surrealist jewels created by famous and talented artists of the day, most notably

*Elsa Schiaparelli at Jacques Fath's Hollywood party in 1925.*

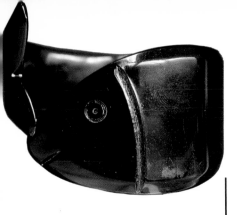

*Stylized fish bangle of smooth amber plastic, designed by Christian Bérard for Schiaparelli, c.1936.*

*Zodiac necklace of naïve, joyful figurative star-signs, in bright innocent colours, designed by Jean Clément for Schiaparelli, c.1938–9.*

Salvador Dali. Her ideas for jewellery were often outrageous, but always witty, and her innate sense of style told her exactly how far to go, and when to stop. Her crazy buttons and jewels were worn with severely simple clothes, their jokes and brash colours moderated by stark lines of chic, tight black suits and strong simple hats. Today they appear as amazingly early forerunners of 'punk' fashion.

Italian by origin, Schiaparelli grew up in Rome, an inquisitive, restless and imaginative child. She came to work in London where she met her husband, Comte William de Wendt de Kerlor. They moved to New York but the marriage failed and she was forced to take many different jobs to make ends meet. In 1922 she made her way to Paris, with her friend Blanche Hays. There she met the great Poiret who was back in Paris after the War, trying to finance the reopening of his business, and fell under the spell of couture. She created her own range of sportswear, and in 1927 made her mark with hand-knitted sweaters, with *trompe l'oeil* designs of bows, handkerchiefs, men's ties or crosswords knitted in. These new and expressive designs were very different from the current cool Chanel look of neat machine-knitted cardigans and sweaters with pure unadorned lines and were enormously successful. By this time, in early 1928, Schiaparelli had taken premises at 4 rue de la Paix, and the Maison Schiaparelli was established.

Schiaparelli had the ability to bring the best out of her collaborators; from the richly varied friends and colleagues who designed for her, she drew the most exciting aspects of their imagination. She was immersed in all the art movements of the day: modernism, futurism, cubism, African art, Art Deco design, preoccupation with the machine. She absorbed all these influences, yet she was a great creator, her ideas daringly original and way ahead of their time. Year after year came fresh and exciting innovations, gradually more adventurous and imaginative, and eventually she moved more and more towards the surreal. On the way, her work attracted rich and famous customers around the world.

One of Elsa Schiaparelli's innovations was turning clothes' fastenings – buckles, buttons, hooks, zips – into important decorative features that became the nucleus of her repertoire of costume jewellery. She always had her own buttons created specifically for her clothes, most of them designed by Jean Clément. Schiaparelli first noticed Clément's talent in 1927 when he was 27, a painter who had just graduated from L'École des Beaux Arts. He also had a degree in chemistry, which explains his understanding and clever handling of the new plastics. Clément was a brilliant designer who was responsible for Schiaparelli's jewellery and

accessories from those early years until his death in 1949. After a while
his designs were made up by the Francis Winter workshop in the rue des
Gravilliers. Specializing in costume jewellery and accessories, the
workshop was managed by Roger Jean-Pierre, and the team included
Pierre Toulgouat and model-makers experienced in the techniques of
real jewellery manufacture. Jean-Pierre went on to great success; he
established his own workshop and produced jewellery for Christian Dior,
Yves Saint Laurent and Balenciaga and became President of the

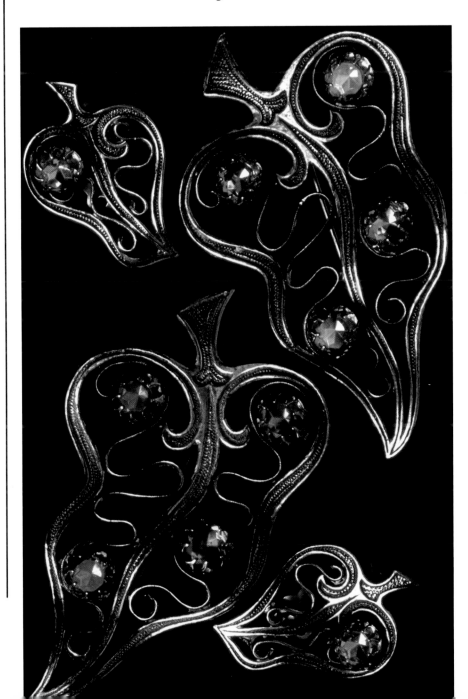

Silver-coloured metal and paste-set
brooch and earrings designed as
dancing openwork leaves, by
Schiaparelli, c. late 1930s–1940.

103

Chambre Syndicale de Paruriers de la Haute Couture. Schiaparelli and Clément used a wide variety of unusual materials to obtain the right effect for buttons: wood, china, celluloid, glass, crystal, amber, white jade, sealing wax. The effect was shocking, totally unexpected, and the list of different shapes and motifs seems endless: buttons looked like shoelaces, spinning tops, padlocks, nuts and bolts, coffee beans, lollipops, peanuts, musical notes, spoons, glass paperweights and a whole assortment of fruit and vegetables. Albert Giacometti designed a set of white metal and blue clay buttons in about 1935, the year in which he also created surreal ornaments for Schiaparelli's new Salon at 21 Place Vendôme.

In 1931 Schiaparelli began to broaden the scope of her costume jewellery in order to complement her clothes and the women who wore them. They were daring, sometimes jarring and bizarre, but they took an important step forward in finally liberating jewellery design from the 19th-century traditions and in allowing women to express their individuality. Schiaparelli had no hesitation in calling it 'junk' jewellery: it still performed the same function of decorating, enhancing and sometimes signifying good luck in a timeless tradition. It was very different from the couture jewellery of Chanel, Schiaparelli's arch rival; in place of pearls Schiaparelli's necklaces were made of porcelain flowers, of feathers or ermine. Motifs were as wide-ranging as those for buttons and very often inspired by Schiaparelli's own personal 'real' jewels which were *avant-garde*, in surreal or organic shapes such as shells and snails and composed of unusual combinations of richly coloured gems. Many came from the Paris jeweller Herz. Inspired very much also by black African art, Schiaparelli designed a range of barbaric-looking jewellery, which seemed also to be ritualistic, amuletic, reflecting Schiaparelli's own superstitious nature. For these 'tribal' jewels she used exotic-looking beads and added many different materials such as porcelain and plastic, aluminium and glass.

In the early 1930s Schiaparelli and Clément devised a whole series of clips, one of the most popular and versatile forms of jewellery. Motifs included shells, fir-cones, vegetables, mermaids, birds, musical boxes. She also produced slightly more jewel-looking costume jewellery set with fake gems and lots of sparkling diamanté on huge ball-earrings and bracelets.

For a few years in the mid-1930s clear Perspex, lucite or Plexiglas was a characteristic feature of Schiaparelli's designs. It was in 1933–4 that she introduced her outrageous glass fabric for dresses and capes, and her

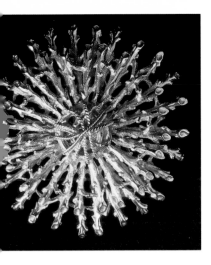

*Gilt metal surreal composition inspired by Dali, in the form of a circle of twigs, at its centre a nest tied with rope. Schiaparelli, late 1930s.*

costume jewels and belts were a clever answer to the vogue for all-white jewels of expensive materials such as rock crystal and diamonds. In 1935 lucite hearts were worn, and shreds of metal or metal insects were suspended into flat, wide necklaces of Perspex.

From this time the jewellery and accessories grew wittier, more surreal with each collection. Louis Aragon, the surrealist poet, designed a necklace that looked as if it was made of aspirins; there were jewels of phosphorescent flowers, lamps that lit up, or passion thermometers to measure the wearer's level of arousal. Dog collars were hung with a mass of jangling gilt and enamelled coins; a vegetarian bracelet hung with bright crude vegetables and jewels of brutal-looking mechanistic motifs appeared in 1935. Earrings were always noticeable and amusing, and again in 1935 a Hindu-inspired range set off Schiaparelli's saris of that year.

Surrealist accessories encouraged by Schiaparelli's association with Salvador Dali were prominent in 1936. Jewels began to look like

*Seaweed necklace of bronze set with glass beads and paste, designed by Serge Matta, made by Toppio e Coppola for Schiaparelli, 1951. The necklace is on a photograph of Bettina Bergery by Chevalier.*

Gilt metal dangling hearts brooch
designed by Schlumberger for
Schiaparelli, late 1930s.

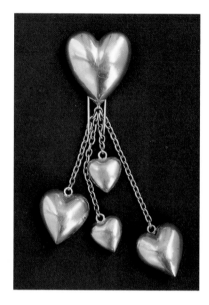

gingerbread pigs, fish, starfish, birds, crayfish. The most classical of jewels – cameos – were taken out of context and worn incongruously with sportswear.

Around this time Schiaparelli discovered the talents of a young designer from Alsace. Jean Schlumberger was working in his atelier in the rue la Boétie, taken over from Picasso, making unusual jewels for a small, select group of aesthetically and artistically inclined society leaders. Schiaparelli noticed a stunning pair of earrings worn by Marina, Duchess of Kent, and admired the jewels made of porcelain flowers set in gold. When she found that Schlumberger was responsible she immediately commissioned him to make a series of buttons. Schlumberger created buttons that looked like Chinese pink starfish, a feathered cap of d'Artagnan, marbled pebbles resembling rough gemstones, rich ruby or jade. Schlumberger worked with pieces of antique jewels or objects, relics of gilt Victoriana, that he picked up in the Paris fleamarket. Over the next few years there were jewels of cherubs holding torches, set with diamanté, metal clips like English Staffordshire pottery dogs, insects, sea creatures, fish that lit up, hearts pierced with swords, swans, ostriches, roller-skates, necklaces representing lush marine life. His mixture of baroque and bizarre, fantasy and fashion was all the rage and Schiaparelli-Schlumberger jewels were a major contributing factor to the popularity of costume jewels in the 1940s.

Gilt bronze, black and pink enamel
bow brooch, set with turquoises,
designed for Schiaparelli by
Schlumberger who predicted, in 1937,
the unexpected, jarring colour
combinations of the 1940s.

Schlumberger came up with ingenious, colourful and fun-loving themes for Schiaparelli's hugely successful Circus collection of 1938: clowns, acrobats, circus horses' heads made of gilt metal or Venetian glass, some set with semi-precious stones. For the Pagan collection of the same year there were jewels made as leaves, vegetables, flowers, thriving plant life and insects, including metal fly necklaces made by François Hugo. The Harlequin collection, based on the Commedia dell'Arte, remembered from Schiaparelli's youth, featured necklaces hung with a fringe of comedy masks and jewels shaped as pierrots or blackamoors' heads.

*Perspex collar embedded with realistically modelled and coloured metal bugs, by Schiaparelli, c.1938.*

Left: Group of rainbow-shaded,
iridescent pink paste jewels,
Schiaparelli, c.1940–50.
Below: Curled leaf brooch of
gilt metal set with iridescent pink
pastes, with a gold metal tassel.
Schiaparelli, c.1940–50.

Étienne de Beaumont joined the list of defecting staff and customers from Chanel and designed a range of jewels for Schiaparelli. Made of enamel and gilt, the best known are the rings made of three pieces that covered the entire finger. Jean Cocteau designed a famous eye jewel of lacquered rope, dating from about 1936. Along with other mad accessories there were belts designed by Christian Bérard and hair combs, sometimes beaded by the Maison Lesage, or moulded to look like geisha-girl pins or carnival masks.

From 1936, as the shadow of gloom was lengthening over Europe, Schiaparelli's colours became wilder, brighter. They were luminous, full of electric drama that sparked off a fashion for shimmering 'rainbow' pastes flashing with blue and green lights. This was another fashion that was taken up by costume jewellery manufacturers all over the world. Dazzling colours led up to the most famous Schiaparelli invention: the shocking pink of 1937 extended of course to jewels, which were lacquered pink or set with bright pink pastes. At the same time, surrealism was heightened and Dali's buttons resembled bees swarming over chocolate, his telephone and mermaid obsessions cropped up as earrings and brooches, while Schlumberger continued to create masterly jewels, including a famous sunbeam brooch in gilt set with pastes. In the 1930s, Schiaparelli began to object to the extensive publicity and attention Schlumberger was receiving and one day she simply asked him to leave. Schlumberger moved to New York in 1940 and went on to become one of the most successful jewellery designers of the century. He died in 1987.

The spiralling madness and frivolity of Schiaparelli's accessories were diversions from the approaching chaos of war, which was to eclipse this brilliant moment of triumph for couture and couture jewels. After the War, the crazy dreamy surrealism had evaporated. Jewels were simpler, more conventional and sculptural, and during the 1950s jewels bearing the Schiaparelli mark, her signature, were made under licence in the United States. Schiaparelli closed her boutique in 1954.

Left: Opulent Fabergé-egg-shaped
earrings in orange plastic with
pastes set in pewter-coloured
metal, by Schiaparelli, c.1940.

# Four

# SOPHISTICATED BARBARISM: THE ART DECO YEARS

The evening of the first performance of Diaghilev's *Schéhérazade* by the Ballet Russe in Paris in 1910 was a turning-point for the future of 20th-century decorative design, fashion and jewels. The exoticism, eastern opulence, the intense vibrant colours of stage sets and costumes designed by Léon Bakst, the passionate boldness and strange sultry beauty of the Russian Ballet had a sensational effect on fashionable Paris. The ballet left a heady magical atmosphere that was to transform the way women looked and dressed.

This provocative eastern flavour of drama and brilliant costumes contrasted sharply with the pale and frilly prettiness of early 20th-century fashions. The chic audiences who gathered to watch the ballet, the latest craze in Paris, were probably dressed in shades of eau-de-nil, lilac, ivory or bluebell, with decorations of frothy lace, hand-embroidered folds and ladylike tucks. Their jewels were either discreetly classical or screeching of worldly wealth. Edwardian elegance must have paled into manicured insignificance next to the bright colours and pulsating movement of the spectacle. The dancers were dressed in swathes of silks and sensuously moving fabrics of jewel-like colours, highlighted with gold ornamentation, their Turkish turbans fixed with gleaming gems and long curling feathers; bare arms and ankles were fettered with ropes of pearls and chains. Along with the Ballet Russe, Art Deco had arrived in Paris, and with it a new flamboyance and a frenzied longing for the unexpected, both of which were to characterize design in the 1920s.

Several elements combined with the colour and excitement of the Ballet Russe to formulate Art Deco, an all-embracing term for the strong decorative style of the years between the two world wars. By 1910 a new and progressive stage of the Art Nouveau movement was developing in Austria, Germany and Scotland. It grew out of and reacted against the excessive curves and emotionally charged figurative themes of Art Nouveau and headed instead towards abstract, linear forms and strong stylization of motifs. The basic aim was to do away with all unnecessary ornament, to streamline shapes and outlines. In 1910 a group of German designers from Munich, working in the new abstract, linear style, showed their work in Paris at the Munich Exhibition of Applied Art, an influential event which attracted unexpectedly large crowds and joined with Ballet Russe-fever to sow the seeds of Art Deco.

It was, however, another 15 years before Art Deco took its name from the Exposition des Arts Décoratifs et Industriels Modernes held in Paris in 1925, after many years' delay. During that time the style had absorbed many different influences, including Fauvism, the method of painting with flat, distorted representations and violent colours, Cubism, Negro

*Advertisement for 'Indra' artificial*
*pearls, 1913, by Stefano.*

art, an opulent orientalism and exoticism, stimulated by the discovery in 1922 of Tutankhamun's tomb. A devastating world war had changed the overall social structure and most lifestyles; the atmosphere of escapism that followed it bred a need for constant diversion and extraordinary novelties, and there was a new obsessive interest in machines, in functionalism, and in travel, speed and communication.

Although Art Deco is usually associated with a look of stylish geometry, the term can be divided clearly into two main stages. Early Art Deco was still figurative, and rather classical, based on 18th-century styles. Its lingering Edwardian motifs of flowers, garlands, swags, were flattened and stylized to look unreal, angular. Sinuous curves were spread into ovals, circles, octagonal panels; colours were strong, materials exotic. The second stage was Modernism, a style which took over after 1925 and was marked by stark severity, with rigorously abstract forms and a total suppression of colour and unnecessary decoration. Both stages were well interpreted in costume jewellery.

One of the main characteristics of Art Deco was its determined application to every aspect of living, its dedication to 'total design' for everything from skyscrapers and ocean liners to knives and forks and ashtrays. Jewellery, as the most expressive female accessory, and particularly zany costume jewellery, was an important part of the new look. Art Deco costume jewellery was generally superbly designed, witty and inventive, reflecting trends from the traditional to the bizarre, from exotic early Art Deco to Modernism.

The influence of the Ballet Russe was harnessed by the most famous couturier of the day, Paul Poiret, whose own sense of the theatre was an important catalyst to the new look in clothes and jewels. By 1910 *Poiret le Magnifique* reigned supreme over Paris fashion. A protégé of the great couturier Jacques Doucet and a former employee of Worth, Poiret took a major step in revolutionizing fashion, by loosening women's corsets and shortening their skirts and by applying his own unrivalled sense of colour. Poiret was also important in bringing the worlds of clothes and jewels much closer together, and in emphasizing the drama and exoticism that jewels could bring to fashion. Through his beautifully illustrated fashion books, Poiret set about publicizing his designs and so changing the way women looked. He dressed them in brilliant colours, richly textured fabrics, exotic ornaments that were very much part of the costume.

But despite the impact of the ballet, the prevailing musky atmosphere of eastern intrigue and Poiret's influence, changes in real life for ordinary

people must have happened rather more gradually. From 1910 until World War I, styles were generally still fairly classical, with more than a touch of 18th-century baroque, although the exaggerated 'S' bend gave way to a straighter, pillar-like look, with Poiret's tunic tops and overskirts sometimes wired like lampshades to stand out from the body or falling loosely to the knee. One of his most famous pre-World War I innovations which was not generally and immediately adopted was the '*jupes-culottes*' or trouser skirts shaped like huge harem pants; he was also responsible for the hobble skirt, aptly named, which hampered women's brave new steps forward, while yet another Poiret hallmark was the turban fixed with a soaring aigrette: a jewel from which sprouted a tuft of feathers. What did change immediately in fashion was colour. Around 1910 sober pearl-grey, lavender and olive gave way to rich and violent hues of yellow, deep pink, vibrant blue and a colour called 'Nuit d'Orient', a deep midnight blue. After clothes and perfume – very evocative of eastern promise – jewellery was most affected by this general transformation.

Good paste jewels continued to be made during this transitional period between Edwardian styles and Art Deco and the costume jewels are interesting reminders of these changes: bracelets, earrings, and brooches were usually still classical in design, with drapes and garlands and little flower baskets, derived from 18th-century design but now often arranged within rectangular plaques, with the occasional geometric sunburst or palm tree motif in which straight sunrays or fronds fanned out behind a simple sun or flower. Flowers were still very popular, but they began to look more stylized: simple, flat, colourful blossoms that started to take on the air of artificiality associated with the 1920s and 1930s. Stars and crescents continued to be in demand, as now they conjured up visions of starry Arabian nights, and could be worn in the hair or obligatory turban with long, dancing feathers. There was a strong oriental look in the use of coloured enamels, lacquer, jade or green glass, with thin jagged outlines perhaps in black enamel tracing here a Chinese geometric design, there a craggy prunus branch. As the silhouette became longer and slimmer, so earrings began to be longer and more slender, ideally suited to the fashion for sweeping hair back into a chignon, or into coils over the ears, leaving the neck bare.

The jewelled aigrette and other strategically placed jewels and gems became an intrinsic part of Poiret's total look for modern women and one of the most popular and generally accepted innovations. At the same time, his designs suggested new and sacrilegious ways of wearing the yards and yards of artificial pearls produced in Paris and intended originally to imitate Edwardian grandeur. *Schéhérazade* had encouraged the wearing of ropes and ropes of pearls, and jewels that looked like hoards of rare and costly gems from Aladdin's cave. As quantities of pearls were now needed to be the height of fashion, it was obvious that more often than not they had to be fake, and then, at the very pinnacle of the value and popularity of real pearls, partly as a perverse whim of the rich, the fake versions began to be ultra-fashionable and respectable. The fake pearl and costume jewellery manufacturers of Paris – Técla, Suclier, Richelieu, Gripoix – were of course poised ready for this fashion, having been commissioned during the first decade to make convincing replicas for stage or for society ladies, and techniques had certainly improved. The glass beads covered with layers of '*essence d'Orient*' looked more and more lustrous and convincing.

In the stylized fashion plates painted by Paul Iribe, Georges Barbier, Georges Lepape, Poiret showed exotic costumes of rich colours and patterns, draped with lashings of pearls, ungraduated for a more 'modern' look. They were hung round the neck, dropping to the knees or hooked over an elegantly poised hand, wound round the wrists or the ankles, or slung under the chin in rows linked to ornaments placed over the ears. Sometimes the entire bodice would be composed of beads or pearls. Flowers, now stylized and artificial-looking, were important decorative features of clothes, too: the diagonal drapes of skirts were usually secured by an artificial rose; fabrics were woven or embroidered with roses. There were also lots of tassels in both jewellery and clothes, usually hanging from the handkerchief points of overskirts. This all added to the sensuality of jewels and clothes that swayed with the movement of the body. Fake glass gems and beads of deep sultry hues, blue, amber, purple, added hot-blooded eastern promise to turbans, and folds of silk, and emphasized the jewel-like colours and shiny textures of fabrics.

From about 1912–13 onwards through the 1920s and 1930s, jewellery, very definitely costume jewellery, became a vital ingredient in fashion illustrations, in advertisements, photographs, publicity material and in stage costume designs. Towards 1920, for instance, a favourite fashion image for prints and posters was a lady at her toilette, gazing into a hand-mirror decorated in Art Deco style, held by a hand with long slender fingers heavy with ostentatious 'modern' rings, large and chunky, her slim wrist ringed with bangles, apparently made of plastics, her cropped hair offset by a pair of outrageously long, looped or slender dangling earrings; face, hair, accessories and jewels conformed to a sleek geometry. Most important, more jewels began to be worn and the emphasis shifted from the small, valuable and discreet to the overtly ornamental. The rich revelled in their ever-growing whim for wearing frankly artificial jewels which stood them in good stead for the hard times ahead in the late 1920s and 1930s, when reduced finances often made fakes a necessity.

If fashion had exploded around 1910, the peace, the morality and manners of the Edwardian era were shattered by World War I. Cut off from Paris, the world of fashion lost its direction; the progress of Art Deco was temporarily halted and Poiret joined the forces. The pre-war years of leisured luxury and well ordered lives, of sheltered young ladies in hand-sewn dresses, were irrevocably lost. The transformation and liberation of women which had started in the 1890s, was given a huge impetus. Men had gone to war, and women took over their jobs and their

*Bracelet and pair of clips of emerald pastes and diamanté; the bracelet in gently geometric buckle-shaped links; the curved clips designed to make use of baguette-cut stones. By Alfred Philippe for Trifari, late 1930s.*

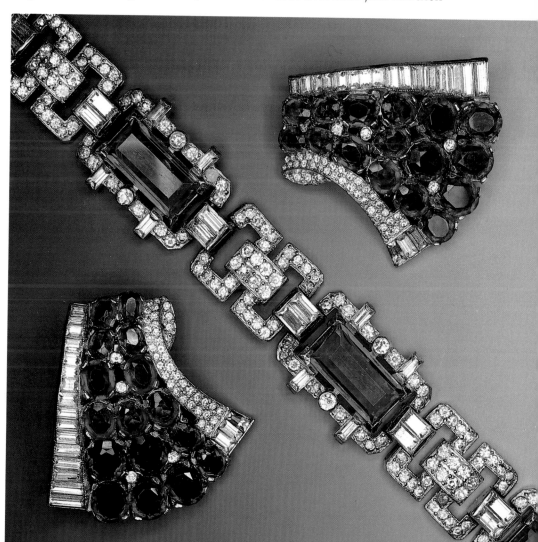

*Gertrude Lawrence, photographed by Paul Tanqueray, in a pose of casual bejewelled elegance. It was the fashion in the 1930s to wear several sparkling bracelets on each arm; c.1930.*

roles; they ran offices, they drove trucks, they had to move around easily on foot. They could no longer afford to wear clothes that hampered their movements and stressed their submissiveness and reliance on men. Added to this, they lived constantly with the idea of the imminent death of their loved ones, which encouraged a new attitude of living each moment to the full and a new sexual and moral freedom.

After the War women around the world could not possibly return to the frothy femininity, to the classical jewels that had become relics of a bygone age. They needed new clothes and new jewels to tell the story of the new age and their new freedom. But despite the drastic social changes wrought by war, it was only in the mid-twenties that the new outwardly visible style of the liberated female began to emerge. At this time, the story of Art Deco costume jewellery becomes more involved with general changes in society, and jewellery was influenced as never before by economic and moral changes, by art and industry, travel and communication.

In real jewellery, the 1920s and 1930s signalled a great age of untempered luxury and innovation in the use of diamonds and precious stones. For the first time, extravagant, capricious designs of the moment were executed in fabulously expensive materials, with a daring irreverence for the classic diamond heirloom syndrome. Jewellers were no longer paralysed by the value of the gems. The prevailing geometric flatness, the slim angularity, stylization and sharp movements blended with an opulent and colourful orientalism in the miraculous creations of the great Paris jewel houses – Cartier, Mauboussin, Lacloche – who catered for royalty, for magnates and maharajahs, for filmstars and the super-rich around the world. For a while in the mid-1920s there was a chic crisp black and white vogue, contrasting diamonds and rock crystal with onyx or black enamel, and in the mid-1930s, there was an all-white Jean Harlow vogue, all slinky oyster satin, silver fox and diamonds, which were usually *pavé*-set (literally paved) in platinum for increased whiteness and fineness of setting. But at other times through the 1920s and 1930s, all the coloured precious stones were often combined in one jewel, in a kaleidoscope of colour and flair.

In the 1930s there was a fashion for little lively jewels set with masses of small coloured gems – rubies, emeralds, sapphires – which came from Madagascar and were carved like leaves or flowers and clustered like succulent berries. This Tutti Frutti or 'fruit salad' style was well mimicked in costume jewellery. By 1934 diamanté jewellery was very much more opulent and colourful. Imitation carved rubies, emeralds

and sapphires were liberally and lusciously scattered amongst the diamanté on the most exclusive clips and bracelets. One bracelet mentioned by the Fashion Editor of *Woman's Home Companion*, New York, in September 1934, was centred with a huge carved cabochon paste ruby, surrounded by emeralds, sapphires and more rubies and diamanté. The design was named Schéhérazade 'because of its brilliant oriental character'. In the late 1930s, Trifari, the leading American manufacturers, came up with a soft combination of opaque jade and coral moulded glass, mixed with diamanté paste in ultra stylish designs for clips, brooches and bracelets. This range was sold in 1937 at B. Altman in New York, where a bracelet cost $7.50 and a brooch $5.

In real jewellery, away from the world of commercial mainstream ideas, there was a group of modernist designers, serious artist-jewellers like Jean Fouquet, Gérard Sandoz, Jean Desprès, who used silver and semi-precious materials to produce stark symbols of the machine age. Both breeds of Art Deco jewel were beautifully interpreted in costume jewellery.

One of the most important aspects of Art Deco jewellery, real and fake, was the use of new cuts of diamonds. The cutting and setting of diamonds had improved enormously and new shapes for stones had been developed to suit geometric designs: baguettes, batons, trapezes, little square cuts known as *calibré* all added movement and a tailored crispness to fine 1920s and 1930s jewels. As in the 18th century, pastes improved correspondingly and successfully imitated and often improved on fancy shapes. The varying cuts of gems could tightly and precisely fill any shape of jewel to give an overall dense sparkle. For increased brilliance and finer settings, diamonds were set in platinum until the economic crises of the 1930s. To capture the same whiteness costume jewels were set in silver, in white-plated metals or in Platinin, the new platinum imitation alloy of the 1920s.

Through the 1920s and 1930s there was still a strong market for glossy, diamanté jewels that looked like the real thing. The best paste jewels were made in France, in the United States and also in Pforzheim, Germany, but in England they were all called French jewels. French jewels in this Place Vendôme style were sold in good jewellers' shops in London, at Asprey for example, and in fine shops and department stores in all the world's capitals. They were grand sparkling jewels, substantial, well made and paved with masses of diamond pastes to present a solid surface of lustre, sometimes with a flash of strong colour or with a line of black enamel or a chunk of fake 'onyx'. Necklaces and pendants were heavy and angular, with rectangular or plaque-shaped pendants hung on wide chains of cable or rectangular links, or of the strap and buckle design, with a baton or rod-shaped motif between. Other pendants were more fluid, based on stylized waterfall designs, neatly curved, dripping with paste drops and hung on slender paste-set chains. Brooches were increasingly angular, circular or plaque-shaped, and bracelets – the most important accessories of the 1930s – were wide ribbons of complicated abstract patterns, sometimes slightly oriental in mood, like a Persian carpet, always glamorous and slinky, worn several at a time for a filmstar effect. Flexibility and movement was of prime importance in design and manufacture, especially as bracelets became wider and more fanciful in the 1930s. The most daring girls wore armfuls of bracelets, from wrist to elbow. All-white diamanté bracelets were often of openwork design, others were solid, *pavé*-set and decorated with a pattern of specially cut coloured pastes arranged into stylized flowers: a prunus branch, or a little picture in the popular Egyptian revival style; reclining Nubian maidens surrounded by hieroglyphics, birds, symbols. Fashionable handbag frames were often set with pastes, and decorated perhaps in geometric or Egyptian revival style. In Pforzheim, the firm of Murrle Bennett (who had a showroom in London, in Charterhouse Street) specialized in top-quality paste in the 1920s. At the same time, the firm of Henkel & Grosse was also creating fine paste jewels in the latest fashion, sold in Paris, London and around the world. This fine-quality paste was certainly expensive; a good pendant might cost about £35.

The supple movement of bracelets, chains, beads and tassels was reflective of the new energetic sporty woman with a long, slim, tubular silhouette. Sports motifs occurred in jewels: the lady tennis player, a lady golfer in mid-swing, tennis rackets and golf clubs or archery equipment, arrows and especially the target emblem, also signifying the winning post in horseracing, which conformed perfectly to new geometric ideals of modernism. In the 1920s beads of glass or wood, fake pearls or paste *sautoirs* were worn very long, sometimes to the knee; beads were even wound around the leg. The new sleek silhouette cried out for costume jewellery and accessories. Pendants, beads and necklaces were all worn longer, to emphasize the lines of clothes and to swing with the new lithe female body. In January 1920 Vogue recommended a 'long strand of convincing emeralds' which hung over the shoulders and ended in two heavy jingling tassels of the same stone. This kind of jewel would hang nearly to the floor. A slender, straight figure was needed to achieve the right kind of swaying movement of clothes and jewels, and in contrast to

Design for a paste necklace by Murrle Bennett & Co. of Pforzheim, showing an Odeonesque waterfall design incorporating stones of different shapes. German, c.1925.

Enamelled metal bell-hop brooch, a cubist-inspired emblem of the 'Grand Hotel' era. French, c.1925–30.

Group of silver and paste jewels created to look like chic and precious diamond jewellery. French, c.1930–35.

the well-rounded females of the turn of the century, the new obsession was with slimness in women as well as in jewels. There was a fad for dieting, and bosoms or womanly curves were entirely out of fashion. The trend was moving towards the active, androgynous boy-girl look, the fast *garçonne* or the fashionable idea of the adolescent, immature body. As well as dieting women used underwear such as wide rubber bands to press their curves into the desired cylindrical shape. Themes and symbols of sleek movement and speed followed through in design and everyday life; the greyhound or Borzoi were favourite pets; the gazelle was a persistent decorative motif, along with the zigzag streak of lightning, all found on costume jewels of the Art Deco period. The motor car, ocean liner, aeroplane all signified the idolized speed and the luxury of expensive travel enjoyed by the post-war *nouveaux riches*. A little souvenir brooch, superbly made of enamelled metal, recalls the bell-hop, evocative symbol of the era of the Grand Hotel, his tiny cubist body laden with suitcases labelled with exotic place names.

Nancy Cunard photographed by Cecil
Beaton wearing her celebrated
African ivory bangles, 1927.

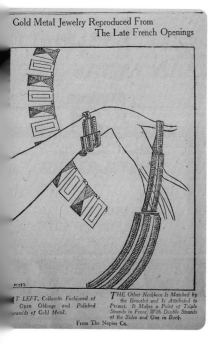

Gold Metal Jewelry Reproduced From
The Late French Openings

T LEFT, Collarette Fashioned of
Open Oblongs and Polished
ramids of Gold Metal.

THE Other Necklace Is Matched by
the Bracelet and Is Attributed to
Premet. It Makes a Point of Triple
Strands in Front, With Double Strands
at the Sides and One in Back.
From The Napier Co.

Stylish advertisement for Art Deco
jewellery made by the Napier
Company, c. 1928.

Decorative sparkle was vital for evening, and looked especially effective on a trim, lithe figure. Paste or jet beads or sequins were sewn to gowns, Poiret was showing lots of lamé and glitter. Headdresses like bandeaux were bejewelled with faux-gems, and worn low on the forehead. Hair was generally still long, fixed with haircombs of tortoiseshell or, yet more exciting and highly prized, of plastic studded with jet or pastes.

For daytime, the clutter of bracelets was replaced by jangling bangles of ivory or jade, real or artificial, and an essential accessory for the 'flapper', the racy modern girl about town of the 1920s, was the ivory bangle, sometimes paste-studded, worn just above the elbow, with a chiffon handkerchief tucked into it. The fashion for wide ivory bangles was encouraged by the Paris Colonial Exhibition in 1922 and its various successors. It was, however, Nancy Cunard, socialite and trend-setter, who did most for this barbaric vogue. She was famed for her armfuls of wide, wild ivory bangles, bone-like, all smooth and worn like ethnic, ritualistic body ornaments.

Not everyone, however, had Nancy Cunard's resources, especially in a post-War Europe inhabited by a new social class, the new poor or *nouveaux pauvres* (to add a dash of Parisian elegance), although anyone with any pretence to being fashionable lusted after an armful of bangles. By the early 1920s advice was creeping into magazines about dressing on a limited budget, and inventive, inexpensive ways of adding sparkle and style were reported in each issue of *Vogue* or *Harper's Bazaar*. In 1922, for example, when an all-silver craze swept the fashionable world and set interiors, clothes, jewels scintillating with a mirrored shimmer, costume jewellery responded with ornaments of nickel or chrome and frosted glass to look like rock crystal. These chrome jewels in the late 1920s and 1930s interpreted ultra-modern geometric Bauhaus doctrine through mechanistic bracelets and necklaces of flexible brickwork: a deep flat collar, for instance, with a stepped Aztec-inspired outline, or a wide slippery bracelet. In 1928 the couturier Lucien Lelong designed a sleek, mechanical silver-finished necklace, reproduced by Napier in New York.

In 1923 women cut their hair, and did away with the long flowing tresses that were another *passé* symbol of the turn-of-the-century female. Women now smoked, they wore make-up, sometimes they even wore men's clothes. The short, sharp, boyish look was in, but another consideration was the fact that ladies' maids had become a thing of the past and short hair was easy to manage. The new bob was daring and geometric, adding angularity to the overall silhouette of the modern woman. It also demanded long, louche and ever more noticeable earrings, even glass earrings that shed perfume as they swung, or odd earrings, one small clip and one long pendant. The first short haircut, popularized by Gabrielle Chanel, was the bob; then came the shingle, cut like a man's at the back, and then the Eton crop, the most extreme style and one of the outward signs of the Lesbian. The cloche hat pulled down low over the haircut allowed great scope for brooches or clips that lit up the dark glistening eyes peering out from under the low hat.

The eyes and the sparkle were very like the eyes that glowed seductively from the mesmerizing silver screen. Hollywood's power over fashions and jewels cannot be over-emphasized. In difficult times, the cinema brought magical escape, entirely new entertainment and fascinating fantasy into everyone's lives, while for some it stood for the rags-to-riches story, the hope for a life transformed from drudgery to divine stardom. Hollywood symbols crept into jewellery design, real or fake: palm trees, a cactus, a gleaming motor car, a woman's face, a top hat and cane. Yet more influential was the impact of glamour, real or false, the sparklers glinting in the glare of flashbulbs, and Anita Loos's unforgettable image of diamonds as a girl's best friend.

In 1922 the tomb of the young King Tutankhamun was excavated by Lord Carnarvon and the treasures unearthed there stunned the world. The Romance of Egypt infiltrated the world of fashion and design and also set Hollywood alight with blockbuster epics of *Cleopatra*, played in 1917 by Theda Bara and in 1934 by Claudette Colbert. The exotic Egyptian ornaments provided an ideal theme for stagey costume jewellery. Designers did not aim at authenticity but translated instead the mystical and symbolic grandeur, with a somewhat indiscriminate but effective assembly of stylized profiles, scarabs, hieroglyphs, winged falcons and the eye of Horus, copying original inlays as bright enamels and interpreting the rich gold as silver gilt or gilt metal. The results looked even more Egyptian than the real thing. Glass took the place of lapis, turquoise, cornelian, although sometimes real semi-precious stones were used on silver gilt jewels. Small brass-winged brooches were decorated with beetle motifs enamelled in metallic blue-green; small, slim rectangular pendants represented wall paintings; larger pendants brought to mind immense pectorals, and complicated necklaces like huge chest ornaments were draped or fringed with lotus flowers, little mummies or hieroglyphs, all enamelled in blue-green or purple and set with imitation or real turquoises. Carefully designed and well-made metal jewels often incorporated the skilful translucent *plique à jour*

*Claudette Colbert as Cleopatra in 1934, wearing exotic and dramatic jewels, the ultimate in Egyptian revival mania.*

enamel for vultures' or scarabs' wings. The best of these jewels were made in silver in France or Pforzheim, Germany. The more up-market paste-set jewels such as those of Murrle Bennett incorporated stylized Egyptian motifs in the manner of Cartier and Van Cleef & Arpels.

In New York the Napier Company, always first with the latest crazes from Paris, where they had an office, introduced a range of jewellery which they described as having the 'Spirit of Ancient Egypt'. The complete line of necklaces, brooches, bracelets and earrings, reflected, according to their advertisements, the 'vivid colours and bizarre designs made popular by the interest in the excavations of the tomb of

Costume Accessories Are Important

*By Helen Williams Vance*

Written and Illustrated Especially for the Globe-Democrat

Newspaper cutting from Women's Wear Daily, October 1926, showing Napier's popular Cobra necklace and slave link bangles, all of Egyptian inspiration.

*Turquoise opaque glass beads with diamanté trim, the two main motifs in strong Art Deco style. French, c.1930.*

Tut-Ankh-Amen'. Stones of imitation turquoise matrix, jade and lapis lazuli, with some flashes of ruby red were mounted in complex patterned settings incorporating the Egyptian lotus, scarabs and hieroglyphics 'rich with the symbolism of the ancient Nile country'. Earrings were long and thickly fringed with dangling motifs, pendants were large and plaque-shaped and also hung with fake stones and drops. For autumn 1926 'Cobra' jewellery was all the rage and Napier's versions were flexible and slinky with a green-gold finish. Cobra necklaces with or without fake gems coiled around the neck, the head clasping the body so that the tail hung down over the neckline. The most popular stones were imitation peridots, perfect with the green-gold finish. Equally Egyptian-flavoured were necklaces and bracelets of 'slave link' design, large open rectangular links made from silver, and plastics looking like crystal.

In the years before 1925, costume jewellery was full of exotic fantasy and capricious escapism, and under the influence of Chanel (see chapter 3) costume jewels began to take off on a path of their own, establishing a new art form, breaking down barriers surrounding materials, values, class and rules of jewel wearing. There was a fast-growing market for all fashion accessories, for handbags, for smoking and make-up accessories; buttons and belt buckles were zany and artistic, and as more and more costume jewellery was worn, outrageous and unashamedly fake jewels became yet more fashionable.

The most important contributing factor to the new freedom and artistry of costume jewellery was the development of plastics, the exciting and revolutionary material of the two decades under scrutiny. Real jewels went as far as they could in terms of *avant-garde* design, the use of luxurious materials and unprecedented combinations of gems. Where imagination was at last defeated by the limitations of cost or of natural properties of materials, plastics stepped in and took over. They imposed virtually no restrictions on the designer and maker and offered a challenge to the real thing: anything you can do we can do better.

It was an Englishman, Alexander Parkes, who had produced the first commercial plastics material in 1855. Parkes sold examples of his cellulose nitrate, which he called Parkesine, for one shilling per pound at the 1862 International Exhibition in London and won a medal for his invention. Unfortunately, at the time the new material was most prized for its ability to imitate horn, tortoiseshell, coral, wood, and it was not until the 1930s that plastics were appreciated for their own highly

*Wide moulded plastic bangle and necklace of cornelian-coloured and black plastic separated by diamanté. Possibly French or German, c.1925–30.*

individual properties. Parkes' company went into liquidation in 1868, and his former manager Daniel Spill invented and registered his own material which he called Xylonite, his company being called the Xylonite Company Ltd. One of his specialities was imitation coral jewellery at a time when real carved coral jewellery was extremely popular in the 1860s and '70s. Lustrous plastic pearls were also popular, made by the addition of particles of lead phosphate to the Xylonite.

Meanwhile, in the United States, John Wesley Hyatt had patented his discovery of cellulose nitrate in 1868, giving it the trade name of Celluloid. A manufacturer of ivory billiard balls, troubled by diminishing supply and rising costs of ivory, had organized a competition to find a substitute and Hyatt had been encouraged by this challenge. At the start of the 1920s celluloid was used for haircombs, and a hand-cut celluloid comb was a very highly prized acquisition, often more so than the tortoiseshell it sought to imitate. The new material was perfect, too, for decorative handbag mounts, carved and coloured to look like ivory or tortoiseshell.

The next important step was taken by Leo Hendrik Baekeland, a Belgian chemist living in the United States. Around 1907 he created the first totally synthetic plastic, a phenolic resin which became known as Bakelite, patented in 1909 and the best known plastics material to be used in Art Deco jewellery.

New types of plastics were developed in the early decades of the 20th century. Casein, milk-based plastics developed in Bavaria in the 1890s, and given an original trade name of Galalith, was later produced in England from 1919 and marketed under several different names such as Dorcasine, Erinoid, Keronyx and Lactoid. Casein looked much like celluloid and had similar versatile decorative qualities suitable for jewellery and small trinkets. Catalin was produced in Britain from 1928, while the United States came up with a huge variety of plastics with evocative names such as Gemstone Marblette, Opalon, Prystal. In the 1930s Napier sold opaque white Catalin jewellery imitating designs by Herz of Paris, as well as Prystal jewellery resembling carved and tinted rock crystal. In the 1920s great improvements enabled plastics to be moulded, cast and brightly coloured, made to different degrees of opacity and translucency, mottled, marbled.

Plastic jewellery marked the epitome of recklessness, the ultimate in freedom of design and manufacture. Plastics could look unbelievably sumptuous, wittily outdoing the most extravagant and luxurious baubles of the Place Vendôme. At the same time, the low cost meant that the

Group of Galalith and chrome jewels
of abstract, modernist design, by
Henkel and Grosse, c.1925–30.

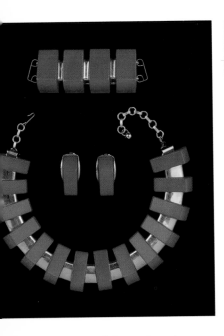

Red plastic and chrome brooch,
earrings and necklace. Probably
American c.1940.

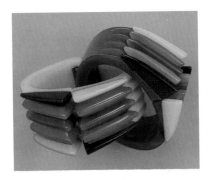

Multi-coloured Bakelite bangles.
American c.1930–40.

jewellery could reflect the fleeting whim of fashion, to be discarded in favour of each new idea. Designers and craftsmen need not be concerned about wastage or mistakes, and experimentation led to exciting results. Colours of gems could be uniform and strikingly intense, their size impossibly huge, a dream come true. Plastics that looked like amber, jade, lapis, could be skilfully carved in a way the real materials could not withstand, and later plastics were machine-moulded to look like intricate carving. Since manufacturers found the temptation to copy precious and semi-precious stones irresistible, much plastic jewellery still followed current designs, yet the best plastic jewels are unashamedly unprecious, proud to be plastic.

The era of plastics coincided with the Jazz Age, with the influx of modernism, futurism, the functional mechanistic mood. In 1925 the new woman looked geometric from head to foot, her outline a cylinder or rectangle. The same year also saw a much greater recognition of African art; black was 'in' as Josephine Baker's *Revue Nègre* caused a sensation: her beautiful black skin sizzled with diamanté and little else. Jazz was played in dark, smoky nightclubs, an atmosphere demanding rather more risqué jewels. Jazz Age jewels, the flapper's frivolities, were made in dark, moody colour combinations almost always including black. Necklets or expanding bracelets were made up of flat geometric slices or chunks imitating gold-flecked aventurine, honey-coloured cornelian or cream-coloured ivory, alternating with black plastic onyx and highlighted with paste; fringe necklaces with flat or wedge-shaped beads were popular and very often the plastics in red, green, mustard or black were combined with chrome for a machine age look. These chrome and plastic jewels are usually particularly geometric, stylish and abstract, typical of the 1930s classy and fashionable costume jewellery. A softer, prettier more conventional effect was achieved by mixing plastics with marcasite, while geometric pendants were well designed, often incorporating carved surfaces with smooth enamels or lacquer. The African mood could be conveyed through beads carved to look like wood or ivory like tribal ornaments.

Bangles *à la Nancy Cunard* were probably the most popular and most barbaric items of costume jewellery at this time, and looked spectacular when made of either misty or vibrant colours, hand-carved and polished to take a very high lustre. Some were clear and amber-coloured, like barley sugar, the finest examples carved from the back so that a motif, such as fish, appears to be suspended inside a glutinous gel. Muddy-coloured fake jade and ivory were very popular, as well as intense

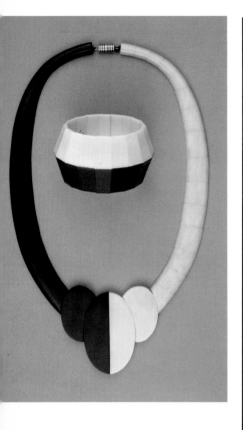

*Plastic modernist jewels of powerful shapes and stark colour contrasts, by Auguste Bonaz. French, c.1925.*

yellow, green and red, occasionally covered with polka dots, and multi-coloured bangles were especially effective. There was a vogue for bangles that looked like jewelled cuffs, with bold buttons or buckles. Bakelite was the most successful type of plastics for this kind of carving, moulding and polishing, as it was rock hard, water and heat proof and lent itself to mechanical processes. Usually the Bakelite was opaque, but without its toughening 'filler' ingredient that produced the opacity it could also be cast in moulds to produce slightly more fragile, translucent jewels.

Brooches showed the greatest and zaniest variety of motifs, colours, textures, forms: hearts, hats, sombreros hung with luscious fruits, cherries and all kinds of fruits and vegetables (Carmen Miranda inspired), shoes or soles with holes, a black top hat and cane, very Hollywood, a woman's profile derived from African art, her crinkled hair flowing backwards. There were liner-shaped brooches, stylishly geometric and celebrating the launch in 1935 of the *Normandie*; there were trains, cars, a variety of dogs, an elephant's head, a parrot. Gradually, with an understanding of the vast possibilities of the material, designs became more and more uninhibited and ingenious, and craftsmen took the same pride in the finished plastic product as in any other decorative work of art. Even the great artist René Lalique worked in

*Group of novelty Bakelite dog brooches, stylized to suit Art Deco design or the theme of speed and streamlined movement. English, c.1930–40.*

*Black plastic and chrome modernist necklace. French, c.1925.*

plastics in the 1920s and 1930s; one well known line of plastic trinket from the Lalique workshops included a square bright red box, moulded with luscious cherries.

The French designer Auguste Bonaz created the most exciting modernist costume jewels, working in Bakelite and Galalith. He used pure, simple linear abstract forms, free of surface ornament, for a very powerful effect. The strong contrasting shapes, ovals, squares, oblongs, show a deep appreciation and understanding of the potential of the glossy material; and despite the angularity of the chosen forms, the results are especially fluid, recalling the movement of a slick machine. Bonaz used equally strong colours, usually red and black, blue or black and white, green and black. The necklaces are most striking but he also made hair combs and bracelets, all rigorously abstract and evocative of 1930s design. Bonaz exhibited at the 1925 Exhibition which gave plastics and costume jewellery in general a great deal of credibility and respectability.

In 1925 there were so many manufacturers of costume jewels that they had to be arranged in different groups such as 'Clothes Accessories', or 'Plastics Materials'. One of the most successful and prominent of Paris manufacturers was Piel Frères (see chapter 3), who had first made inexpensive art jewels in the Art Nouveau style of 1900. The firm specialized in high-fashion ornaments and fine enamels on copper and base metals. In 1925 Piel was working in close association with the couturier Patou, amongst others, and excelled in belt buckles of engraved and patinated glass and enamels in chic, modern geometric patterns. The firm of Greidenberg specialized in jewels and buckles of coloured metals, oxidized or plated in silver or gold, and their designs were very Cubist inspired. Gradually after 1925, with the encouragement of an annual exhibition organized by the Chambre Syndicale, French costume jewellery was more and more innovative, less and less reminiscent of real jewellery. The growth of costume and plastics jewellery was partly in answer to a growing need for novelty for its own sake, a constant search for anything out of the ordinary, for fantasy as an escape from the stark functionalism of the modernists and from the growing mood of disillusionment.

The 1920s ended with the Wall Street Crash; the 1930s began with an uncertainty in general; people had less money to spend but a greater appetite for escapism, for anything diverting, out of the ordinary. The luxury trades suffered from the Depression while costume jewellery blossomed. New materials brought a constant stream of surprises. In

Group of jewels using black and marcasite or black and paste to conform to chic colour schemes of the 1920s and 1930s; the two brooches (left) mix a lingering Art Nouveau or Edwardian style with contemporary geometry; the circular brooch (right) is made to imitate a real onyx and diamond brooch. German or French, c.1930.

Two silver and paste set brooches; (above) formalized geometric diamanté scrolls incorporate baguette-cut stones and fake rubies; (below) in the shape of a horse chestnut; the broken spiky case reveals the shiny diamanté fruit. French, c.1930.

May 1930 Vogue said 'Costume jewellery becomes more and more extraordinary, but the chic of one's necklace does not always depend on the remarkable nature of its materials. A conservative but very charming idea now being used is to have the necklace made of beads covered with crêpe-de-Chine to match one's frock.' At the same time, in the late 1920s, femininity was creeping back into fashion and with it a craze for slinky curves, for glamour, satin and diamanté. Paste became more opulent and more noticeable, while a less expensive daytime alternative to paste was marcasite and silver jewellery, which fitted in well with an all-grey vogue stimulated by displays at the 1929 exhibition of jewellery in Paris at the Musée Galliéra.

The best of this marcasite jewellery, very typical of inter-war popular jewellery, was made in Pforzheim, in high-fashion or amusing novelty designs. It was turned out in huge quantities, glinting softly as bows, little drapes of fabric, as circles, arrows, flowers, animals, birds of paradise with curling feathers, dogs' heads such as bulldogs with drooping jaws, climbing monkeys or perhaps trifles inspired by the East such as an elaborate enamelled Chinaman carrying a yoke of water buckets or pulling a rickshaw. Abstract steely compositions were sometimes enlivened with enamels, pastes or with coloured semi-precious stones. Theodore Fahrner, a Pforzheim manufacturer, was the leader in this field. Fahrner had specialized in mass-producing well-designed inexpensive jewels at the turn of the century in the prevailing Art Nouveau or Jugendstil manner, converting idealistic important designs into trinkets to appeal to the tastes and pockets of a much wider audience. The firm continued on this successful track through the Art Deco period, and was famed for silver and marcasite jewellery.

Clips were increasingly popular in real jewels as well as in costume (see chapter 5), and many examples can be found in marcasite, as well as in paste, plastics and chrome. Their stylish versatility meant they could be pinned to necklines, belts, pockets, lapels, cloche hats. Fahrner's range included a wide choice of clips, along with very attractive and distinctive ranges of geometric jewels, mixing the marcasites with semi-precious stones in the popular soft colour schemes of brown, lavender blue and mustard. Necklaces were generally of the stepped Odeonesque style, with matching clip or drop earrings and bracelets or rings.

In the mid-1930s, the geometry of some costume jewellery was already displaying a certain curvaceous softness and giving way in many cases to figurative ideas. There was a vogue for 'antique' costume jewellery, as the new poor rooted around antique and flea markets for individual, inexpensive treasures from past ages, such as Victorian gilt metal or early 19th-century Pinchbeck jewels. Old or modern jewels, expensive or humble, which depicted disembodied hands or parts of the body, were much worn, a ripple from the wave of surrealism of the 1930s.

The big jewellery manufacturers cast back into history for inspiration and romance. Alongside the modernist, abstract jewels from Paris, the Napier Company devised successful reproductions based on the antique: their filigree range, for example, called Rosace jewellery, finely hand-worked with spirals, coils, rosettes which they considered Graeco-Roman in feeling. The jewellery was set with synthetic onyx, jade and cornelian and given a special dull finish known as 'Georgian Silver', which they described as their 'light antique silver finish'. In 1926 they had introduced their Viking jewellery, based on a simple spiral motif, which was apparently found on the boldest of all plundering Viking ships in the ninth century. The pattern symbolized the dynamic vitality and strength of the Viking race. It was recreated in silver or gold plate.

Nineteenth-century gilt metal or Pinchbeck hand clasps and brooches were sought after. Cartier made a famous brooch like a hand holding a rose; Ciro made a bejewelled gilt hand, its long, slender fingers with brightly painted nails.

In the United States, the 1920s and 1930s saw the establishment or growth of many of the greatest costume jewellery firms. As in Europe, the shift in social structure, the extremes of new wealth and new poverty with the Wall Street Crash, the growth of Art Deco design, particularly in New York, and the glory of Hollywood had all conspired to bring about the changes in values and lifestyles that made costume jewellery the most important fashion accessory. While Paris still led the way for women's fashions, the American jewellery trade, inspired by what was happening in Europe, took off on its own creative and technical route.

The firm of Trifari was founded in 1925 by Gustavo Trifari, Leo F. Krussman and Carl M. Fishel. Trifari and Krussman had together been manufacturing diamanté jewellery since 1918 under their own names. Fishel had been Vice President of Rice & Hochster, important manufacturers of shoe buckles, hair combs and hair ornaments, including tortoiseshell and fake tortoiseshell and the popular decorative celluloid and paste haircombs. The comb industry was very much more important than the costume jewellery industry at that time. Fishel had

*Silver and marcasite novelty brooches were popular between the wars: a pig-tailed Chinaman, set with paste turquoises and marcasites, a sign of the Oriental craze of the 1920s and 1930s. Probably German, c. 1920–30.*

met Trifari and Krussman when they too had been associated with Rice & Hochster: Krussman worked for the firm and Trifari was a small independent manufacturer. In 1924 Fishel made his annual trip to Paris, but he came back with the shocking news that the comb and buckle industry was doomed: high-cut shoes were out of vogue, and Chanel had persuaded women to cut their hair and wear fake gems. It was at this point that Fishel met with his two friends, over lunch at the Waldorf Astoria in New York, and they decided to start their own costume jewellery firm.

They specialized in diamanté jewels of extremely fine quality, and were soon known as the Rhinestone Kings. Trifari was the technical man, and also supervised designs; Krussman was a superb organizer, and Fishel was the dynamic salesman. In general, the early jewels were made by a method of sand-casting, although often dies were made for more successful lines. The metal settings, silver plated, were always immaculately finished and polished, and designs were complex, composed of several different shapes and parts. The early jewels, marked with the initials TKF, aimed at a real, precious look.

In 1930 Trifari took a major step forward when they employed the young designer Alfred Philippe, who had studied at L'Ecole Boulle in Paris and had worked for a fine jewellery manufacturer, designing magnificent, stylish jewels for Van Cleef & Arpels and Cartier. Philippe was sent to work in the United States, but shortly afterwards, the Crash of 1929 adversely affected the fine jewellery trade, and Trifari persuaded Philippe to leave the world of real jewels for that of fantasy jewels. Recognizing his talent and value, the three founders of Trifari made Philippe virtually a partner in the business. He continued as their chief designer and then a Vice President until 1966, by which time his son Jacques was also working at Trifari. Philippe's designs were adapted from and inspired by his work with precious jewels, but his new designs for Trifari were highly original, daring yet convincing, and always made the most of the exciting materials and techniques at his disposal. The jewels expressed the fantasy and freedom of costume jewellery, and yet showed the control, the dignified elegance of the most aristocratic of precious jewellery. Exquisite, imaginative design was at the core of Trifari's early success. Trifari, Krussman and Fishel all contributed ideas, and one simple line or shape, or a particular swirl, spotted and sketched by Philippe in Paris, might then form the basis for a whole collection. Production was limited at this time; there were about 100 workmen at the factory (which was in New York until 1939), and the quality was strictly supervised to reach the desired degree of perfection. All the paste stones were made to order by Swarovski in Austria. Trifari jewels were sold to the finest stores in the United States, but they did not penetrate the British market until the 1930s, when enduring non-tarnishing rhodium-plating techniques were introduced. The crisp, clean finish appealed to the British market, and Trifari jewels were sold at Harrods and Ciro.

Early examples of Philippe's designs are distinguished by the same expensive softness as very finely made real jewels. Bracelets and necklaces are fluid and supple; designs represent the best of Art Deco characteristics, quietly stylish, uncontrived yet geometric, incorporating a rich use of colour and unusual cuts of stones. Trifari excelled at using small carved coloured stones, typical of Cartier and Van Cleef & Arpels. Sometimes these took the form of convincing paste rubies, emeralds, and sapphires clustered within a framework perhaps of baguette diamanté; other designs made use of opaque carved turquoise and coral pastes for a very individual, soft look. This was followed by a quite different rather whimsical range of exuberant jewels of the 1940s imitating the fashion for chalcedony, a semi-precious stone, stained lavender blue. Trifari's versions used pastes of the same bluebell or 'heaven' blue, as it was called in their advertisements, carved as leaves and flowers, mixed with

*Silver and paste-set hand-pierced openwork bracelet by the Napier Company, decorated with tiny filigree and wirework rosettes, in a pastiche of Regency goldwork. American, c.1925.*

Group of exquisitely made paste
bracelets, wide, flexible and luxurious,
of exciting, inventive design. Trifari,
c.1930.

diamanté and gathered into huge and lively bouquets, or spilling out of wheelbarrows (see chapter 5). Small *calibré* or specially cut pastes were a speciality of the firm in the 1920s and 1930s, again echoing their use in Place Vendôme jewels, and later in the 1930s Philippe created a Trifari range that brilliantly challenged Van Cleef & Arpels's jewels in the emerging cocktail style and especially those incorporating the famous invisible settings (see chapter 5). For instance, he introduced large silky blue paste sapphires, geometric and eye-catching, set either with gilt metalwork or surrounded by specially cut diamanté, very often as stunning matching sets of various jewels. Huge rubies and specially flawed emerald pastes were used in the same way. In 1937, Philippe created his first 'gold' or tailored collection, intended for day-wear and as a departure from the diamanté look. This increased the scope of the firm considerably and exciting, innovative ideas became the hallmark of Philippe's designs for Trifari in the 1940s and 1950s.

The TKF mark was discontinued around 1936–7 and replaced by the name Trifari in full, accompanied by the crown, their trademark. This coincided with the introduction of an extensive national advertising campaign by Trifari, the first of its kind in the costume jewellery industry. Like the jewels, the advertisements were very fashionable, expensive-looking and elegant, usually featuring a photograph of a beautiful bejewelled woman in a vignette surrounded by detailed photographs of the jewels and highly descriptive copy. The catchphrase was 'jewels by Trifari', which accounted for the change in signature from TKF.

The firm of Eisenberg also rose to fame and success in the 1930s. Eisenberg & Sons Originals, established in 1914 in Chicago by Jonas Eisenberg, sold exclusive ladies' clothes. One of the special attractions of the dresses and coats was the addition of paste clips, buttons or trimmings. Apparently the alluring sparklers were so often stolen from the clothes that Eisenberg was persuaded to begin a separate production of paste jewellery. It is not clear exactly when this began, but the jewels were first marked 'Eisenberg ORIGINALS' around 1935, a mark that was used until 1945. These jewels, large and heavy, have a very distinctive, aristocratic appearance with a strong 18th-century flavour. Deep settings of white metal, very like those of 18th-century paste, hold large shaped old-cut pastes set at varying angles. The pastes were probably foiled to add a deep, misty charm. Designs were seemingly random patterns, some within strong abstract outlines, others more fluid such as ribbon bows or soft swirls of old-looking stones enclosing a pearl softened with a golden patina. The overall effect was one of sophisticated timelessness, the mellow moody colouring blended with a certain boldness of size, shape and a lavish gem-encrusted surface. The largest part of the range consisted of clips, probably intended to be worn on furs, and most of the other jewels are brooches. During the Second World War, silver was substituted for base metals which were required for the war effort, and the jewels became slightly sharper, less baroque and more modern, moving towards the tougher, sparkling diamanté of the 1950s.

The Napier Company originated in 1875 in the jewellery manufacturing centre of N. Attleboro in Massachusetts. Whitney & Rice, as it was then called, manufactured huge fire-gilt gentlemen's

*Group of early Eisenberg diamanté jewels showing a distinctive, baroque opulent softness, reminiscent of 18th-century grandeur; c. 1920–40.*

watch chains. Eventually the company was taken over by E. A. Bliss, the salesman, who later hired a new designer William Rettenmeyer. By the 1890s, the company was flourishing as virtually the first of its kind to be producing non-precious costume jewellery, along with an extensive range of giftware and silver novelties. James Napier joined the firm in 1914 and under his leadership the company was revitalized and given an entirely fresh high-fashion approach, employing new staff, buying new machines and equipment, planning new campaigns of advertising and promotion. During World War I the company turned to manufacturing war materials, but by 1922 its reputation as a fashion jewellery house was greater than ever. Its name was changed to the Napier Company and Napier continued as president until 1960.

It was surely due to Napier's talent and foresight that during the 1920s the company specialized in producing replicas or American versions of the new and exciting Paris couture jewels by famous names such as Chanel, Lucien Lelong, Premet, Patou, Jenny, Agnes, Worth, Schiaparelli. Napier was the first to bring these new designs to the United States, although it is not known whether this arrangement was under contract or licence to Napier. As early as 1927 Napier was manufacturing replicas of the simple gold jewellery designed by the couturier Premet. The jewels were made of gilt chains of the springy close-knit Brazilian linking, a necklace composed of twisted strands, a wide bracelet of several rows of chain, the earrings long and simple drops. They were advertised as blending 'modern sophistication and Florentine splendour'. Premet's new design in the same year was a laurel leaf necklace and bracelet, the gold-plated metal pattern set with simulated jade or lapis at the centre. Various copies of couture jewels were available in different price ranges. In 1928 modernistic jewellery from the house of Lucien Lelong ('a decided sophisticate') included a Moon-Glo necklace made of Pentagon blue crystals separated by flat silver discs. Lelong's range of 'Modern Art' featured a metal and ivory bracelet in superb geometric and abstract design, a simple mechanistic silver-finished necklace and a wood and gilt metal bracelet, equally geometric and Cubist-inspired. Patou's necklace of 1928 reproduced by Napier was considered to be 'utterly modernistic' in design: a circlet of flexible metal sections finished in front with a loop or a bow-knot. This, too, came in a gold or silver finish. In 1928 and 1929 Lelong continued to thrill customers with jewellery 'inspired by the French Modernistic Spirit' and for good measure he threw in some native or exotic elements. In 1928 Napier was selling a Lelong necklace designed as Cleopatra's

Advertisement for Napier's version of
Schiaparelli's globe circling bracelet,
in non-tarnishing gold plate.
American, 1937.

Illustration from an article in Life,
January 1938, discussing the growth
in popularity of costume jewellery;
the article stated that in 1937
department stores had doubled the
space devoted to costume jewellery.

asps and a fringe necklace called 'Africana'. The barbarism of Lelong's jewellery was sometimes likened to that of a South Sea Island 'Chieftess'.

To counteract the ferocity of the modernistic spirit from France, Napier continued to come up with interesting traditional lines, particularly in filigree work, which was a speciality in the 1920s and 1930s. Their skill has always been in metalwork, in intricate wire bending and folding, all hand worked. In 1925 long necklaces, 48 inches in length, worn bandolier style, over the shoulder and under the arm, were made of large beads of filigree with mock lapis stones or fake pearls in between. The Napoleonic bee brooch in gilt metal was popular in 1925, worn on hats, shoes, belts or handbags, and the same year saw the fashion for 'Trianon' bracelets, now known as Russian wedding bands. The Trianon range of bracelet and matching ring was marketed as a new French fashion, the interlocking bands plaited in green, red and white gold, symbolizing respectively health, wealth and happiness. By 1927, when modernism was making its mark, Napier also promoted their Rosace jewellery (see page 133), with its gentle filigree, soft distressed colouring of metal and fake stones, and an innovative line of imitation crystal jewellery in two new colourings: Canary topaz (yellow) and Rosavel (pink). In 1928, the year Napier marketed Lelong's abstract and barbaric wide Egyptian bracelet, and Chanel's beach beads, they also produced a range of medieval jewellery inspired by armour – massive, metallic with shield motifs.

Chanel-type necklets of the late 1920s with small geometric patterns in coloured crystals, in a layered Odeonesque design, were called Cascade, one of a series of delectable names dreamt up by Napier for their own ranges. Chrystobal graced their chrysoprase and silver line; Sun-Tan described their new bronze finish, which suited the new vogue for looking sunburnt. Aloma was the name for sapphire and amber jewels, conjuring up blue skies and yellow sunshine, 'a tropical combination'. Typical Art Deco colour combinations of jade and sapphire and jade and amethyst were exotically labelled Hawaiian moonlight; Solaray summed up the amber and gold jewels, and Montmartre was the name given to amethyst and pearl combinations, as Napier claimed, in tribute to 'a well known place in Paris where many of the best-dressed women gather nightly. Entertained by the well known artist Raquel Meller, who favours amethysts and wears them always'. Capucine was the colour sponsored by Patou; it made an excellent contrast to Chinese jade jewellery popular at the time. It was in 1929 too that Napier launched a new range called Casanova Coral 'named for that bold Italian adventurer

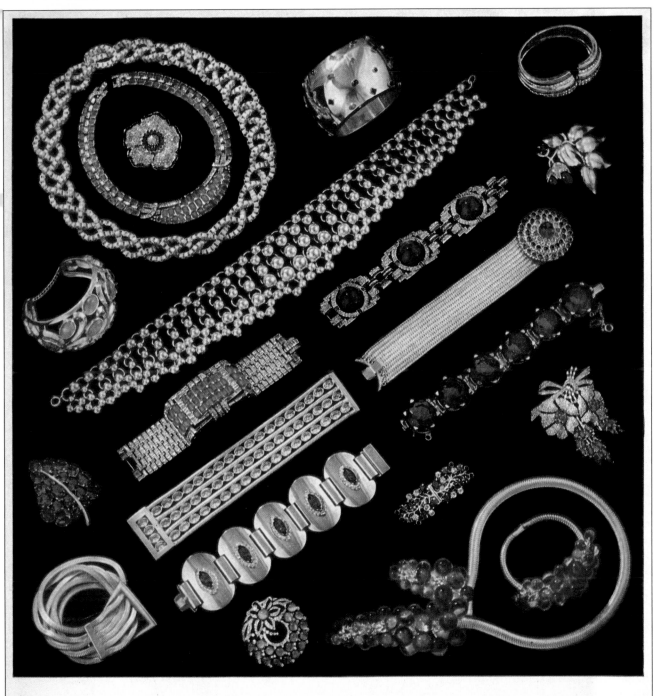

# JUNK JEWELRY: A FLASHY FAD FOR SIMPLE STYLES

The twenty-one sparkling trinkets in this photograph are the pick of the 1937–38 winter crop of what the trade, with neither malice nor shame, likes to call "junk jewelry." During the past year sales of "junk" reached new highs. In the boom days of 1929 dollar sales may have been greater, but never have as many pieces been sold or worn as during the current season.

Jewelry manufacturers thrive when dress fashions are simple. Last August, at the Paris Openings, wise ornament merchants whooped with joy at the dresses with plain high necklines or V-shaped *décolletages* with short sleeves, and generally without fancy buttons, elaborate collars and frills. Schiaparelli and Chanel called several of their creations "jewelry dresses." The mannequins modeling them were bowed with the weight of the jewelry they wore. Cameras clicked, cables carried the news to the U. S. and the stampede was on.

By November, leading American department stores had doubled space devoted to junk jewelry. Fashionable shops on 57th Street, New York, and comparably exclusive stores over the country which had never stocked "junk" before, succumbed.

All jewelry made of nonprecious metals (except silver) and stones is called "junk." A decade ago "fake" was the qualifying term. Then the aim was to make the imitation look real. Several years later the more polite phrase "costume jewelry" was adopted. Last year when heavy gilt jewelry became so popular, the trade aptly labeled all nonprecious jewelry "junk." No attempt is made to fool anyone into believing it is real. The six clear, perfectly matched pieces of glass in the bracelet (*centre right, above*) obviously couldn't be emeralds.

"Junk" can be expensive. The rhinestone and simulated emerald bracelet (*top, right*) costs $100. The ruby and rhinestone necklace (*inner circle, top*) costs $75. Biggest sales of "junk" are for pieces from $5 to $10. The least expensive item in the collection above is the gold and emerald spray (*lower left*) which costs $5.

of the 18th century who styled himself a lover of coral', so the advertising copy ran. Casanova Coral featured a chunky ribbed gilt geometric design, veering towards the mechanistic mood, set with smooth mock coral beads. There was a necklace, bracelet and drop earrings.

In the 1930s Napier instigated a unique finish to their 24-carat gold plating process. Called Naco, the special finish guaranteed to prevent articles from discolouring or tarnishing. By the mid-1930s Napier was making the most of exciting plastics, Catalin and Prystal, their opaque white bangles designed with popular sporty motifs of hurdles or stirrups. Before long, however, the vogue was shifting very much towards massive gilt jewels at which Napier could continue to excel.

Many other New York firms developed around this time, including Marcel Boucher, manufacturer of some of the very finest jewellery of the period. From the 1930s to the late 1950s Boucher, together with his wife Sandra, produced exceptionally fine 'real'-looking jewels in geometric motifs, similar to those of Alfred Philippe but usually bolder and more extravagant. His jewels are usually marked 'BOUCHER'. Like Philippe, Boucher had trained as a fine jewellery designer, working for Cartier. In the mid-1930s he began making paste shoe buckles and fancy goods and progressed to superb costume jewellery.

Back in Paris, in the late 1920s and 1930s, a new wealth tax meant that women could be taxed on the value of the jewellery they owned. Determined not to give up their adornments, nor to be heavily penalized for them, ladies of fashion turned more and more to costume jewellery, which was free of tax. Along with paste and fake pearls, they wore the new glass beads and jewels that came either from the Orient or from the genius of glassmaker René Lalique, who had been the leader of the Art Nouveau jewellery movement before turning his attention to glassmaking around the time of the First World War. In the 1920s, as part of his range of modern glass, Lalique produced pendants, rings, bracelets, necklaces and brooches of scintillating colours and forms. Many of the shapes were derived from Japanese decorative arts, but he added his favourite organic motifs: flowers, birds, insects, wasps, grasshoppers, butterflies, along with serpents, Medusa heads, satyrs' grinning masks. Beads were made of moulded glass; other jewels were created from clear or frosted glass backed with intensely coloured gleaming foil which shot luminous fiery colours through the icy crystal.

Long beads were shaped as lily of the valley flowers in opalescent yellow-green, as heavy-petalled lotus flowers or as little veined green ivy leaves or ancient cylinders, strung on silk. Brilliantly coloured pendants shaped like circular or rectangular *Tsuba* or Japanese sword guards were also hung on silk and finished with the fashionable tassel. Necklaces were often of clear glass, and shaped like ancient fringe necklets with formalized motifs of owls or lotus flowers. Bracelets consisted of discs like flowerheads, plaques or cylinder shapes, threaded on elastic. Rings were large and bombé, smoothly domed and incised with a pattern, clear or deeply coloured.

Everywhere in jewellery, colour, life, richness of form and stylized 'modern' decoration were taking precedence over intrinsic value. In the same way that women were enjoying their new fun and freedom, despite the economic gloom, costume jewels too made the most of an unrivalled period of liberation and excitement. The 20th century had finally arrived for women and their jewels.

*Blue glass pendant with frog motifs, in the form of a tsuba or Japanese sword guard, by René Lalique. French, c.1920.*

# Five

# THE COCKTAIL STYLE

Costume jewellery flourished in the dark and gloomy years of the late 1930s and 1940s, and brought a veneer of golden glamour to fashion and the women who followed it. These were years of rapid expansion and progress in the costume jewellery industry, particularly in America where the effects of war were less pervasive. Amongst the enormous variety of costume jewellery made in the 1940s, there is one particularly strong style that is most evocative of the period: the Cocktail Style. Sometimes known now also as Retro Modern, 1940s cocktail jewellery was equally at home in the realms of both real and costume jewellery. It has a robust, distinctive look of its own: bubbly and extravagant like the alcoholic concoctions from which it took its name, it was assertive, bossy, jewellery to show off in.

You can recognize cocktail jewellery by its bursts of pink gold and rubies, folds and drapes of buttery-yellow gold or gilt metal, huge hunks of citrines, icy aquamarines and ribbons of tiny square-cut sapphires. It was a look based on outward impressions of massive wealth that lent itself particularly well to interpretation in costume jewellery, so much so that fashion jewels must surely have often led the field of design, perhaps even inspiring the real jewels in this style.

This exuberant and prolific era of jewellery took off in the United States, where the bold and effervescent look was much admired. Cut off from Paris during the war years, the United States was forced into exploring its own talent and developing an American style. Despite the economic crises from 1929 to 1939, or rather because of them, there was a need for luxury, for brightness, cheerfulness and escapism wherever possible, at all levels of society. There was a need for a last surge of

*Diamanté and sapphire double clip, the original design fluid but formal, showing the gradual return to a curvaceous movement. Designed by Alfred Philippe for Trifari. American, c.1935–45.*

energy, a last lunge at life and style before the dark times ahead. Working girls longed for movie-style Hollywood glamour and found it in their clothes and accessories. For the growing new-rich, costume jewels as ever fulfilled an important function as outward indicators of fashion and style.

Once again the story of costume jewels was affected by social changes: the numbers and status of working women had increased considerably, and the market in ready-to-wear clothes and accessories was flourishing. Popular magazines brought high fashion and style into ordinary lives, and everyone could aspire to making dreams come true, through work and careers, through mixing in different circles, through rags to riches stories of stardom. Fashion and style became a leveller. The gap between the fashions of the very rich and the middle classes had narrowed considerably, and very good affordable copies of couture clothes were readily available off the peg. This was another innovation for which we owe a great deal to Chanel; she found plagiarism of her designs one of the most flattering of compliments. Naturally, the right high-fashion look in jewels was needed to accessorize these clothes, and costume jewellery fitted the bill perfectly, providing pizazz, style and designer names at the right price. Now in the late 1930s, the lifestyles of the rich were also being imitated, as more and more women realized that they too had a right to a social life that involved parties, dances and cabarets.

Everywhere, on both sides of the Atlantic, the cocktail party had become a popular form of entertaining at home, less expensive and less formal than a dinner party and a way of accommodating more guests at once. A whole new cult of dressing for the 'cocktail hour' began: the little black dress, pioneered by Chanel, was the perfect solution and its simplicity cried out for exciting jewels. For cocktails, ladies could still dazzle with after-dark glamour but need not conform to the conventions of formal evening wear.

Almost all women had some kind of evening or cocktail dress, which was more often than not inspired by something they had seen at the movies. Dressing up was an important part of life, and the right jewels were needed to go with these dresses. The enormous impact of the movies, in which lavish jewels (often fake) were worn, helped raise the status of costume jewellery. The movie star's style of real jewels was copied, or famous designers, like Hobé, commissioned to design costume jewels for specific movies.

Costume jewellery was now exceedingly chic. Ever since Chanel had employed ducal designers, Schiaparelli had commissioned fashionable artists, and both enjoyed rich and royal patrons, designing and wearing costume jewellery had become a high-society occupation. In America too the socialite Miriam Haskell, following in Chanel's footsteps, was creating expensive hand-made jewels that were quite the rage amongst the cognoscenti.

As frankly fake jewels had gained respectability, the manufacture of fashion jewels, particularly in America, had become almost an art form; it was also big business and a competitive one. Top designers were lured away from 'real' jewellery firms, and the fancy goods trade in New York, swollen by immigrant European artisans and embryo businessmen hungry for success, grew rich in talent and labour, and therefore

*The Hollywood influence: glamorous photographs of stars such as Lana Turner and Marlene Dietrich showed that jewellery was an integral part of the Hollywood image from the 1930s to the 1950s.*

profitable and fast-expanding. A great deal of attention and money was lavished on finding just the right up-to-the-minute designs, and the quality of manufacture was very high at the top end of the market.

Cocktail jewels have a strong recognizable style of their own, but many other types of costume jewellery were being made during the period. Individual designers were developing their own particular styles, while the next fashion was always slowly evolving, so that sometimes it is hard to know if a piece originated in the late 1930s, or in the 1940s or even 1950s. However, the strong cocktail look of the 1940s has an immediate appeal and is easy to recognize and place in jewellery history.

The Cocktail Style was itself a cocktail of various ingredients of 20th-century design. The main characteristics come from aspects of late Art Deco, from modernism and the machine age, with a strong emphasis on movement and especially on the rhythms and components of the factory assembly line.

Modernist jewels of the 1930s had been based on stark, architectural geometric lines: unlike the purely ornamental and sensual early Art Deco, modernist jewels stemmed from a more intellectual approach. They were serious jewels. Stripped of all unnecessary ornament, their design was influenced by the high-minded theories of the Bauhaus, Futurism, Cubism, by ideas of suitability of form to function. The streamlined abstraction created a cold, severe look so far as female ornaments were concerned, suppressing feminine traits. It seemed to consolidate the feelings of women about themselves and their new-won strength and independence, their roles in a tough masculine world of industry and machines. For a while women had dressed to look like men; there had been a tubular look hiding the curves of the body, short haircuts and the Eton crop, mannish trouser suits and women known as 'garçonnes' (after a novel by Victor Margueritte, published in 1922). But although their influence was strong, these abstract modernist jewels probably appealed only to a small proportion of women. The easier, more glamorous paste or diamond 1930s jewels, just gently geometric in concept, were popular throughout the decade. Most women did not conform to the mannish look; extremes of fashions that are best remembered are only rarely representative.

Basically what happened to jewellery in the late 1930s was that flat architectural forms were softened into more voluptuous curves, inflated into plump three-dimensional designs, coaxed once again into quirky, fun and figurative shapes and then injected with colour and a flirtatious

*Group of gilt ribbon or wirework jewels, the speciality of the Napier Company; the strong cocktail designs illustrate the 1940s characteristic of frozen movement, American, c.1937–40.*

Group of gilt metal, paste and plastic
bracelets in the effervescent Cocktail
Style of the late 1930s and 1940s.
French, c.1940.

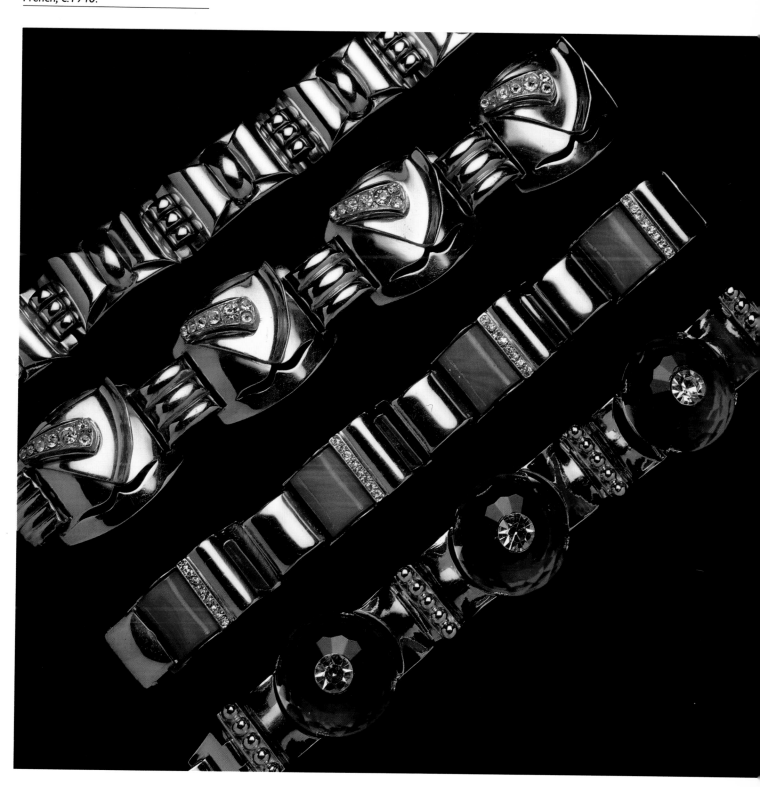

*Stylized wasp in silver gilt, diamanté and citrine pastes, the fluted gilt metal wings capturing the fluttering movement of the insect. Designed by Alfred Philippe for Trifari. American, c.1940.*

femininity. In a way this followed what was happening to women; now that their independence was more generally accepted, a new femininity could safely creep back, and the jewels reflected the new idea of this femininity, no longer subservient or weak, but full of life and strength.

The most entrancing characteristic of 1940s jewellery design is the balance of opposing elements and ideas; side by side you notice motifs that are both natural and artificial, stiff and fluid like a slice of frozen movement; shapes that are either soft like draped velvet or rigid and tough with the metallic coldness of machines. The appearance of so many 'fabric' motifs – folds, drapes or pleats – and the use of textured metals also referred to the new artificial fabrics such as jersey or rayon, which were particularly soft and fluid. This juxtaposition of contrary motifs also had a parallel in 1940s women: they were characterized by a seductive blend of masculine and feminine traits; they wore severely tailored clothes, trousers with turn-ups, square jackets with padded shoulders. They owned up to their sensuality. By day an air of crisp efficiency mingled with the softest of long wavy hairstyles; by night the slinkiest of satin evening clothes showed off the freedom and strength of curvaceous bodies.

The image of women projected through the 1940s was very much influenced by Hollywood and the movies. The stars of the 1940s, Rita Hayworth, Lauren Bacall, epitomized the new woman, still slinky and provocative, with gleaming eyelids, long silken hair but strong, vibrant, independent and determined. As opposed to the diamond-adoring frilled and flounced Belle Époque female, the new woman prized jewellery for its daring and powerful design rather than for its intrinsic value. She could buy her costume jewels for herself.

Outside Hollywood, Paris still led fashions as the centre of *haute couture*. Christian Dior's radical 'New Look', launched in 1947 with the revitalization of Paris couture, seemed also to epitomize the New Woman; the revolutionary Dior suit was still tailored, uncluttered, yet softer and feminine with a nipped-in waist, and a longer, fuller skirt with more softness and movement. It was soon after this that the House of Dior began to manufacture its own range of costume jewellery, to tie in with fashions but, most important, to appeal to the independent lady of fashion who bought costume jewels as vital accessories. Christian Dior has been a leading name in fashion jewellery ever since.

When the new styles of cocktail jewels first began to evolve in the late 1930s the new costume jewellery equivalents, usually made of gilt base

*Joan Crawford wearing a stylish cocktail bangle, c.1940.*

*Starfish brooch, pavé-set with paste citrines and diamanté; a Schiaparelli-inspired motif, c.1940–50.*

metal set with pastes or the new synthetic stones, looked just like bulkier versions of abstract Art Deco designs, pumped up into more sculptural and massive forms. You can see the transition clearly in the rings, which were particularly popular and plentiful at this time: square-edged knuckledusters for clenching round a glass of champagne, with layered edges like steps and square-cut stones stretched into a line over the corners and down the sides. Changes in designs can also be traced through double clips which were probably the most popular items of jewellery in the 1930s and 1940s. Their shapes moved from sharp geometry to something slightly more curvaceous; straight lines softened into shell patterns and straight sunrays rolled up into snail-like coils. Slowly, the 1930s look took on 1940s characteristics.

In real jewellery slim platinum settings and the crisp sparkle of diamonds and coloured precious stones gave way to a wider use of gold or metal surfaces. This was of course as much due to economic necessity as to style, but it created a mood that worked particularly well in gilt metal, which could be even more generous and voluptuous in its interpretations of fashionable swirls, windmill-like whirls, drapes, circles, bows. Times were bad, platinum was an expensive indulgence, and by eking out gold to give an impression of weight and substance and adding small, cleverly cut stones or large semi-precious stones, designers created a look that had immediate impact for less cash. Costume jewellery could do even better and easily produce the desired impression of glossy wealth. Base metal could be die-stamped or cast to look solid and heavy, then plated using new improved techniques to the required shade of gold.

The trend towards massive gilt jewels began in the late 1930s. Trifari's range of tailored golden jewellery was launched in 1937, Napier made the most of their speciality of handmade gilt wire jewellery, and by December 1938 the vogue was definitely heading towards more and more gilt ornaments and accessories. In 1941 Macy's in New York advertised their 'Gold Rush', promoting fabulous fake gold jewels.

Techniques of stamping or casting were much improved at this time. At the end of the 1930s gravity casting was the most usual method of manufacture, but centrifugal casting techniques were being developed also. This meant that quite complicated and intricate patterns could be produced in quantity, and the settings were well finished with clear, sharp detail. French workshops still excelled in die-stampings, an extension of their goldsmithing expertise, and separate vital components of cocktail design, chunky geometric gilt metal motifs, for example, were stamped out and hand-assembled into stylish French jewels: wide bracelets, perhaps, that looked like linked machine parts or like tank tyre tracks.

In 1937, the firm of Monet in New York began to make costume jewellery. This company, originally called Monocraft, had started in 1929 manufacturing gilt metal monograms for the fashionable envelope-type handbags. Their wearing qualities and their expensive look were so successful that Monocraft was asked to produce costume jewellery of the same quality. The company, owned by two brothers, Michael and Jay Chernow, set about researching metals and plating processes and came up with a long-lasting triple-plated product that closely resembled 14-carat gold. Encouraged by department-store buyers, they aimed to produce a range of jewellery with the look and feel of real jewellery but at a price that would tempt all fashion-conscious women. This mood of research and development in a growing industry affected many companies in the New York fancy goods trade. However, from about 1941, the base metals suitable for new casting techniques were needed for the manufacture of armaments and most costume jewellery was set in silver. During the War years Eisenberg jewels, for instance, previously set in pewter, were set in silver as were those of Trifari. All of Trifari's tools and dies were contributed to the War effort. Often the silver had to be cast by the lost wax method, which made the jewellery more expensive but still popular. After the War, as manufacturers reverted to using base metals which could be gold- or rhodium-plated for durability, Trifari produced an alloy called Trifanium to add glamour and prestige.

Some of the best and strongest costume cocktail jewels were made by an American firm called Pennino. The designs are extraordinary, full of surprises, and although very much in the cocktail mood they have an individuality that proclaims the success of costume jewels. The gilt metal, either rose pink or yellow, was cast into strong 1940s shapes of confident and emphatic movement and pride. The compositions and shapes are all finely proportioned, showing a serious and talented approach to the mood of fun and freedom of costume jewels.

Pennino set the jewels with paste, either bright diamanté or in deep strong colours, often creating floral forms, unnaturally bulbous or sprouting chaotic shoots or blooms in heightened colours of fuchsia pink, zircon, turquoise-blue or emerald green. The firm used unusually cut pastes in other jewels to form petals and flower centres. Bows and ribbons were especially energetic, as were thrusting flower bouquets bursting with life, while other designs were abstract and curiously suggestive of organic forms, often incorporating a huge mound pavé-set with pastes.

This wild colour reflected the new importance of colour generally. After the black and white craze of the 1920s and 1930s it was needed again, not the theatrical exoticism of Art Deco but an overall abstract use of colour that was a more intrinsic part of the jewel, like a metallic glow of pink or yellow gold or the mixing of unusual stones. By 1937 or 1938, a new colourful and exciting opulence was the most significant fashion trend. Fashion writers traced the mood to a revival of Louis XV splendour or to French Exposition fireworks. Clothes were trimmed with coloured sequins, tinsel and embroideries. In real jewellery fashions, the soft translucency of semi-precious stones such as aquamarines, amethysts and citrines in all tones from blond to deep sherry could be worn in huge chunks at relatively low cost. Small diamonds and coloured stones were

*Group of gilt and paste jewels by Pennino, expressing the dynamic movement and strong stylization of natural forms associated with this maker. American, c.1940.*

Two variations of the bow motif: a bow and flower spray brooch of diamanté and aquamarine and sapphire blue pastes, made by Mazer. American, c.1940–50. Traditional openwork diamanté bow, probably based on a Royal favourite worn by the new Queen Elizabeth in the 1950s. English or American, c.1950.

added for emphasis, as trimmings to the large array of semi-precious gems. This was good news for the costume jewellery manufacturers, whose pastes could outdo the grandest show of rocks, whose well-cut small pastes or synthetics could look like the most affluent trail of *calibré* rubies or sapphires. The finest pastes still came from Swarovski in Austria or from Czechoslovakia, and mechanized cutting was producing more adventurous shapes, particularly the popular baguette or rectangular-shaped stones. During the War the glass stones were in short supply so that designs were developed to make better use of gilt metal, or silver gilt requiring fewer pastes.

The movement so well conveyed through Pennino's jewels was the keynote of cocktail jewellery design. This was another reaction to the static geometry of modernism. The images of mechanical movement were especially important in 1940s jewels, providing the artificial, tough elements to counteract the more feminine aspects. The theme of machinery in motion spilled over from the 1930s and became the dominant influence on real and costume jewellery. In 1937 Macy's in New York was advertising an avant-garde, machine-age bracelet from the house of Schiaparelli who 'strings pistons and fretted metal balls on her latest vagary'. In the 1930s it had manifested itself in abstract geometric shapes or in jewels shaped like motor cars or ocean liners. In the 1940s design focused on individual parts of engines or machines: ball bearings, screw-heads, girders, pipes or rods, flexible linking like brickwork or tyre tracks, brilliantly engineered clasps and hinges, gilt roundels with paste-set edges like glamorous cogs or washers or chunky nuts and bolts. Smooth rolls of metal curved over a solid rod-shaped motif, often repeated in rows to give the impression of the bumping, rolling rhythm of the production line. The jewellery moved too: bracelets slipped through buckles and ended with a swinging tassel, or a thick gold chain slipped through sphere-shaped slides, and little pieces of gas pipe chain bobbled at the centre of brooches and necklaces.

Concern with movement extended to the 'working' parts of jewels. Chains, links, clasps and hinges not only had to function ingeniously but also became decorative features. There was a fascination with the way jewels were made and both real and costume jewels are fabulous feats of engineering at this period, worth collecting for this reason alone. Real gold bracelets were often so well articulated that they were slinky and supple on and off the wrist and could sometimes be folded up into a compact little concertina. Very wide gilt metal bracelets in this flexible style were composed of heavy-looking mechanistic motifs that gave the

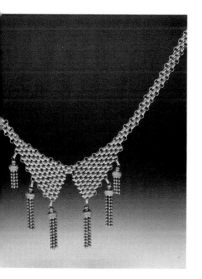

Collar-shaped necklace of flexible gilt metal 'brickwork', hung with tassels for extra movement, the metal tinged pink in imitation of the fashionable pink gold. French, c.1940.

impression of clanking armour. The effect was superb. Stamped components were hand-assembled to look like a moving staircase, like a series of fat stiff bows or like the ever popular brickwork design.

This brickwork pattern of rectangular flexible links was also popular for necklaces made as costume jewels, as it could be well made, by inexpensive available hand labour, in gilt metal. Necklaces were sometimes given unusual jagged outlines like a pointed shirt collar, for instance, or like the terraced step pattern that is an important feature of cocktail jewels in general. The brickwork could be small and tightly knit, ideal for slim and slippery bracelets that perhaps slotted through a gem-set buckle, or it could be large and chunky with more space between the links. There was a particularly successful cheap version of the brickwork design created in England in chromium plate and used for necklaces and bracelets under the trade name 'Radior'. Chain for

Brooch and bracelet of gilt metal and paste, featuring a strap and buckle design, made of flexible 'brickwork' linking, a perfect expression of the machine age. Made by Schreiner. American, c.1940.

necklaces was often ribbed or folded like a concertina in a style known as gas pipe for obvious reasons; this was particularly popular in real jewels and echoed in fashion jewels. Another metalwork speciality that was cleverly copied by costume jewellery manufacturers was the Van Cleef & Arpels technique of 'honeycomb' designs: a perforated pattern of little hexagons or little overlapping semi-circles, like scales. Very often each little shape was embedded with a diamond, sapphire or ruby – pastes or synthetics in the case of copies – set into a star-shaped recess. This setting was directly borrowed from High-Victorian jewellery, a sign of the popularity of earlier and antique jewels.

The preoccupation with movement gradually began to take on different characteristics, particularly in the case of metal wrought into the contrived stiffness of folds of fabrics, pleats, swirls and flounces. In New York Napier specialized in pink-gilt metal brooches, the wide, flat wire curled and folded and tied into stylish rosettes. Pennino and many other firms, notably Mazer, manufactured ranges of jewellery exactly like the real jewels with these fabric motifs and pastes that imitated the use of precious stones. Certain favourite motifs based on movement soon become familiar to the collector. There were swinging chains and tassels with pointed cone-shaped tags on the end that tumbled out of the centre of a windmill or propeller motif or were draped through circles or through a complex spiral design at the centre of a necklace. Flowers came back into fashion, and they had a stylized naïveté about them, a thrusting dynamism of growth in the curve of the stems or leaves. Petals were simple, with hard edges and sharp points, like cut-out flowers, a style that was easy to interpret in base metal with pastes for stamens and flower centres. Mazer excelled in a strong cocktail style for brooches incorporating a motif very like a twisted leaf, with a deep central vein or sweeping chunks of gilt metal, ornamented, perhaps, with a curved row of five rectangular stones or carved glass motifs.

In real jewels, Van Cleef & Arpels made the most sumptuous flowers using their invisibly set square-cut rubies or sapphires. The invisible setting or '*serte mystérieuse*' was one of the jewellery triumphs of the age. Square-cut stones were set *en masse* to look as if there were no metal mount. In fact they were held at the back by a trellis-like framework of gold. The front presented an unbroken covering of colour, which was used to create jewels like ribbons or curled petals of luscious flowers. The effect was copied in costume jewellery with square-cut pastes stuck close to each other, usually in a closed-back setting which was engraved to evoke the trelliswork mounting of the precious equivalents. Trifari and

*Luscious paste flower brooch using Trifari's version of invisible setting, pioneered by Alfred Philippe in the 1940s and continued with great success into the 1960s. American, 1961.*

*Brooch in the form of a blossom-laden tree, in metal, resin enamel and paste, made by Trifari. American, c.1940–50.*

Alfred Philippe led the way with imitation invisible settings. Trifari had groups of stones specially made, the little squares produced in one piece. This fashion had an effect on costume jewels towards the end of the 1940s when the gilt metal 'trendsetting' look began to be replaced by the grandeur of a 'real' look in which flowers and other motifs were completely paved or covered with cleverly cut pastes, improved pearls or turquoises. Necklaces and bracelets were entirely gem-set to look like precious parures. These were the speciality of American firms, notably Trifari as well as Marcel Boucher, whose flower jewels in particular offered a very rich and sensual overblown effect that was to remain popular during the 1950s.

In the 1940s and 1950s, large brooches were worn high and wide on the shoulder, in line with the collar bone. Flowers looked attractive worn in this way, and so did the bows and knots that were distant echoes of 18th-century ornaments. Usually they took the form of energetically tied ribbon bows of rippling pink-tinged metal, with fat knots paved with pastes. More forward-looking motifs for brooches reflected another obsession of the age, this time with outer space and science. Cocktail jewels could look like shooting stars or fireworks, sputniks or atoms.

By the mid-1940s costume jewellery was doing so well and attracting such talented and individual designers, for example Marcel Boucher and Trifari's Alfred Philippe, that it is sometimes hard to know which came first, the real or the fake. Amusing Disney-like figures and gawky cartoon animals gradually crept into real and costume jewellery designs in the mid- to late-1940s but costume jewellery seems to have had its own more individual repertoire of insects, animals and flowers. Designs for costume jewellery butterflies or bees in mid-flight, a pink-gilt shaggy-edged leaf on which crawls a charming diamanté-set ladybird, wings slightly parted ready for flight, or a paste wheelbarrow overflowing with flowers and leaves, are all so strong and so well executed that it is tempting to believe these jewels must sometimes have led the way.

In spring 1948 one of Trifari's leading ranges featured clusters of moulded light blue glass fruits and flowers, in the manner of the Fruit Salad jewels of the 1930s (see chapter 4). The light sapphire stones, known as spring sapphires, were the fashionable powder-blue colour of stained chalcedony, and were fashionable for springtime. The little stones ornamented all sorts of designs, bursting from the centres of orchids, tumbling out of bouquets, spilling over wheelbarrows, but one of the most popular lines was called 'Floraleaf', a design based on plump

*Matching brooch and earrings of stylized butterfly motifs, with soft, bow-like wings, of silver gilt set with pastes. Trifari, c.1945–50.*

and curvaceous heart-shaped leaves. Each leaf was half clustered with stones, half of gilt metal scattered with tiny diamanté, separated by a diamanté stem. They were made as a brooch or clip with matching earrings. An advertisement in *Vogue* for March 1948 pictured and described 'Floraleaf': 'exquisitely carved flowers of heaven-blue chalcedony* and pale, opalescent moonstone* combine with golden Trifanium and rhinestones in this newest tribute to Springtime by Trifari.' At the bottom of the page the asterisk pointed out that the gemstones referred to were simulated.

Birds, animals and figures were all adapted to the stylized chunky lines of the cocktail style. Favourite whimsical figures included scarecrows, clowns, a gardener with watering can, a flowerseller, Cinderella, a parachutist, figures from the Arabian Nights and particularly the

'Floraleaf' was a popular design in Trifari's spring 1948 range, as advertised in Vogue, March 1948. Made in golden Trifanium, set with clusters of moulded glass stones and diamanté. American, 1948.

158

*Trifari Clear Belly silver gilt and lucite jumping fish brooch; a white metal brooch set with a huge aquamarine paste and diamanté, in a strong cocktail design; abstract gilt metal and ruby-paste clip, by Trifari. American, c.1940.*

*Amusing, cartoon-like frog brooch, of gilt metal set with a paste cabochon sapphire centre, by Trifari. American, c.1940–50.*

ballerina. All sorts of animals and especially birds like highly stylized parrots on their perches joined in the cartoon show. During the War when paste-stones were in short supply Philippe and Trifari produced a famous and ingenious collection of animals using large polished mounds of lucite that looked like rock crystal treated in the Renaissance manner to create creatures around these fake gems: fish, swans, birds, bees, a delicious poodle, penguin, lizard and a range of exotic flowers were made in this vein. Wildly successful, these celebrated jewels came to be called 'Clear Bellies'.

These fun-loving ideas all confirmed the continuing influence of Hollywood and the movies, of Walt Disney and his endearing characters based on clever observation of animal movement. The jewels share the same emphasis on one particularly revealing characteristic. The ballerina is perhaps the most evocative of these symbols: stiffly poised on points, skirts of fluted gilt metal in imitation of famous jewels created by Cartier, Van Cleef & Arpels and John Rubel in New York. One of the most impressive versions of the ballerina jewel was made by Marcel Boucher in the 1950s, with a Cubist-shaped skirt and smooth, egg-shaped head.

Funny creatures and perky birds of paradise began a trend that was to reap great benefits in the 1950s and 1960s, when bright enamels, whimsical birds and cute animals came into fashion. In the 1940s, at the beginning of this fashion, there was a strong connection between the great ladies of fashion and design: Jeanne Toussaint of Cartier had bred this animal cult and must surely have been influenced by Schiaparelli's sense of fun and surrealism, by Chanel's sense of the barbaric and exotic. Coco Chanel had been a customer at Cartier from as early as 1919. It seems that she chose jewels of particularly rich colours: an enamelled ring, a brooch with an unusual mixture of sapphires, rubies and topaz. If Chanel was inspired to make larger-than-life pastiches of the real things, Toussaint was tempted to turn the whims of fashion jewels into expensive treasures for the rich, which were later turned back again into costume jewels. Parrots and birds of paradise à la Toussaint were often quite outrageous in costume jewellery, with jarring colour combinations, feathers in garish enamels around a body set, perhaps, with an absurdly huge paste sapphire. They were and still are humorous attention-seeking conversation pieces.

Wallis, Duchess of Windsor was one of Jeanne Toussaint's most famous and most talked about customers. Since the mid-1930s she had appeared in society wearing fabulous jewels that came under close

159    THE COCKTAIL STYLE

scrutiny as barometers of her romance with the Prince of Wales. Through the 1930s and 1940s, as she became a fashion leader, her jewellery remained a focus of attention and an influence on both real and fashion jewels around the world. Wallis had an unconventional and adventurous taste in jewels and she wore them with exceptional panache. She had a strong sense of her own style, which was parodied in brilliant costume jewels of the period. A regular customer at Cartier and Van Cleef & Arpels, and at Harry Winston in New York, she loved fine gems but also figurative jewels, exotic sensual animals and birds. She revelled in colour and texture and championed the major innovations of 1940s jewel design, including the move towards yellow gold jewels and surprising colour combinations of gemstones.

Each age has its favourite forms of jewellery: the double clip was the best-loved jewel in the 1940s, particularly appropriate to the machine age for its clever mechanism by which one large brooch could be separated into two clips which could then be worn individually. It expressed ingenuity, versatility and economy, and its form allowed for freedom of design. Many jewels of the period were made so that they could be taken apart and worn in different ways: a bracelet or necklace would have a detachable central motif which could be worn as a brooch. The double clip was very suitable for costume jewellery because it demonstrated the close liaison between jewels and clothes at the time. This double clip had come into being in the 1920s, and during the

*White metal and diamanté double*
*clip in a classic arrangement of swirls*
*and geometry. American, c. 1945.*

Every exquisite piece designed by TRIFARI is a triumph
in the art of costume jewelry.

*Jewels by* TRIFARI

1930s, clips began to replace conventional brooches. Instead of a pin, the clip had a spring fastening that gripped the edge of the lapel, neckline or pocket. As they were usually worn in pairs, it was natural for them to be fitted together to make one brooch. Usually the two pieces had identical motifs, rather like mirror images. Designs for double clips range from the pedestrian to the scintillating. There are endless permutations of flowers, scrolls, circles, girating geometry. Some of the most exciting and colourful designs are found in the costume jewellery versions which today can still seem 'chic' while the real jewels tend to look old-fashioned. The metal mounts would be cast and then *pavé*-set with pastes, often with the addition of plastic to imitate onyx or other semi-precious carved stones.

Rings had an important part to play in the repertoire of cocktail jewellery. Their advantage is that both the wearer and the onlooker can see and admire them and they have always been especially popular and easy to wear. At this period they could make rich and dramatic gestures, and they could add considerably to the overall look of extravagance, as many could be worn at once. Ring designs were also ideal for incorporating the mechanistic block shapes and for interpreting the massive three-dimensional look. Cocktail rings were raised high from the finger in eye-catching shapes. They most often echoed the wide square-shouldered look of fashions in clothes, as well as the spiral motifs of draped fabrics and turban-shaped hats, and of course the machine age motifs. A turban-shaped ring was made of interlocking spirals or voluptuous ribbed swirls tied in an elaborate knot. The enormously popular 'bridge' ring had two scrolled shoulders joined by a paste-set central motif, and a similar design looked like a square chunky bow with an ornate central knot. Designs were, however, often asymmetrical. Generally speaking, these styles of rings followed those of real jewels and can be very effective and convincing.

The world of costume jewellery was rapidly expanding at this time and major names and characters were beginning to come to the forefront of attention. Today's collectors of 20th-century costume jewellery concentrate on the 'named' designers and manufacturers who were flourishing at this time and who set the scene for the later 1950s and 1960s production. Outside the realms of the idolized couturiers, 'names' had been previously of small importance. In France, commercial manufacturers were largely anonymous; small workshops like Semana and Fried produced couture jewels, and Framex supplied the world with metal stampings which were assembled into jewels bearing the trade names of other companies. Some individual artist-designers such as Bonaz signed their *avant-garde* plastic creations.

It was the revival of Paris couture under the strong guiding influence of Christian Dior that established 'designer' jewellery and started the name-chasing phenomenon of the 20th century. The ideas for the jewels came from Dior himself and from the house's latest collections but the couturier had to find a suitable factory to transform the ideas into reality. In 1955 Dior turned to the busy jewellery centre of Pforzheim and the accomplished firm of Henkel & Grosse for the production of his costume jewellery, but before that time Christian Dior jewellery was produced under licence by a British company called Mitchel Maer.

American-born Mitchel Maer left New York to come to London in the late 1930s. Together with his brother-in-law, who had been in the fancy goods business in New York, he decided to set up a costume

*Exotic Byzantine-style jewels by Mitchel Maer for Christian Dior, made of gilt metal, decorated with enamels, set with pastes and imitation pearls. British, c. 1950.*

163

jewellery firm, and took offices in the run-down district of the Barbican. They advertised for craftsmen and Horace Attwood, an engraver and die-caster in the Birmingham jewellery industry, came to London for an interview and took the job, despite slight reservations about the two Americans in overcoats and Homburgs in a dingy Dickensian office. Attwood had the skills required to start producing fashion jewellery, while Maer was blessed with an abundance of charm which worked wonders with his staff and with store buyers. The firm was called Metalplastics at that time. They experimented with gravity casting techniques employed in America, using a soft metal with a high tin content so that the designs were rather flat, in low relief. The business made an auspicious start through a very good connection with Woolworths, who sold large quantities of costume jewellery, and as the turnover grew, the firm moved out of London to larger premises in Wales. During the War Attwood, with his special skills, was recalled to London to make tools, parts for cannons and gun belts. However Metalplastics was still allowed to make a small quota of jewellery and Mitchel Maer took on an agent to sell to the stores. He was Adrien Mann (who is today a major manufacturer).

After the War when business was gradually getting back to normal, Mitchel Maer decided to try the American technique of centrifugal casting, and it was Attwood's job to experiment with these techniques. The main problem came in making the rubber moulds and the initial models carved out of metal, which was again a highly skilled job. Another branch of the fast-expanding company, now called Mitchel Maer, made the casting machines and hydraulic presses. Attwood found a talented model-maker, Alun Roberts (who is still head designer at Attwood & Sawyer), and they began to create very fine costume jewellery in complex designs, all pastes set by hand, demanding the same skills as the real jewellery trade. This range was added to their normal Woolworths lines. In the early 1950s their factory employed some 250 people, with 15 casting machines and four presses to make the rubber moulds.

Early Mitchel Maer jewellery was made in a wide range of designs and styles. Some of the most distinctive is particularly baroque in character, with a Byzantine flavour, its softly coloured metal in elaborately curved shapes such as hearts or dolphins, hung with fringes of deeply coloured pastes, red or green, mixed with the softness of pearls and occasionally set with Limoges plaques. All stones were hand-set into claw mounts. Goldwork is intricately textured, sometimes to look like eastern filigree work. The typically 1940s use of movement in designs was emphasized by moving parts: bracelets that hung down over the hand, necklaces with fringes of chain or pastes. The jewellery is marked MITCHEL MAER.

In 1952 Mitchel Maer was approached by Christian Dior to make costume jewellery to designs chosen from specially commissioned freelance designers in Paris. Dior granted a concession to Mitchel Maer, who was later allowed to mark the jewels 'Christian Dior by Mitchel Maer'. Horace Attwood recalls that Dior demanded an exceptionally high quality; all the stones were hand set; extra staff were employed and trained to do this work, and a whole section of the factory was devoted to Christian Dior production. The jewellery was successful and very fashionable; in the 1950s Mitchel Maer jewellery for Christian Dior was often given names such as Rambouillet, Chenonceaux, Aubade.

Unfortunately, despite Maer's charm and a highly successful product, the company fell on bad times. Cash flow problems and one rather poor selling year meant that the firm went bankrupt in 1956. Horace Attwood,

*The classic, sophisticated side of 1940s and 1950s design: a finely proportioned, immaculately made fringed diamanté necklace. Trifari, American, c.1945.*

*Machine-age bracelet in two-coloured gilt metal, of superb design and manufacture by Henkel & Grosse. Germany, c. 1937–8.*

who was working at this time with his brother Douglas, decided to set up his own business in 1957. Attwood & Sawyer (Sawyer was a sleeping partner) was operated at first from a disused garage in Porthcawl. Since they were most interested in fine fashion jewellery, they decided to aim only for the top end of the market. Horace Attwood's ideas and sketches were turned into immaculate designs by Alun Roberts, and other designs were bought from Tom Durant and from Yves André, who produced designs for Dior. Durant's ideas were fantastic, largely unsaleable but always a talking-point. He was much influenced by space travel at this time and designed sputnik earrings, star-shaped necklaces, a pair of earrings with some 20 rows of chains that fastened with a pin to the shoulder. The jewels were very difficult to make. Meanwhile Attwood & Sawyer continued to produce classic fine paste jewels, working against the current fashions and selling mostly abroad. They concentrated on a 'real' look throughout the 1960s, creating, amongst other diamanté treasures, the crowns for the Miss World competition.

Henkel and Grosse took over the contract for Christian Dior jewellery in 1955, working closely with designers in Paris, and their pieces have become some of the most highly prized collectors' items today. They have a distinctive look and quality, and are stamped *'Christian Dior'*, with very often the year of manufacture, which is a great help in trying to trace trends, fashions and colours.

The company was established in Pforzheim in 1907 by Florentin Grosse (1878–1953) and Heinrich Henkel (1876–1941). Henkel, the brother of Florentin's wife Eleonore, had set up his business as a goldsmith in Pforzheim, following in the footsteps of his grandfather who had been a successful manufacturer of watch chains and jewels made of hair (see chapter 2). When Henkel expanded his repertoire of jewellery, he invited his astute brother-in-law to become his partner, and the firm of Henkel and Grosse was founded in 1907. Their business made steady progress, and after World War I Grosse encouraged his three sons to come into the business. The two oldest were sent to America, to 'see the world', while the third son Artur was an artist and sculptor who fell very much under the progressive influence of the Bauhaus. His paintings and sculptures hang in the offices of the factory in Pforzheim today. Artur's early jewel designs were sculptural and modernist, and his extraordinary artistic talent formed the basis for the company's dedication to innovative, high-fashion jewels in which design has always taken precedence over materials.

After the difficult years following World War I, Henkel & Grosse made a deliberately fresh start in the late 1920s, concentrating on fashion jewels in the jazzy modern style that was emerging. They decided to use new materials, particularly Galalith (a brand of casein: see chapter 4) and a new metal called Platinin, a platinum imitation with an ultra chic, cold and mechanical colour and texture. Their modernist jewels based on Artur's ideas were too avant-garde for the commercial market, and they proved difficult to sell, so that the firm turned to making softer, more feminine, slightly more conventional paste-set designs. Henkel & Grosse enjoyed great success in the 1920s and 1930s, selling to speciality fashion shops in Europe and even to Chanel and other Paris couturiers such as Lanvin and Schiaparelli. World War II interrupted the rapid progress of the entire Pforzheim industry. The Henkel & Grosse factory was destroyed, along with all its contents.

In the late 1940s costume jewellery manufacture was revived in France, England and Germany, and Christian Dior began to play an important role as the leading couturier.

After the War, Henkel & Grosse resumed business on a very small scale, mostly reproducing earlier pieces. The market for costume jewellery was growing along with a general need for decoration in the post-war years and Henkel & Grosse continued to make pastiches of earlier jewels until they formed their long-lasting business relationship with Dior in 1955. In Paris, this controversial contract with a German firm was frowned upon in many quarters, but Dior was searching for the best manufacturers for his products and was never prepared to compromise on quality. From the start, he had very firm ideas about the way the jewellery should look, insisting at first only on rhodium-plating rather than gold-plating which he felt looked too much like an imitation. In the early years, the designer employed by Henkel & Grosse worked in Paris at Dior's headquarters in the Avenue Montaigne in order to interpret Dior's ideas. Gradually the designer spent more and more time in Pforzheim and eventually Henkel & Grosse took over the supervision of design, always keeping in close contact with Dior. Now, they still meet once a month with Marc Bohan or his right-hand assistant.

Dior dominated the world of Paris fashion during the 1950s, and his curvaceous yet tailored designs for women encouraged the wearing of opulent-looking jewels, bold and full of character, making good use of unusual high-fashion colours in pastes which were very different from the current fashion for real jewels. The early costume jewels were expensive couture accessories. In real jewellery, at the end of the 1940s,

*Rhodium-plated and diamanté
necklace with loop motifs; in the
centre a flower brooch by Marcel
Boucher, exquisitely made, using the
finest paste cabochon rubies to
achieve a 'real' look. American,
c.1945–50.*

the cocktail style was turning into a new all-diamond look with designs still based on movement. Diamonds were cut in fancy shapes but especially in baguettes to emphasize the lines of the design of drapes, folds, loops, hanging tassels, waterfalls of gems that tumbled out of twists, bows and knots. Heavy necklaces were much in fashion to make the most of deep necklines.

In the 1950s costume jewellery often paralleled and echoed this dripping diamond look, but Christian Dior introduced many different fashions, different colour schemes, sometimes working on the 'real' look, sometimes creating an entirely idiosyncratic fashion accessory, mixing pastes of fancy cuts with striated glass cabochons and elaborately chased metalwork. There was a gradual return to a feminine, regal grandeur, rather 18th century in its mood. Rococo settings, soft rich colours, draped necklaces, brooches with drop-shaped pendants were often set with what Henkel & Grosse refer to as Maharajah-sized fake gems, luscious cabochons of rubies or emeralds making the most of their falseness. One particularly appealing characteristic of Dior jewels of this period is the use of petal-shaped faceted pastes, often arranged as flowerheads or as a fan shape in the midst of a more abstract design. These shaped pastes are highly reminiscent of fine French 18th-century paste, and have an expensive and aristocratic charm, especially when made in white paste or soft lemon. Also during the 1950s there was another revival of Queen Alexandra's dog collar, interpreted in varied forms in which for instance the classic pearls might be replaced by smoky grey or brown faceted glass beads, and during the late 1950s and 1960s there was a craze for 18th- and 19th-century style diamanté flower spray brooches, often set *en tremblant* so that the flower trembled with every movement of the wearer. In the manner of the French Second Empire style, they were huge glittering and nodding extravaganzas, their classic appeal again winning popularity. Perhaps it was this 19th-century passion for realistic flower jewels that inspired Christian Dior to produce a huge and stunning wisteria ornament in pearls and amethyst pastes in 1961.

Dior jewellery of the 1950s is distinctive also for immaculately made pastiches of real, classic jewels, particularly festooned and clustered sapphire and diamond necklaces, ruby and diamond suites or wonderful arrangements of subtly coloured pastes, obviously in the current fashion colours, and these pieces are the most fun to collect and wear. Around 1958, Henkel & Grosse introduced a very successful colour scheme of soft greys and smoky browns, with some amber or soft creamy beige with brown striations. Others were in corresponding shades of soft pink, ranging from shell pale to a deep raspberry ripple.

Miriam Haskell is one of the most collected names in 20th-century costume jewellery and her jewellery is at present enjoying a huge revival of interest. Most of the pieces available today were made by her workshop in the 1940s and 1950s, the heyday of period Haskell. Her style was not in the prevailing cocktail style, instead she developed her own individual look, of Indian or Byzantine inspiration. It was based on masses of tiny seed pearls, rich filigree metalwork with an 'antique' patina to produce a soft, subtle yet rich colour scheme. Miriam Haskell was a lively, versatile talent, and although she is best known for this pearl and filigree look she made various ranges of costume jewellery. Clearly she possessed a charismatic personality and this charisma, reflected in her jewellery, has charmed today's collectors.

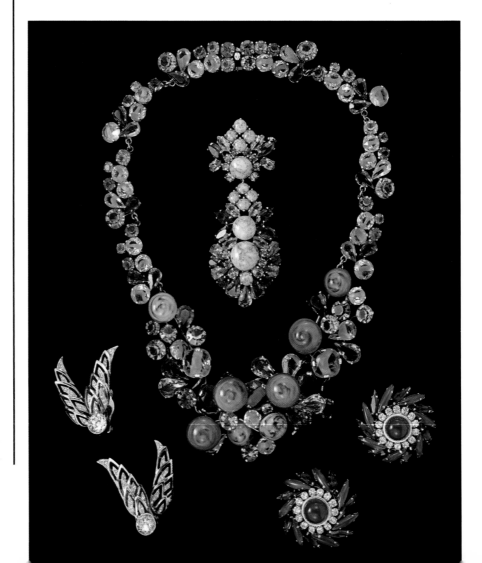

*Group of 1940s and 1950s jewels, the necklace and brooch of glass beads in soft marblized colours by Henkel & Grosse for Christian Dior, 1958; white metal and diamanté wing-shaped earrings, Mitchel Maer for Christian Dior, c.1952–6; deep blue-green cluster earrings, Christian Dior, 1969.*

She was born in Indiana in 1899 but very little apart from hearsay is known about her life. It is not certain how she came to be involved with jewellery but it is said that she started her business in New York in the mid-1920s. Haskell appears to have been very much influenced by Chanel, and it is likely that she was inspired to begin making costume jewellery by the fashion movements in Paris as they hit the headlines in New York around this time. Fabulous fake jewels, loose sporty clothes, short hems, short haircuts and independent working women were all the rage. Miriam Haskell recognized the need in the America of the mid-1920s for a very different kind of decorative jewellery; it had to be high fashion, flattering, geared towards independent women and their clothes. It had to be of fine quality but at a price that would enable smart women to change their jewels with their clothes. Real jewellery was stale and unexciting in design and concept and so prohibitively expensive that most people could only afford one piece, if that.

At first Miriam Haskell may well have designed and made the jewellery herself, by hand, but soon she sent her designs to be made up by an outworker in New York. The business went from strength to strength and in the early 1930s she moved her atelier to a loft on Fifth Avenue and began working with Frank Hess, who helped to convert her plentiful ideas into a marketable range of costume jewellery. Miriam Haskell was known to be a great socialite, sophisticated and attractive. She travelled a great deal, was friends with Coco Chanel, with the Gimbels and Rockefellers and was reputedly in love with John Hertz (of the car-rental firm). She was devoted to her business and regularly visited the factories in Providence, Rhode Island, to watch production and play with the jewels and their components.

Miriam Haskell was keen to maintain the high quality of her jewellery and travelled around the world to find the finest components: machine stampings, pearls, pastes and hand-made glass beads from firms such as Rousselet and Gripoix, who made Chanel's jewellery. For pleasure and inspiration she travelled further afield, visiting the Far East, including China, which seemed to inspire a range of jewels made in ox-blood red and jade green, the glass beads imitating jade carvings. One can only guess at Miriam Haskell's original inspirations; they must have come from faraway lands and eras, from ancient Greece, India, Byzantium, as well as from the Far East, while the subtle colour combination of the pale silky seed pearls and burnished metalwork suggested an antique look of faded opulence. It was also an intensely feminine and rather sensual look. The warm reddish patina of the metalwork was achieved by a

*Group of gilt metal, paste and imitation pearl jewels by Miriam Haskell, the shell and flower motifs adapted to her distinctive style, the metal with a rich burnished 'antique' finish. American, 1940s.*

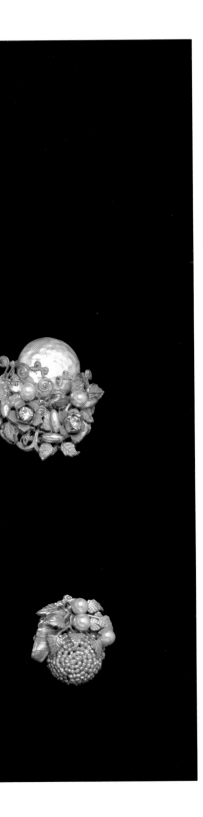

special electroplating process carried out in Providence and the special finish is called 'antique Russian gold'. Bright paste was added to the pearl and old gold combination, or the entire colour scheme would be altered by changing creamy pearls for silvery pewter-coloured pearls or warm golden bronzes. With the pewter look Haskell would often mix coloured pastes of pale pink and green that picked up the glints in the pearls: topaz pastes mingled with bronze pearls. Motifs were sometimes based on floral designs or classical shapes: a cornucopia or sea shell, butterflies, seed pearl apples or a rococo filigree arrangement. A spectacular beaded necklace of 1937 was designed with Calla lilies and green transparent leaves. The jewels are always backed with an openwork filigree metal plate, later bearing the Haskell mark, most usually an oval plaque embossed with her name in capital letters.

As with so many firms the evidence of marks and dates is far from conclusive. It would seem that early Miriam Haskell jewels were not marked and that the earliest and rarest mark is a horseshoe-shaped plaque bearing her name in capitals, but even this was probably only first used in the late 1930s or 1940s. During the War Haskell marked some of her jewels with a flying bird motif, symbolizing the dove of peace. The first regularly marked pieces with the oval plaque appeared only in the 1950s.

As well as the seed pearl jewels, Haskell created a number of very different ranges; there was the summer 'Palm Beach' or 'resort' look in the 1950s, with white shiny glass beads mixed with mother of pearl and imitation coral. There was a summery fairylike range of tiny shimmering opalescent beads, strung perhaps as a deep multi-stranded choker with a delicate floral central motif, or a range of deep green glass beads and fiery red jewels with opaque hand-made glass beads mixed with leaf and berry motifs. Huge green glass beads echoed Chinese jade cabochons or carvings with a smooth, worn surface that conjures up centuries of fond handling, and a curious celadon and mustard-coloured range of summer jewels assembled from organic-looking shapes. She also used opaque turquoise and shiny black Bakelite with filigree clasps and trimmings.

Haskell's great success and popularity meant that her style was widely imitated by big manufacturers such as Corocraft and by her co-workers such as Robert de Mario, who sometimes signed his jewels 'Robert', and by a colleague called 'Eugene'. It is possible that these pieces, which are all well made, were produced with her approval. Today there are attractive and effective copies or revivals of old Miriam Haskell jewels but the modern lookalikes are usually more chunky, the pastes and pearls have a harder sparkle, the overall tones are less subtle and silky.

In the early 1950s Miriam Haskell became ill and sold the business to her brother Joseph Haskell, who in turn sold to Morris Kinzeler; and then Sanford Moss, who had worked with the firm for many years, bought the business and is currently President and owner of Miriam Haskell.

The jewellery continues to be made to the same high quality and in the same spirit. Miriam Haskell jewels were and are still hand-assembled from stampings bought in Paris, from Framex, from Pforzheim or produced in Providence. All the jewels are put together in the New York workshop, where there are 65 workers including designers and sample-makers who help produce the five collections and some 5,000 pieces each year. Miriam Haskell is unusual for being one of the few individually owned, self-contained manufacturers of fine costume jewellery in the United States.

Since 20th-century costume jewellery has become a true collectors' area, names and makers have become increasingly important and collectors concentrate on one favourite or divide their collections into makers' groups. Designers and names bring a subject to life, but in a way this is a collectors' disease and as with all collecting the labels should not be over-emphasized or used as a crutch for critical judgement of design and manufacture.

From the late 1930s the United States industry benefited enormously from talented French and Italian craftsmen and jewellers who were leaving Europe. American firms flourished, helped by the closely related clothing and fashion industries and by the 'real' jewellery market whose centre shifted during the War to New York. There are too many names of New York manufacturers in the 1940s and 1950s to mention here but favourites amongst collectors include Kramer, Mazer Brothers and Joseph Mazer (whose mark was JOMAZ), Pennino, Eisenberg, Weiss, Trifari, Napier, Monet, Vendôme, Coro (later Corocraft), Marcel Boucher and the more individual designers and couturiers, Maclelland Barclay, Josef of Hollywood, Hattie Carnegie and Nettie Rosenstein.

Albert Weiss had worked with Coro and eventually in 1942 set up his own firm which continued until 1971. During the 1940s and 1950s Weiss produced fine-quality diamanté jewels, classic in design, as well as a range of enamel floral jewellery. For a short time Weiss commissioned designs from the fashionable dress designer, Charles James, English-born but working in New York during most of the 1940s and 1950s.

The most spectacular Hobé jewels were also created during the 1950s. The firm had first been established in Paris in the mid-19th century as fine jewellers, and the tradition was continued by successive generations. During the 1920s, a descendant, William Hobé, who was a partner in a firm making beaded stage costumes, received a commission from Ziegfeld to make expensive-looking and dramatic stage jewellery, in the family tradition of real jewellery but using inexpensive materials. Subsequently the Hobé jewellery business developed a distinctive style of fashion jewellery, all exquisitely hand-made by traditional techniques of

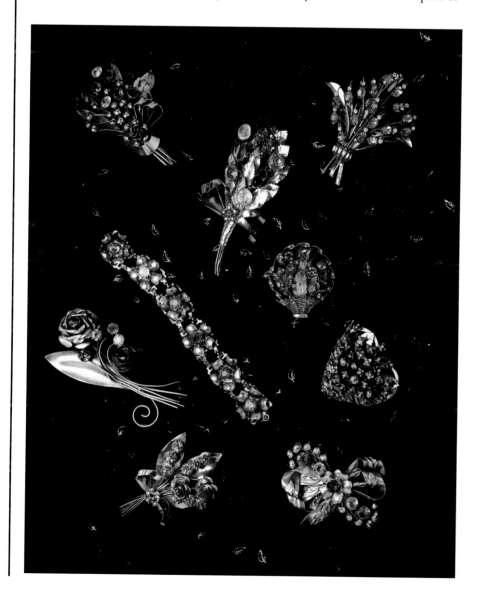

*Group of gilt metal and paste-set flower jewels by Hobé. American, c.1940–50.*

metalworking and gem-setting, and until the 1950s mixing semi-precious stones with pastes, and silver with base metals. The most distinctive Hobé jewels are the stylized and colourful flower sprays blossoming with tiny closed silver buds of closely overlapping petals and large curved leaves with curling tendrils of filigree work and tied by softly waving bows and ribbons. Large pastes of deep rich colours were individually hand-set in deep bezels of metal to achieve one of the strongest and most creative styles of costume jewellery of this era.

Hattie Carnegie and Nettie Rosenstein were both dress designers in New York. Hattie Carnegie (1889–1956) was born Henrietta Kanengeiser in Austria but the family moved to America and changed their name. Hattie began working in the hat department in Macy's and in 1909 opened a hat shop; later she bought out her partner who had developed the dressmaking side of the business and took over the dress designing. During the 1930s and 1940s her clothes were much in demand as smart status symbols, tailored and tidy, with an emphasis on the little black dress. It is interesting that, like Chanel, the jewellery she designed was in sharp contrast to the clothes: colourful, quirky, boisterous. Many designs have a strong primitive, native flavour, based on African art which was having an intense effect on designers in Paris in the 1930s. She used plastics, enamels and gilt metal rather than all-pastes and avoided imitations of real gem-set jewels.

Nettie Rosenstein set up her own business as a couturier in New York in 1917, and in the late 1930s was also known for conventional smart clothes accessorized with dazzling, paste-set costume jewellery.

Maclelland Barclay was a successful artist, illustrator and poster designer who turned his talent to costume jewellery design in the late 1930s and 1940s. His jewels are recognizable by distinctive Art Deco geometric arrangements of pastes within sculpted or bevelled gilt borders, most often on brooches and bangles.

In the early 1950s, the costume jewellery industry began to boom all over the world. There seemed to be renewed interest in novelties, in fashions and particularly in fashion accessories, in the frivolities of everyday living that had to be forgotten during the War. In England the traditional 'old money' look of marcasites and subtle greys with an antique silver finish was very popular for wearing with tailored suits and classic sweaters during the first half of the decade. Light, bright and often white beads were worn instead in summer and colourless pastes for the evening. These glamorous evening jewels were made in the American

manner of the real jewels, yet with a flair and extra verve of their own, and styles were dominated very much by the baguette-cut stone, a little oblong of light used to create sweeping or trickling movement: waterfalls, swirls, loops, drapes. In the mid-1950s came a return to colour, to gilt jewels and the start of a fashion for rainbow pastes with pink or blue lines or tinges.

In America, the emphasis in the early 1950s had been on specially cut stones, on wonderful paste baguettes swept up into ribbon-like loops and swathes. Pastes from Austria and Czechoslovakia were once again available, and base metals suitable for fine settings could now be used again. Marcel Boucher jewels are of exceptional quality and design and represent the best of 1950s costume jewellery. Based on a 'real' look, Boucher's style was very much a post-war phenomenon with the emphasis once again on cleverly cut and set pastes. These jewels, however, were far from straightforward imitations or fakes; they had their

Group of paste and plastic jewels
by Hattie Carnegie, the designs
influenced by primitive African jewels
and motifs; c. 1940–50.

own sophisticated and original designs but aimed at a serious, expensive image, rather classical, with all the cachet of the Place Vendôme. Boucher made good use of specially cut stones, baguettes and cabochons in pigeon-blood ruby red, convincing kashmir sapphire blue and deepest emerald, intense turquoise mixed with pearls and diamonds, and all set in new improved castings. In the industry his work was considered a breakthrough in terms of creating such a convincingly real style that still showed great pride in its own art and a highly individual elegance.

At the same time, Kramer, Mazer, Coro, Trifari, Monet, Napier, Albert Weiss, Eisenberg all increased their production of jewels in the prevailing real look. During the 1940s the firm of Eisenberg, based in Chicago, was producing very sparkling diamanté jewels, in machine-made settings, bearing the stamped mark of either 'Eisenberg' or 'Eisenberg Ice' to describe the jewels' icy whiteness. In the 1950s they used smaller, brighter pastes to create snowflake brooches with spiralling movement and this classic all-white jewellery was joined by a new range of enamelled pieces.

Marcel Boucher had worked for the firm of Mazer, which started in the 1920s, following the tradition of high-fashion, high-quality merchandise. Mazer specialized in hand-set flower jewels that often used opaque glass petals and clusters of flowers in deep, dark colours, even black with a turquoise centre. Brooches were widely worn and regarded very often as conversation pieces, large and conspicuous, or small and

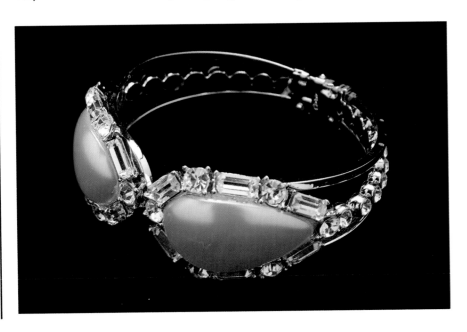

*White metal, diamanté and imitation pearl bangle by Kramer. American, c.1950.*

Two novelty or 'conversation jewels'; the receding back view of a coach and horses in textured gilt metal and a bouquet of purple glass violets, the glass leaves moulded in imitation of jade, set against a gilt doyley. Both by Mazer. American, c.1950.

amusing and witty, such as a series of musical notes. Mazer also created stunning examples in the Cocktail Style. Necklaces, however, became fashion's most important accessory, especially the 'bib' necklaces with deep fringes of stones at the front which were popular through the 1950s, along with chokers which enjoyed yet another revival. Sweetheart necklines or low-cut evening dresses made way for the triumph of swirls and ribbons of glistening and dripping diamanté.

In the United States a seal of approval was put on American costume jewellery when First Lady Mamie Eisenhower wore a Trifari pearl choker, earrings and bracelet to her inaugural ball in 1953. She broke with tradition twice that year: she was the first wife of a President to wear a pink gown to her inaugural ball, and the first to wear a set of costume

Two sets of imitation pearls and diamanté jewels designed and made by Trifari for Mamie Eisenhower to wear at the inaugural balls of 1953 and 1957.

179

jewellery. Her gown was pink satin covered with diamanté and she chose pearls and diamanté for her jewels. The set was designed by Trifari's Alfred Philippe. He used the finest quality imitation pearls, with diamanté baguettes and created a three-strand necklace with matching pearl and diamond earrings. To present the commissioned set to her, Philippe had a white leather case tooled in gold, bearing the inscription, 'Mamie Doud Eisenhower, January 20, 1953'. Only three sets of this custom-made jewellery were made: one for Mamie Eisenhower, one for the Smithsonian Institution, where it can still be seen, and a third for Trifari's archives. Four years later in 1957, Mamie Eisenhower commissioned another set of jewellery for her second inaugural ball.

*The cover of the* Society Pictorial, *January 1956, shows the Duke of Windsor dancing with Sonja Henie who proudly wears a convincing paste bracelet by Napier.*

This set consisted of a triple strand of graduated pearls with very small diamanté roundels, a matching bracelet and a pair of cluster earrings. The necklace was finished with a fringe of nine pear-shaped pearls.

During the 1950s America was undoubtedly the centre of the fashion jewellery trade. In 1953 Corocraft announced a turnover of $22 million; in 1955 a British trade paper dealing specifically with costume jewellery reported that the fashion jewellery trade in the United States had a turnover of some £180 million a year. Paris often led the way for ideas and colours but the United States had the ability and technical expertise to translate jewel fashions into popular and glamorous accessories.

The tailored gold look was still very strong in New York in the 1950s, and designers were anticipating the 1960s taste for textured gilt surfaces. Napier created large eye-catching sets of brightly gilt necklaces, bracelets and earrings. A very feminine gilt mesh necklace and bracelet were each set off-centre with a huge bow, while massive fringe necklets were made from ribbed and ridged gilt metal. Napier's bent-wire jewellery continued to sell in huge quantities, and new ambitious ranges were added, one of linen-textured jewels, the design imitating softly folded ribbon, and another designed in a basket-weave pattern called 'Golden Rhythm' which was advertised for Napier in 1956 by Doris Day, who wore the jewellery in her film *Julie*.

Trifari's tailored gilt range, pioneered in 1937 by Alfred Philippe, continued to enjoy success after World War II and well into the late 1950s. Immediately after the War, Trifari created a brilliantly flexible die-stamped gilt metal honeycomb necklace which proved an enormous success. Alongside the gold jewellery, however, Trifari's best-loved jewels included large and luscious paste-set flowers, a dramatic diamanté rose with densely packed curling petals, and a huge colourful blossom with blood-red flowers, a long curling stem and deep emerald-green paste-set leaves – a triumph in 1950. Trifari often produced simple tailored gilt models for daytime wear, adapting the same design for nighttime by adding diamanté. Stylized animals and birds combining pastes with textured or polished gilt metalwork continued to be made in the stylish cocktail taste but Trifari advertisements now showed such animals being worn together with the 1950s sophistication of a pearl choker perhaps. In 1959 a set of three birds in flight made use of earlier castings for the smooth curved gilt wings and tails modelled to give the impression of soaring movement. The plump bodies were set with mock moonstones and fake 'black diamonds', the owl-like heads with deep round eyes.

The crown motif, which featured in Trifari's trademark, was one of their most famous successes. Devised during World War II when it was produced in silver, the crown jewels – a brooch in two sizes and earrings – continued to be best sellers in the 1950s and received a huge impetus in 1953 with the coronation of Queen Elizabeth II. Trifari manufactured a rich gilt and bejewelled range called 'Coronation Gems' made of 'golden Trifanium' set with deeply coloured pastes. The crown set was joined by an orb set and a sceptre set, all greeted with enthusiasm by the buying public on both sides of the Atlantic.

*Trifari's advertisement for their Coronation gems of 1953, including a set of their famous crown-shaped jewels, created to celebrate the coronation of Elizabeth II.*

In Paris and Europe in the mid-1950s, the emphasis remained very much on pearls. In 1955 Jacques Fath, leading creator of couture costume jewellery, showed long, multi-strand necklaces of outsized pearls, as well as chokers with coloured stones at the centre or iridescent beads. Fath also used huge cuff-links of pastes to ornament his clothes or deep latticed paste cuffs and huge buckles that recalled the glory of 18th-century France and the glitter of Versailles. Dior featured paste hearts and horseshoes. The A line dress came to the forefront of attention, followed in the later 1950s by the Empire line, and these simple moulded lines called for elaborate collars and necklaces of many strands, sometimes pulled outwards and clipped in place to give breadth over the shoulders. Dressing up was very much in fashion for the evening, when huge full skirts and low necklines were worn; for daywear the subtleties of coloured semi-precious stones were becoming popular, soft tweedy greens and browns for the business woman, with bright flashes of high-fashion colours such as acid green and tangerine, and cabochons of jade green and deep golden brown. In England, the Queen's Commonwealth tour inspired a brief flurry of eastern exotic motifs in 1954 and 1955; gilt jewels were made in the form of African heads wearing huge creole earrings, and there was a rage for big slave bangles, some with African head motifs. Wide gold surfaces of jewels like this were given textures, hammered or etched to look like woven fabric which hinted at the styles to follow in the 1960s.

Perhaps the last fashion deserving mention in the 1950s was the revival of an Edwardian look. Shades of classicism had been ushered in with the strong Empire line, creating jewels with glass medallions or intaglios, but now the classical mood had gradually changed to one of Edwardian gentility and femininity. Queen Alexandra chokers graced fashionable necks, and manufacturers concentrated on finely made hand-set diamond-paste jewels in delicate lacy designs. It was a step backwards into the past before the onslaught of aggressive newness that was to mark the costume jewellery of the 1960s.

# Six

# GLAM ROCK: THE 1960S ONWARDS

In the 1980s costume jewellery became wittier and more exciting than ever. Freed from restrictions of design, manufacture and, particularly, social prejudices, non-precious jewellery for fun and fashion came to be elegant or playful, innovative or imitative, the single most important fashion accessory. Costume jewellery became totally acceptable for all social occasions, for all times of day; the new couture jewels by Chanel or Yves Saint Laurent were worn for the smartest of formal day or evening wear, while glorious glitter paraded the streets during the day, mixed with gabardine or denim, and there were even signs of a move towards the 1920s fad for paste on the promenade, baubles on the beach. The Princess of Wales, influential fashion leader of the day, is known to treasure her costume jewellery, much of it from Butler & Wilson and worn on official occasions. Perhaps the most famous royal fake was the diamanté lizard brooch, slithering in the limelight of an official tour of Canada, on the lapel of a black evening jacket.

After some years of hovering like a poor relation in the background of the jewellery world, costume jewellery became highly respectable again. By the end of the decade there was a boom worldwide in every corner of the industry, the choice enormous, ranging from one-off creations of great vitality and originality to opulent and convincing copies of real

*Through the 1980s Butler & Wilson promoted a new image for women and costume jewellery. This photograph of 1985 featured twisted ropes of pearls and a huge 18th-century style topaz-paste bow.*

gems and smart Bond Street, Place Vendôme or Fifth Avenue jewels. The range of materials, from paste, mirror and resin to wood and plastic, and manufacturing techniques, from electroforming, centrifugal casting to stamping, had never been greater. The most significant change in the market lay probably in the realm of adventurous, highly individual ornaments, some made by designer-jewellers who have occasionally moved from real jewellery, others totally factory-made and commercial but highly inventive and sold in glamorous specialist boutiques around the world. By its very nature, costume jewellery by and large is commercial, mass-manufactured as a product not as 'art'. But as the field is quickly expanding and changing, some exceptions have been included in this chapter by virtue of their sheer fantasy and ornamental value.

Women in the 1980s opted for fabulous fairytale fantasy and for jewels that added instant glamour, wit and excitement, to suit their moods, clothes and highly varied roles in life. With many of the battles for emancipation and equality behind them, they could return to an image of luscious femininity without fear of compromising their hard-won independence. It is interesting too that in New York, London and Paris a growing interest in early costume jewellery began, especially in the vintage models of the 1930s, 1940s and 1950s by American makers such as Trifari, Boucher and Miriam Haskell.

In the 1950s, jewels and costume jewels – like women – were resolutely grown-up: diamonds represented the ultimate in sophistication, and just as daughters longed to look like their mothers, so costume jewellery had aped and worshipped the swirling, tumbling arrangements of 1950s diamonds. Fifties women had aimed at a soignée look, expensive and well-groomed, somewhat untouchable. Make-up looked obviously like make-up, eyes were thickly lined, lips were hard and deeply coloured, womanly figures were exaggerated, waists pulled in, hips rounded out, hair was pulled up into smooth chignons or French pleats. Apart from dressy jewels, beads were enormously popular, usually worn in several short strands and formal-looking even when made of colourful Venetian glass. Young girls dreamt of being grown up and sophisticated as soon as possible for there was nothing for them in the wasteland in between. They practised with make-up, they tottered around in mother's high heels, and played with rows of cultured pearls, with beads or the new plastic poppets, little pull-apart plastic beads brightly coloured or pearlized. Although it was a brilliant conception, poppets made from injection-moulded plastics had the effect of debasing and finally killing the huge fashion for beads.

As everyone knows, the 1960s brought all kinds of revolution, a renaissance of design and above all a youth cult. Teenagers tired of waiting to grow up and demanded a culture of their own, grabbing the 1960s for themselves and creating a suitably tempestuous style that rebelled against hairpins, buns and beehives, against roll-ons, stockings, pointed breasts, pearls and twinsets and dutiful sophistication. The fashions, like the music, remain nostalgic and evocative relics of a memorable era. The deep social and moral changes needed outward signs of change, and there was a massive demand for new, young and exciting clothes and accessories to absorb and reflect the many influences and 'happenings' that brewed the new mood.

In the late 1950s Mary Quant opened her first shop, Bazaar, in the King's Road. First she sold clothes bought from manufacturers, but then began to design them too, producing low-cost high fashion that was an instant success. In London, Mary Quant became the quintessential designer of the decade; she championed the mini-skirt, the geometric haircut, PVC clothes, hipsters, coloured tights, skinny ribs, crochet dresses. In Paris too, new designers set out to break away from the traditions of haute couture, moving towards ready-to-wear fashion. In 1964 André Courrèges thrilled young fashion-crazy customers around the world with short, sharp, white clothes: angular, futuristic, uncluttered and body-skimming with the shortest skirts of the century, worn with mid-calf white open-toed boots and white goggles with slits.

In 1965, Paco Rabanne, the true *enfant terrible* of Paris couture and former architecture student, went one step further and introduced yet more space age, more anti-fashion ideas: mini dresses of plastic discs, chainmail clothes, handbags and accessories. Paco Rabanne's most famous and earliest contributions to the new look were in fact his bold, bright plastic jewellery and buttons, which he sold to Balenciaga, Dior and Givenchy. By 1960 Paco Rabanne had created the perfect anti-jewellery to suit the emerging fashions. The earrings were especially startling to set off the new, sharp geometric haircuts and bobs devised by Vidal Sassoon. They were made in geometric shapes, squares, circles, psychedelic spirals, and were totally uncompromising in their newness. Rabanne says that he wanted to create something mad, wild, that he wanted to break away from the rules of precious stones, even from Chanel's imitations or parodies which still recognized the supremacy of traditional gems. He was very much influenced by the new geometry of art and architecture, and by the Op-Art movement. 'I wanted to create jewels,' Rabanne said, 'that looked like the paintings of the period, huge,

*Sixties models wearing Paco Rabanne plastic disc clothes and huge swinging earrings.*

mad and uninhibited. Women too wanted to change, to reject past values and traditions. Their jewels were to be part of the whole new aesthetic. I made jewellery for the alternative side of women's personality, for their madness.' He experimented with new materials, with wood, paper and the shiny space-age plastics or PVC, choosing the least valuable materials possible and the least jewel-like colours. He worked in glaring black and white or in clashing fluorescent colours: orange with red, vibrant pink, acid yellow, purple. The plastics, produced by the traditional plastics industry in the Jura region of France, were cut into wafer-thin cubes, discs like gambling chips, circles, loops

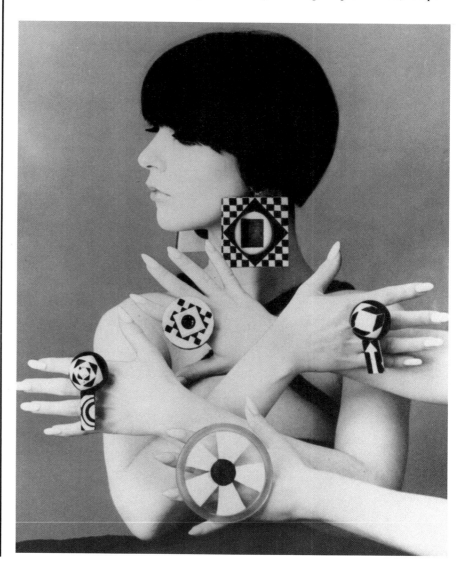

*Clean, architectural lines in bold black and white, influenced by Op-Art, applied to 'Architec-jewels' made of Lucite and designed by Ingeborg Sant' Angelo for Richelieu, Paris. French, late 1960s.*

*Pierre Cardin gilt metal and plastic bracelet in the prevailing geometric style of the 1960s.*

and squares. They stood for new technological progress, and the oncoming computer age was heralded by Rabanne's use of the 'disc', the watchword of the 1970s and 1980s. Earrings moved like psychedelic mobiles, spheres turned within circles, loops within loops, spirals twirled and discs were clustered layer on layer. There were also huge rings, arm bands, leg bands and, in 1967, when the Israeli Six-Day War brought Moshe Dayan to the forefront of world attention, Rabanne introduced a plastic disc eye-patch jewel.

The young outsiders of Paris couture, Rabanne, Courrèges and Emanuelle Khanh exerted a huge influence on fashion with a look that was easily and effectively interpreted by mass manufacturers around the world. Shiny Op-Art plastic earrings – huge parrot perches, squares, discs or daisy-like flowers (the daisy was Quant's motif) – suddenly appeared in every boutique and department store. Eventually Op-Art was followed by Pop Art with its little plastic brooches shaped as biscuits, chocolate, slices of lemon. Trifari introduced a young Op-Art inspired range of jewels made of cast metal spray-painted shiny white. There were wide cage-like bangles in the manner of Courrèges, necklaces made up of sections like geometric openwork webs, with white wiry spirals or swirls, all linked together like Rabanne's chainmail. Henkel & Grosse for Christian Dior came up with a range of geometric, chunky gilt jewels incorporating plastics and bright abstract enamels, alongside their ranges of romantic and opulent gem-set 1960s models to suit more sophisticated clothes. Mainstream Christian Dior jewels took the guise of tempting shiny clusters of fine glass beads in softly marblized colours, opaque faux-gems in muted tones of bronze, purple, beige and plum offset by baroque gilt metal. An impressive range of luscious paste-set flowers continued a popular 1950s fashion. The flowers were complicated and exotic, with deep centres out of which curled sensuously licking petals and leaves.

In London, the swinging centre of 1960s fashions, a boutique called Biba opened in Kensington in 1964 and was an immediate and sensational success. Conceived by Barbara Hulanicki, the cult shop moved in 1966 to Kensington Church Street, then in 1969 to a huge store in Kensington High Street and came to epitomize the distinctive style of total dressing of the design-conscious decade. The clothes were inexpensive enough to appeal even to schoolgirl fashion followers – a fast-expanding market – and they were whimsical, high-fashion garments intended to be discarded whenever the next craze took over. Biba was famed for narrow-shouldered, tight-sleeved empire-line mini dresses in

On the Hippie trail, these Indian-inspired earrings, worn around the ear, are hung with cascades of crystal beads. Made by Napier. American, late 1960s.

muted shades of beige, plum, burgundy and olive; there were smocks, maxi coats, trouser suits and all sorts of accessories including make-up and furniture. The Kensington Church Street shop was atmospheric, dark, gloomy and nostalgic, with potted palms and mahogany counters and coat-stands laden with dresses, hats and feather boas. The later High Street shop was dark, dramatic and Art Deco in design and atmosphere. At this time, the overall Biba image looked back to the 1920s, 1930s and 1940s, converting the 1960s' pale mask-like face, with pearly lips and dark, smudgy eyes, into a 1930s-style vamp tinged with a Victorian sweet innocence. This nostalgic and retrospective tendency of the 1960s signalled the end of the futuristic new look.

By the late 1960s the harshness of minis, of PVC and bright whiteness, was giving way to a craze for old clothes, for muted colours, soft velvets, Paisley, granny shawls, braid and brocade, old uniforms from Portobello Road and Chelsea market, gilt buttons and masses of beads and chains and antique jewellery. As a reaction to the mid-1960s' self-conscious sharp streamlined newness, a faded, worn limpness was now in fashion, based on unstructured, rather cluttered dressing. Oriental, ethnic and Indian influences superseded the aggression of the space-age spell. It was the start of the Hippie Trail, the journeys to Afghanistan, the sheepskin coats; the Beatles went to India to seek spiritual richness, the kind of age-old richness invoked by the latest clothes and accessories. Indian jewels were all the rage, gilt metal earrings, necklaces and bangles with little tinkling bells or sequins, or richly coloured oriental-inspired opulent jewels, with enamels coloured like jade or cinnabar, with huge pastes like legendary emeralds or rubies. In 1966 Trifari revived a massive and impressive Indian range, themselves copies of 1930s copies of the great Indian Cartier jewels, with carved paste gems and lavish gilt metalwork.

In New York, the ingenious jewels made by Kenneth Jay Lane in the 1960s flaunted a similar massive opulence, brilliantly tongue-in-cheek. Lane had worked for the art department of *Vogue* in New York in 1954. Even then, Diana Vreeland had sent him to Hattie Carnegie with his designs and ideas. After two years, Lane moved from *Vogue* to work with the shoe designer Roger Vivier. As part of this job, Lane spent some time in Paris where he produced shoes for Dior. As traditional handicrafts gradually disappeared, rhinestones replaced hand embroidery, and as a sideline, in the early 1960s, Lane began to experiment with the diamanté he used for evening shoes, turning it into glittering jewellery. In 1963 he was designing shoes for the couturier Scassi, famous for his glamorous evening wear, and he decided to make buttons to match the shoes and then thought of earrings to match the buttons. He bought cheap plastic bangles, covered them with diamanté and gave them to his fashionable lady friends to wear several at a time. The *New York Times* noticed them

Celebrated 1960s model Paulene Stone wears Kenneth Jay Lane jewels, many of them in the exotic Maharajah mood of the 1960s.

and found them interesting; Bonwit Teller and Henri Bendel sold a few jewels and re-ordered so that within a month or two they were all down Fifth Avenue. This was happening at a time when costume jewellery was very definitely out of fashion and déclassé, used by designers only for their collections and fashion shows; otherwise, as Lane points out, in real life it was jewellery to give to the maid. Kenneth Lane must be credited with totally changing that attitude, for making costume jewellery in the 1960s an acceptable and sought-after accessory in high society and in glamorous or showbusiness circles. He knew his contemporaries in the rarefied design world, his friends were the 'beautiful' people of the New York of the 1960s. Attractive women in their late twenties and early thirties, who did not have the real jewels but were always in the limelight, started to wear his jewellery, bringing it to the attention of fashion writers and store buyers. One friend asked him to make a ridiculously long pair of earrings which would drape over the shoulders. They were photographed at a social gathering and became instantly fashionable.

In the meantime, Lane was learning about manufacturing techniques, about casting, soldering, setting, while continuing to make shoes. At first he made *pavé*-set diamanté jewels in classic shapes: spheres, teardrops, triangles, all three-dimensional and mounted on stiff lacquered cotton. As an extension of shoemaking ideas, Lane then bought wholesale plastic components and simple, cheap bangles from a factory in Rhode Island and covered them with cobra skin and leather, studded them with pastes: 'I had no fear, no preconceived ideas about what was right or wrong. I was like the fool that rushes in,' he said later. The jewellery was such a success that after a year the jewel-making turned into a full-time operation. Lane explains that he was also very attracted by antique and period real jewellery that he had seen and liked, for instance Victorian slinky articulated snake bracelets and necklets of gold or bone, coral, ivory and jet. He remembered seeing one lady whose arm was covered with stunning Victorian snake bracelets, all studded with turquoises. Lane found an old example in ivory, mounted on spring wire. He took it to a meat stringer and they concocted an imitation with string and plastics. Always inventive and full of curiosity, Lane would search out little Viennese bronzes in order to cast animal heads and, constantly watchful of new and exciting materials, he used Cuban tree snails and seashells in the manner of the New York designer Fulco Verdura.

Lane soon became famous for his witty copies or interpretations of the most fashionable, expensive jewels of both his own and earlier ages.

David Webb, the famous and influential jewellery designer of the 1960s and 1970s, was starting at the same time as Lane, so that their styles were mutually inspiring and Lane's costume jewels continued for some time to show the strong influence of Webb's rich and often bizarre animals, his powerful sculptural ideas. Verdura was a friend and an important influence, and Lane was a great admirer of Jeanne Toussaint's jewels of the 1930s and 1940s, fabulous animals and birds and the Big Cat jewels first made for the Duchess of Windsor. He had often seen the original Cartier jewels being worn in high society, and he set out to create a tongue-in-cheek range of costume jewels in the manner of Jeanne Toussaint. 'Except, mine were funny,' Lane points out. 'I made white leopards with polka dots, and I got away with it because it was costume jewellery.' The Duchess of Windsor started wearing Kenneth Jay Lane jewels in the 1960s and 1970s. Lane always dealt personally with her and he believes that his jewels made her feel younger. 'For a young woman, real jewellery is very ageing; and people wonder where she got it. An older woman who has an enormous amount of valuable jewellery feels younger wearing costume jewellery,' he commented.

The rich gilt wild animal jewels, compellingly barbaric, prowling yet benign, quirky yet classically inspired, became Kenneth Lane's hallmark and remain staple sellers in his boutiques around the world. He made sumptuously sculpted and cast gilt lions, leopards, panthers, tigers stretching around the wrist, their proud massive gilt heads overlapping torque-like, striped or dotted with enamels, studded with gems of glass, carved or smooth. There were rings, brooches and famous heavy earrings like door knockers.

Other distinctive and popular designs incorporated bizarre bulging organic-looking clusters, swelling budlike shapes combining outrageous mixtures of colours and textures, using coral, turquoises, amethysts and lots of imitation Burmese rubies, Lane's favourite stone. The Indian or oriental inspiration of the late 1960s was very strong – Lane often travelled to India and still does – and in this mood he created his famous vast fringed chandelier earrings, dripping with imitation rich gemstones or, for summer, startling white coral. There were deep fringe necklaces of massive clusters of fake gems fringed with little bobbling stones. The jewels were huge, funny yet sophisticated at the same time, satisfying what Lane calls the Cinderella syndrome in women, allowing them to relive the delights of the little girl delving into the dressing-up box.

Lane lent the sixties fetish for beads a special sophistication by mingling glass stones and beads with diamanté roundels or discs

between, while the statutory 1960s fistful of rings was easily
accomplished with huge, mocking knuckledusters rising from the hand
in rounded layers of clustered stones. He always liked the dignity of
Court jewellery, and set out to conjure up an aristocratic air about his
jewels. He used foiled diamanté, while amethysts, aquamarines and
semi-precious stones were left unfoiled and clear. He instigated an
antique silver plating which set off the diamanté to perfection, adding a
regal softness to the stones.

Soon Kenneth Jay Lane jewels were worn in aristocratic circles on
both sides of the Atlantic. The Duchess of Windsor, Gloria Guinness,
Sarah Churchill all wore 'Kenny Lanes'. Jackie Kennedy personified the
sophisticated side of 1960s elegance, with her bouffant hairstyle, pillbox
hats, suits, her handbag with gilt chain and rich baroque jewellery. Her
own style inspired Lane and she too wore his jewellery, on occasion
commissioning copies of specific jewels which were then included in
Lane's range with several variations.

Real jewellery in the 1960s had also undergone a transformation, a
revolution and renaissance of its own. The formal conventions of the
1950s had been rejected by a new generation of designer-jewellers, as
well as by a new wealthy self-made clientèle. There was less and less
need for very expensive, heirloom jewels, tiaras and diamond suites, and
a greater demand for a different kind of jewel, less formal, more modern
and a symbol of the swinging affluent decade. There was more money
around, disposable income to buy holidays, cars, new homes, gadgets,
machines and luxury goods in which jewellery played an important part.

In 1961 the Worshipful Company of Goldsmiths held an influential
milestone exhibition of modern jewellery in London which uncovered
the potential of jewellery design as a vehicle for artistic self-expression.
The exhibition, organized by Graham Hughes, drew public attention to
jewellery; it encouraged new designers and attracted artists from other
areas of decorative design; it set the new designer-jeweller on his path
towards the 1980s. Amongst the leaders of the new movement were
Andrew Grima, John Donald, David Thomas.

New jewellery design appropriately was all about freedom and
movement, but a chaotic, explosive movement, with themes, textures,
shapes that were organic yet scientific, based on nature yet somehow
unnatural. Jewellery began to look like the mysterious potholed surface
of the moon, like exploding molecular structures, like an oily bubbling
cauldron of molten metal, piles of twigs, spiky sea urchins or the rotting

bark of trees. It was a brittle style whose most distinctive innovation was the use of natural minerals, craggy crystals of frosty amethyst or foamy emerald; swirling glazed and glittering quartz, tourmaline, peridots, topaz. The goldwork that set off the crystals was heavily textured, like semi-molten nuggets of gold, like rough tree bark, arid rock formations, barnacle-like encrustations. Gold wire was always ribbed, coiled, twisted, spiky and spitting. Such was the impact of the exhibition and of the new ideas that much costume jewellery was made in the new freeform style, as it was known, but the costume jewels were not a huge commercial success. The new jewellery of the 1960s is instantly recognizable and amusingly self-conscious in its efforts to achieve a modern style. Stores and boutiques sold curious copies of the new jewellery, with broad, tangled ribbons of silver or metal wire, tortuously twisted to entrap vast, deformed crystals in rather dingy colours. Fashionably enormous rings waved a slice of hazy quartz at the world; pendants and vast misshapen brooches could incorporate the wildest freedom of design wrapped around the biggest slab of mineral.

Trifari made a range of jewels based on this style: spiky brooches and huge gilt bracelets with jagged textured golden surfaces made from stampings soldered together in layers and set with turquoises; a necklace of rocky gold with unstructured, shredded outlines set with coral. Although the success of this style in costume jewellery was limited it does symbolize the 1960s' reassessment of traditional values, questioning whether jewels should have intrinsic worth. The idea of textured goldwork spilled over onto the new ranges of smart daytime jewels,

*Bangle and earrings in bright gilt metal, space-age designs inspired by atomic structure. Monet, American, c.1960.*

*Necklace and bracelet of autumn leaf design, the gilt metal decorated with enamel and diamanté. Trifari, American, c.1970.*

casual but controlled, and the tailored gold look was one of the strongest features of 1960s costume jewellery. The greatest success story was the use of fine Milanese mesh chain, fine gold links knitted together to form a flexible ribbon, soft like gauze. Gold necklaces, bracelets, brooches and particularly knot earrings were extremely popular in Europe and the United States. Necklets were light and simple with a central bow motif set with imitation turquoises and garnets or aventurine and garnets; bracelets were either slim and delicate and set with little gems or left plain and very wide, fastened with a buckle or slide device so that the size was flexible. Both Trifari and Henkel & Grosse excelled in this look. Trifari went on to make jewels in textured and polished gold, either in free abstract designs safely redolent of 1960s freedom or in the ever-popular leaf or flower motifs, the flowers becoming strange, even slightly sinister, the leaves stylized, curled or fluted, with crenellated edges. Oak leaves and acorns were especially popular. Trifari triumphed with a charming range based on peas in a pod, the peas made either of green beads or fake pearls, bursting out of pods made of textured gold and hanging from diamanté leaves and stems. There was a very attractive fashion at this time for a softer type of diamond paste, known as black diamonds, which looked very much like 18th-century tiny rose diamonds with a soft, greyish, expensive sheen. Castlecliff, another New York manufacturer of the 1960s, specialized in using black diamonds to great effect, mixing them with coloured pastes and textured satin-finish gold.

With the 1970s came a gradual return to all things natural. In fashion this meant flowery and dreamy prints and mixed patterns, soft, layered clothes, lacy petticoats, long, hazy Pre-Raphaelite hair. Clothes began to cover up the bareness of the 1960s. Health, fitness and sport began to be important and there was a move towards natural foods and a corresponding back-to-nature Crafts Revival. Just as the Arts and Crafts movement of the late 19th century had idealized untrained, expressive handcraftsmanship, so this crafts movement emphasized the individual artist-craftsman working without the support of the commercial network of his or her particular trade; it promoted the use of humble materials, traditional tools and hand-working techniques, and inevitably encouraged a homespun look without the slickness of the machine-made product. Jewellery was very much part of this new crafts ethic, and a new generation of artist-jewellers who had emerged from the art schools of the 1960s began to work somewhat idealistically in communal workshops

*Streamlined 1970s jewels looked back to Art Deco and modernism for inspiration. Christian Dior, 1972.*

and studios using new materials such as titanium or polyester resin, partly for aesthetic reasons, partly because of the high price of gold. This inexpensive 'crafts' jewellery was sold in the new galleries (as opposed to shops) that were springing up all over Britain and Europe. Sometimes regarded as costume jewellery because of its concentration on non-precious materials, this jewellery in general does not fall into this book's definition of costume jewellery. It was artistically or 'design' biased and had little to do with fashion or with ornamenting femininity. It was, however, a very important stepping stone to the more professional creativity of the 1980s.

Outside, in the world of real, commercial jewellery, the 1970s ushered in an impoverished era of gold chains, small or large, to pander to the medallion man and woman. Neglected semi-precious stones took over from crystals, and tiger's eye, coral, lapis lazuli, black onyx were all keynotes of 1970s jewels. Textured gold was still popular and more colour was injected into design through the use of enamels. The costume jewellery industry took to copying and enlarging the fashionable bright medallions and oversized 'Hippie' crosses in arresting colour combinations. Huge gilt circular medallions hung on large chains were covered with resin enamels and centred perhaps with an abstract motif, a psychedelic pseudo-oriental pattern or perhaps a moulded glass or plastic blackamoor's head. Tiger's eye and lapis lazuli were imitated in plastics on very chunky pendants, usually with textured nuggety gilt metal gripping the edges and creeping over the surface of fake stone. There was a fashion for pendants and brooches of abstract, geometric Aztec design, and also for a rich satirical Renaissance grandeur, especially about the crosses.

As the price of gold soared, jewels became smaller, reaching the infinitesimal; ornamentation was starved to death, and on the whole jewels looked like paltry shadows of their former selves. The 1970s brought devastating non-fashions of minute flimsy gold chains, worn several at a time, around the wrist or often alarmingly tight around the neck, with stamped-out stars or hearts or fixed with a single diamond in the centre. Tiny diamond earstuds were popular and in New York Elsa Peretti instigated Diamonds by the Yard. According to Kenneth Jay Lane the 1970s may well have been the only period in history when ornamentation was out of vogue. Costume jewellery suffered badly in the 1970s, and then, as gold prices went down, so costume jewellery and decoration gradually perked up. Jewels became bigger and bolder, strikingly simple and modern, chunky plastics motifs joining the bright or rich colours of the early 1970s enamels. Kenneth Lane was the first to revive the Art Deco style, around 1977, which led to streamlined, almost mechanistic designs. The sleek shapeliness suited the new career-minded women concerned with 'power' or 'executive' dressing in which good-looking co-ordinated accessories played an important part. These women had to dress to succeed in a man's world, and they rejected any obvious signs or symbols of femininity.

The firm of Trifari once again were the mass-market masters of the new look, as they specialized in plastics at this time. They used a great deal of black with gilt metal chains, as well as plastics in jade green or bright summery blue, mellowing to winter tones of burgundy, jet or horn. A typical mid-1970s necklet would have a central plastic motif, a

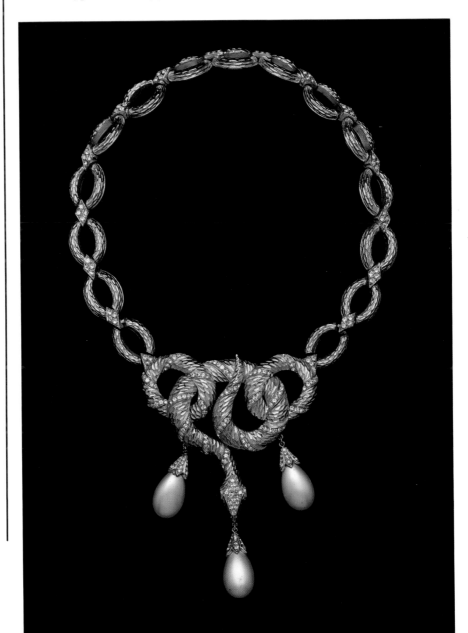

*The ubiquitous serpent makes a late 20th-century appearance, based on a Victorian prototype, in textured gilt metal, entwined with diamanté and hung with imitation pearls. By Trifari, American, 1960–70.*

square or geometric shape with softly rounded edges, hung on a gilt chain of springy Brazilian linking. A summer version might consist of a jade green square pendant hung on white frosted glass beads, with oriental overtones. Enamels became bolder, swirling clouds of rust, peach or sea blue-green, mixed with milky opalescent enamels and occasional feathery strokes of black. Matching sets of somewhat torrid jewels, bangles, earrings, stiff necklets, were large and forceful, formed as russet enamelled autumn leaves, as foaming turquoise waves. Another abstract design strongly evocative of the period consisted of little fat oval slices, of cream, blue or rust enamel, clustered at random and studded with pastes. At the same time, Cartier's status symbol triple-twist Russian wedding rings and bangles inspired hoards of simple shiny knots and twists and plain bangles in two-tone gilt metal.

An account of the 1970s would not be complete without a mention of the punk fad, which brought with it a variety of popular jewellery with unpleasantly violent overtones. The flagrant aggression of the movement was reflected in ugly, anti-ornaments that were clearly anti-beauty. Bicycle chains were wrapped round arms, legs or necks; brooches and earrings took the form of razor blades or iron crosses, and safety pins were pinned all over clothes or body. Metal studs decorated black clothes and leather wristbands as further emblems of violence.

The meteoric rise in the costume jewellery industry happened after 1981. In the 1970s there had been a great divide between real and costume jewellery, which was usually regarded as a cheap and cheerful substitute for the real thing. Corocraft with their low-priced accessories dominated the market. In the early 1980s, the accessories market in general was healthier, and costume jewellery began to improve in quality and rise in price. Almost overnight, it seemed, prices jumped from £5 to £50 or £100 for a good piece of fashion jewellery.

Several factors were involved in the turnaround. The 1980s brought a new freedom to jewellery, and an intense interest in adornment and in femininity. In Britain, the New Romantic look was sparked off by the wedding of the Prince of Wales to Lady Diana Spencer in 1981, giving us a much-needed royal fashion leader, just as Alexandra had been a century before. The new Princess of Wales quickly had a far-reaching effect on fashion and appropriately there was an immediate revival of an Edwardian frilly softness that harked back to the beautiful Princess Alexandra. Echoing Princess Diana's initial fetching coyness, young women wore white blouses with high collars with little frills and ruffs, and huge, extravagant off-the-shoulder ball gowns, not so coy, made of gleaming swirling taffeta with lots of flounces and bows. It was clear that jewels were needed to complement the new dressed-up fashions. Diana began with borrowed heirlooms and introduced a very different type of soft, grand but romantic jewel. In true Edwardian taste, pearls came back into fashion with a vengeance: the Princess's going-away outfit launched a thousand chokers from Corocraft to Collingwood. It was a very flattering and very feminine style that lasted several years. The pearl passion survived several seasons in the real jewellery world too, with constant variations of black pearls, tiny Bewa or freshwater pearls, knobbly twists of silky pale-coloured misshapen pearls, all with seemingly endless ideas for clasps or motifs. Fake pearls, lustrous, creamy and convincing, featured prominently in every costume jewellery collection, short single-strand necklaces with central diamanté and coloured paste bows, butterflies, flowers, clusters. During the 1980s the best fake pearls came from Japan, Hong Kong and Spain. Henkel & Grosse produce their own pearls in a factory in the South of France. The glass beads are either engine-turned or, in the case of the 'baroque pearls', moulded by hand, coated with twelve layers of *essence d'Orient*, and hand-polished.

While jewellery, real or false, piled on layers of lustrous pearls and new romance, there was a dramatic upsurge of glamour, a return to a new brand of tough and sexy filmstar femininity. Figure-hugging clothes replaced loose layers; Madonna shook the world with her brazen, raunchy bejewelled sexuality and *Dallas* and *Dynasty* lured their audiences with a heady escapism.

The fantastic fast-changing fashions of the glamorously troubled women of television's Denver and Dallas struck a chord in the public imagination. Love her or hate her, the image of Alexis Colby has been hard to ignore. Alexis is as tough and invincible as diamonds, with the same mixture of fire and ice, and just as dazzlingly expensive. Shrewd and ruthless in a man's world, she plays up every inch of her femininity with dramatic clothes, make-up, luscious furs and jewels. Costume jewellery delivered a slice of that make-believe world.

Women soon discovered that masses of diamanté, as opposed to one small diamond, could transform the way they looked and felt about themselves. The emphasis in jewellery suddenly changed; the original purpose of jewels as flattering adornments was rediscovered; they were no longer simply vehicles for displaying intrinsic value. The stigma previously attached to fakes evaporated and wearing costume jewellery no longer meant you couldn't afford the real thing. Freed from another

The quintessential Bulgari look of the
1980s, the imitation ancient coins set
in gilt metal. Made by Alpha, London,
and a bestselling line at Fior in London
around 1985.

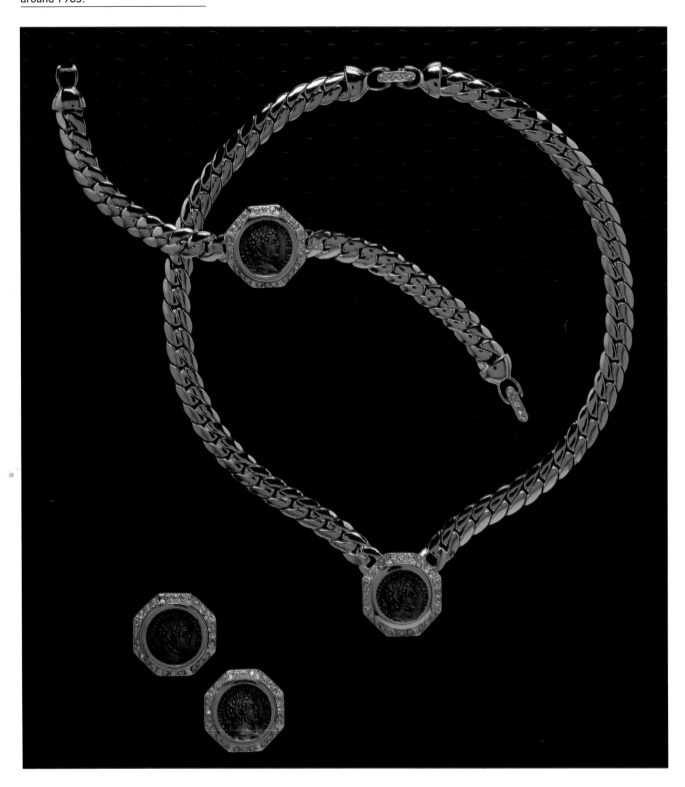

convention, women began buying costume jewels for themselves, on a whim, to suit a mood or an occasion. Dressing up enjoyed a new burst of popularity, and sparkle came back into fashion, not only for jewels but also in fabrics like silk taffeta and shimmering Lurex. Beading and sequins were eagerly welcomed back even on denim and T-shirts. This new era of costume jewels unleashed a primal instinct for personal ornament which seemed unlikely to go out of fashion.

At the same time, the cost of buying, keeping and insuring real jewels became prohibitively high, and as crime rates soared, it was no longer advisable to wear conspicuous displays of gems. The field of fashion jewellery was wide open to new talent and inventiveness, and as costume jewels became more exciting, suddenly precious gems could not compare with the sumptuous spread of fabulous fakes readily available.

Basically, the market was still divided into proud and preening copies of precious jewels, and fantasy jewels, pure whimsical ornaments to fashion and femininity. In between these two categories came the new couture jewels, revived with great success by houses such as Chanel and Yves Saint Laurent, and at the middle to lower end of the market, quietly fashionable ranges by Monet or Trifari were sold in department stores.

Imitation jewels took on the guise of the glossy Italian real jewels, with designs dominated very much by Bulgari of Rome. During the 1980s, Bulgari's distinctive ideas were mercilessly copied by costume jewellery manufacturers; there were flat wide gold chain necklets hung with gold-mounted ancient coins, necklaces of plaited ropes of coloured silk. It was Bulgari who instigated the vogue for neat and clawless yellow gold 'rub over settings', for fancy-shaped coloured sapphires of hot pink, yellow and light blue, set in ribbed gold or surfaces *pavé*-set with diamonds. This young, continental style of real jewels has lent itself very well to copies and interpretations that look unnervingly like the real thing. Ken Lane has wittily mimicked Bulgari ('If I haven't copied you, you're not worth copying', he says) and his 1987 collection included updated versions of the coin jewels, combined with long strands of pearls or set in diamanté. He and Michael Grosse of Henkel & Grosse particularly admired the instantly recognizable style of Marina 'B', Bulgari's sister, who created strong ultra chic, ultra Continental jewels of striking combinations of colours and textures.

Anonymous factories around the world, in London, New York, Hong Kong, Taiwan, Milan and Valenza excelled in fine-quality 'real'-looking jewels. In Great Britain, the firm of Attwood & Sawyer produced some of the finest quality elegant imitative jewellery, easily and often mistaken

*lack and red enamel necklace and* *angles in the form of branch coral.* *ves Saint Laurent Couture, Spring* *980.*

for the real thing. Attwood & Sawyer employs full-time designers, and like many other manufacturers uses the centrifugal method of casting white metal which is then plated with 22 carat gold and all pastes glued in by hand. The jewellery has an immaculate long-lasting finish. Attwood & Sawyer designs are generally classic, with an occasional touch of whimsy and a great deal of glitter that keeps in line with the very latest Continental fine jewellery. So spectacular and convincing are the copies that Attwood & Sawyer supplied much of the jewellery for the stars of *Dallas* and *Dynasty*. They are also particularly successful with more traditional, rather grand jewels, based loosely on regal 18th- and 19th-century splendour, with draped and garlanded necklaces, long drop earrings. In 1987 for the first time Attwood & Sawyer introduced an entirely different range of bigger and bolder diamanté jewels, set with huge crystals that could never be mistaken for the real thing.

Fior, a fashionable London retailer of costume jewellery and accessories, sells a vast and varied stock of scintillating fashion jewels.

*Two designs for a set of jewels by Alun Roberts for Attwood & Sawyer, based on classic designs and pavé-set diamanté. British, 1986.*

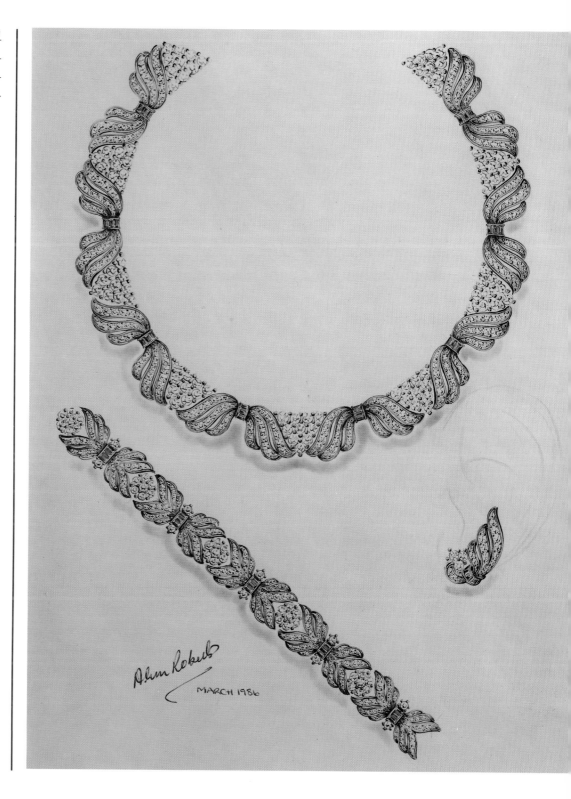

The business was established in 1892, when it originally sold precious jewellery, switching to costume jewellery during the 1920s when there was suddenly a huge demand for frankly fake jewels. In 1950 Mr Sonny Feldman named the company Fior and moved to an avant-garde boutique in Burlington Gardens. Now there are two London branches, and the business is still run by the Feldman family, Lawrence Feldman supervising the jewellery side of the business for over 25 years, buying from factories all over the world and often commissioning exclusive designs. They specialize in fine-quality, well-made work that looks just like precious jewels. For the last 50 years Fior has kept back selected pieces which now form an unrivalled collection of 20th-century costume jewellery, all in mint condition and representative of world-wide fashions and manufacturers. One of the earliest specialist boutiques of its kind, the shop has the allure of an Aladdin's cave crammed with gems and jewels of seemingly inestimable value, treasures beyond belief, piles of gems that slither through the fingers like an irresistible illusion. The shop has always drawn a wealthy, glossy clientèle. In the 1950s regular visitors included Joan Collins, Elizabeth Taylor, Lucille Ball and David Niven. Today this tradition of celebrity customers continues at Fior.

In 1987, the two worlds of real and fake jewels shared the same fever-pitch excitement over the sale of the Duchess of Windsor's jewels, held by Sotheby's in Geneva. The jewels and their intimate association with the love story that changed history were totally captivating, and attracted worldwide attention to jewellery in general, especially to jewels of fantasy and artistry. The Duchess wore her real jewels like costume jewels, with a daring irreverence. So rich and extravagant were the designs and the use of gems that onlookers at the time thought they must be fake. The most important pieces in her collection were those designed by Van Cleef & Arpels and by Jeanne Toussaint of Cartier: the sleek, articulated Big Cat jewels, panthers and leopards, the fabulous flamingo, with its plump, diamond-set body and tail feathers of riotous colours. After the sale, costume jewellery manufacturers everywhere turned out Windsor jewel copies of varying quality.

Couture jewellery, oblivious to other jewellery events, continued on its own Parisian path, led as ever by the house of Chanel, now under the inspired direction of Karl Lagerfeld. Lagerfeld magically invoked the original courageous spirit of Chanel, transforming the classics into a modern jaunty elegance. Recalling Coco's obsession with fabulous fakes, Lagerfeld glorified his designs with masses of gilt, chains, buttons, belts,

*Twisted imitation pearl choker with a diamanté Big Cat motif, by Kenneth Jay Lane, inspired by the sale of the Duchess of Windsor's jewels in 1987.*

jangling coins and bracelets, even *trompe l'oeil* embroidery. Pearls grew to massive proportions, in silky colours. Lagerfeld brandished barbaric bangles, wide as a cuff, heavily embossed and gilt or spelling CHANEL in bold openwork. Earrings dangled with miniature gilt quilted Chanel handbags, or emblazoned the crossed 'C' monogram on the wearer's ears, while purists could still choose classic button earclips in pearl and gilt, but far larger than discreet to recapture the original shock of Chanel's fakes. In the autumn of 1987 Chanel introduced jewels of leather and gilt, chain entwined with leather to make striking earrings and wristbands in a faithful but updated version of an original Chanel detail. To complement the season's dashing Highwayman mood, there were huge gilt fobs or cloak clasps, worn with a brooch pinned to each lapel and linked by a massive gilt chain or length of pearls.

England led the way in fantasy jewels. The London shop of Butler & Wilson, a mecca for costume jewellery addicts, was instrumental in

*Costume jewels from Chanel, created under the guidance and inspiration of Karl Lagerfeld, keeping the spirit of Coco Chanel, in the use of ropes of pearls and gilt medallions. Spring 1988.*

209

creating the new climate for fashion jewels. The shop, owned by Nicky Butler and Simon Wilson, overturned entrenched British attitudes towards fake jewels and on the way created an entirely new jewellery phenomenon. Butler & Wilson turned costume jewellery into the most respectable, most fashionable accessories and single-handed in the 1980s made diamanté acceptable for wear during the day. Perhaps the most important fact was that Butler & Wilson showed women how to wear their jewels. Through magazine editorials and superb traffic-stopping billboards outside the Fulham Road shop, they promoted a fabulous but fun-loving femininity: sexy and daring but intelligent and witty.

*Extravagant and extrovert diamanté from Butler & Wilson, Hollywood style, 1983.*

*Faye Dunaway wearing favourite Butler & Wilson jewels, including a surreal, giant hand brooch, 1986.*

*Red Indians and the planets were two popular themes at Butler & Wilson, modelled by Charlotte Lewis in 1987.*

Butler & Wilson started as antique dealers in the late 1960s in Portobello Road, moving to the Chelsea Antique Market and then to Antiquarius, in the King's Road. At that time antiques, antique markets and in particular genuine Art Nouveau and Art Deco jewellery were becoming very popular, and Butler & Wilson developed a reputation for selling the most stylish and unusual jewels. Magazines and fashion editors came to them to borrow pieces for features, but by the time the features appeared, and customers flocked to the small stand in Antiquarius, the particular jewels were invariably sold. Butler & Wilson realized the potential for a wider market. It seemed a natural move to try to make the jewels to cater to this demand. Originally Art Nouveau had appealed most to them but gradually their preference shifted to the styles of 1925, which were the inspiration for their earliest manufactured jewellery. At first they produced small cast brooches in cubist Art Deco figural forms: little angular swinging golfers, tennis players in silver and enamel. They began manufacturing in a very small way, using repairers to make jewels and enamel restorers to do the enamelling. Just a few new jewels were sold alongside the old pieces. Starting in this modest way, they were always able to control design and quality. The project grew and in 1972 they took their present shop in the Fulham Road, filling it with deliciously tempting and glittering baubles and adventurous, amusing jewels. Certainly their knowledge and experience of old jewels and 20th-century design was a major factor in their massive success. They understand jewellery design, its proportions, colours, shapes and textures, so that even their most enormous jewels are visually pleasing and successful, and effective to wear. Period pieces, from huge Georgian paste bows, through Victorian buckle bangles and entwined serpents, to extravagant bossy 1940s jewels, continued to be inspirational; yet the final result is resolutely 1980s.

By 1987 they had two shops, shops within shops in department stores in London, Chicago and San Antonio, and ran a wholesale business selling their jewellery to retailers around the world. Their dedicated clientèle included some of the most beautiful women in the world: Faye Dunaway, Charlotte Rampling, Catherine Deneuve, Lauren Hutton have all posed for famous Butler & Wilson photographs taken by top photographers such as Terry O'Neill and Terence Donovan, in the tradition of great Hollywood publicity stills. In 1985 they were commissioned to make jewellery for the Pirelli calendar, all with tyre track motifs. The jewellery was donated to London's Victoria & Albert Museum.

The heavy metal look of 1983 at Butler & Wilson, the steely silver-coloured metal ribbed and buckled and set with massive diamanté.

Throughout Butler & Wilson's growth in popularity, publicity, posters and landmark photographs played a very important part in changing attitudes by showing women how to pile on the jewels and look expensive and desirable. Early in their career influential editors such as Grace Coddington at *Vogue* were quick to understand Butler & Wilson's approach and used jewellery in features which had a tremendous effect on public awareness. Pictures of luxurious and enormously wealthy stars wearing fakes added an expensive new dimension to the idea, and the royal patronage of the Princess of Wales set the final seal of approval on their mad masterpieces.

All the jewellery is made in England, at various factories in London and all over the country. Butler & Wilson produce two collections a year and find that styles evolve from one collection to the next. Amongst their most notable innovations were the sensational snakes of 1985. Based on a popular Victorian theme, and blown up larger than life, snakes draped round the neck or slithered one or three at a time over the shoulder, bust, lapel. In the same way, lizards matured from restrained Edwardian creatures into oversized, sinuously curved ornaments, dazzling and darting over the smartest outfits in 1986. Around the same time, Butler & Wilson based a collection on the theme of medals, gorgeous gilt heraldic brooches and pendants, enamelled and encrusted with massive faux-gems, accompanied in the range by crowns and swords and crosses. In contrast there was a popular distressed and tough fashion for steel with paste, wide cuff bracelets and heavy chain necklets. Since that time there have been friendly elephants, large disembodied hands, cuddly teddy bears, Wallis-inspired leopards and panthers and a whole repertoire of creatures. For autumn 1987 Butler & Wilson's jewels were yet more unfettered in terms of whimsical novelties. Massive diamanté jewels ranged through aristocratic 18th-century style bows, Victorian gem-studded serpents and jet and diamanté jewels, huge stars and classic crescents, more teddy bears, a champagne glass spraying bubbles, as well as more reserved daytime jewels in two-tone plated metal.

For spring 1988 the emphasis was on travel and time. Brooches, bracelets, and earrings took the form of fake watches, a reminder of the 18th-century fad for *fausses-montres*. The glorious years of grand travel were recalled by jewels designed as early aeroplanes, a pilot wearing goggles and flying hat, a stately ocean liner set against the New York skyline, a suitcase covered with place-name labels. Simple sculptural jewellery shaped as planets and stars took the travel theme to an extra dimension, while Butler & Wilson's classic diamanté was accompanied for the first time by a new, rather grown-up range of real-looking imitation jewellery.

Monty Don is another English maker of fantasy fashion jewels, working with his wife Sarah Erskine to design frivolously decorative ornaments, mostly paste-encrusted, which are sold around the world and in their shop in Beauchamp Place, London. Monty Don had studied fine art,

Butler & Wilson's slithering diamanté snakes were all the rage in 1985.

while Sarah had concentrated on textiles, but both were interested in design in general. Uncertain of which direction to take Sarah was offered the use of a jeweller's workshop and they experimented with non-precious fashion-orientated jewels. After some months they hit on the design of a crystal or pearl-drop earring topped with a pretty silk bow. The timing was perfect; the affordable, romantic bows and drops hit an eager market. The style lasted for several seasons. Later Monty Don and Sarah Erskine worked with fashion designers, notably Bruce Oldfield and Chloë, making jewels for fashion shows, and they extended their range enormously, most recently making vast diamanté jewels in much the same spirit as Butler & Wilson. Some of their best known designs included long and slinky earrings like fish skeletons, mammoth flower baskets, brooches like Scottie dogs with diamanté fringes for whiskers, giant sparkly crustaceans, vicious lobsters, butterflies, huge parrots and

*Monty Don's famous ribbon and crystal drop earrings; varied by drop pearls and an 18th-century style in diamanté, 1982.*

birds of paradise with flexible tail feathers in a riot of colours. There were plump, curly shells, many more bows and drops, a huge corsage ornament and a belt designed as a swan gliding amongst trailing droplets of water, and a Zodiac range emphasizing the new figurative mood in costume jewellery: a benign bull sporting a leafy twig clenched in its teeth, an elegant ram's head profile with a decorative collar, a water carrier or amphora spilling streams of articulated diamanté water. Amongst the Monty Don repertoire there have always been classically inspired models, enlarged and modernized, with a hint of history without being pastiches. This line included flowerhead jewels, chokers, bracelets, brooches, 18th-century-style bows and girandole or chandelier earrings. Made in British factories, the diamanté is for the most part set in rhodium-plated stamped and soldered metal settings. Contrasting metal jewels made of cast silver and plated brass have been given a distressed metallic finish which lends itself well to figurative, sculptural themes. For a while, such sultry metal jewels looked like a chatelaine's keys, like medieval chains or like worn fragments of statuary. Huge brooches were designed as masses of flowers sculpted in high relief, their imagined colours repressed into monotone.

The giant companies of the industry have made the most of the 1980s explosion of fashion jewellery. Companies are constantly experimenting with techniques for faster and efficient mass manufacture without sacrificing too much quality, although a surprising amount of labour-intensive work – designing, model-making, setting, enamelling, and some polishing – is done by hand. The engineering techniques that could in principle be applied to costume jewellery manufacture are not financially viable in a business concerned with fast-changing fashions.

In Germany Henkel & Grosse's reaction to the boom has been to ensure that they are as self-sufficient as possible. Fine machine-cut diamanté can still only be provided by Swarovski, who supply virtually the world with paste gems. Henkel & Grosse, however, produce their own coloured stones in a factory at Kaufbeuren in Germany and their pearls are made at their own factory in France (see page 203). Apart from the Christian Dior jewels, Henkel & Grosse produce their own range and several other lines. For the late 1980s, Henkel & Grosse concentrated on improving cold enamelling techniques aiming at the brilliantly luxurious look and feel of Fabergé's exclusive turn-of-the-century trinkets, in which jewel-coloured translucent enamels were applied over engine-turned goldwork. Along with other major manufacturers, they also predicted that a sophisticated, tailored look was most likely to succeed the frenzied finery of oversized diamanté.

Subtle, moody colours and graphic shapes were the key elements of many of the larger American-based manufacturers in 1987 and 1988. Napier maintained their speciality of gilt metalwork, adding the warm tones of tortoiseshell and starkness of jet to autumn 1987, while spring 1988 advocated the fun and formality of 'faux marble'. Colours were soft and natural, the gentle tones of stucco and marble, called 'sea spray salmon', and 'celadon green'.

Trifari too were working towards a sleek, subdued sophistication. Spring 1988 brought abstract shapes, still fluid and feminine, combined with the soft neutral colours of ivory, beige and sandstone. Several other ranges catered for the various changing moods of women, from the triumphant career woman to the romantic or the flirt.

James Northrop, President of Trifari, says that women in the 1980s use costume jewellery to reflect the many different facets of their personality and their increasing self-confidence. This was certainly a contributing factor to the revival of the industry in the early 1980s after 10–15 years in the doldrums. Now, however, he sees no end to the new acceptance and enjoyment of fashion jewellery. 'In fact we see an acceleration. We have just tapped the surface of the potential for buying and wearing jewellery as an accessory. In the 1980s costume jewellery has become very much more honest about what it is and has been able to play its fascinating role as an accurate representation of changing fashions.'

Around the world, amidst the classic or couture jewels and the style-setters, costume jewellery today is almost indescribably individual. Each new idea is unexpected, uninhibited, intended to delight and thrill its wearers. Costume jewellery has attracted many artists, designers and craftsmen from so many different fields that it is only possible to mention a cross-section of makers and ideas within this book.

In London, Carolyn Stephenson decided to swap gold and diamonds for papier mâché and paste when she turned to costume jewellery after a career as a precious jewellery designer. Her sculptural and fluid jewellery cleverly blended all the finesse and elegance of the real thing with the fun and freedom of new colours and materials.

Having spent ten years designing real jewellery she could not find the opportunity to create the designs she wanted. 'Sadly, real jewellery is being overpowered by the huge, bold statements of today's costume jewellery,' she says. Working with costume jewellery, she could make the jewellery as she always envisaged it: exciting yet classical and sophisticated, beautifully proportioned and generously sculpted, with luscious use of pearls and gems for maximum sensuality. She adapted traditional methods to new materials, working first in papier mâché then progressing to resin for a more professional and uniform finish.

The resin jewellery was entirely hand-made and hand-painted but she then moved to a metal range which could more easily be mass-produced without sacrificing quality. Gold leaf which looks like pure gold was used generously to envelop massive gold beads, to trail over glossy black beads or on a monumental geometric bangle with lashings of diamanté. Strong, stylized but natural organic forms predominate: snails, spirals, fossils or shells wrapped with smooth coils, flaring bats' wings, ribbed angels' wings and, best of all perhaps, the bone motifs, smooth, sculptural and substantial curves, pleasing primeval shapes. Earrings

*Brooches coated with gold leaf and a frill necklace, by Carolyn Stephenson, 1987.*

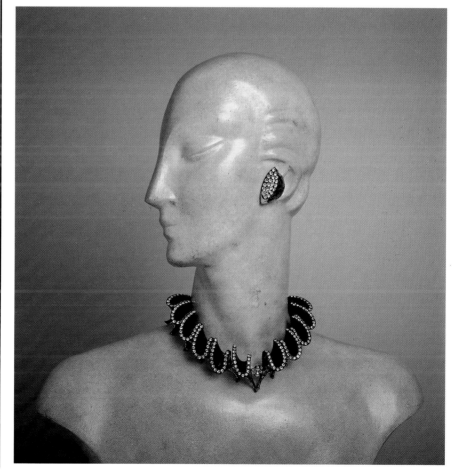

sweep onto the face and brooches are huge, round and domed with textured or mottled surfaces oozing diamanté.

Carolyn Stephenson and other individual designers sell jewels in an increasing number of small specialist boutiques which have sprung up in the capital cities of the world. In London in 1986 Janet Fitch, formerly a design journalist, opened a West End shop selling an exclusive choice of hand-made clothes, objects and accessories including captivating outrageous jewellery. Believing clothes had become too standardized, reduced to a fashionable formula and in need of the individuality supplied by jewels, she stocked up on work by English, Italian and American makers who seemed able to put anything and everything into a piece of jewellery. Jewels composed of *objets trouvés* have had a great following in the 1980s. Some of Eric Beamon's creations are appropriately called kitchen-sink necklaces. Simply but effectively made of beads and baubles and bits of gilt metal or charms shaped like anything from forks to hearts, his necklaces are luxuriant deep fringes of colour and texture, beads strung together with strips and tiny knots of suede. Wide bracelets are constructed with beaded fringes that swing over the top of the hand. Some examples from Beamon's repertoire have a 'native' feel about them, some from the mid-1980s show a punk tendency in their clashing shades of bright orange red and green; others are dark and moody, coloured like bruised and glimmering green-black shadows. Eric Beamon is American, but a workshop in London produces British versions in his style.

Michael DeNardo is another American living in London whose jewellery is sold at Janet Fitch. His 'junk' jewellery looks as if it is made of scrap metal in unexpected combinations of cogs, nuts and bolts, all clustered together like scrapheaps of memories, miniature wiry and shiny sculptures in neutral metallic non-colours. John Wind is another American maker, Philadelphia-based, who assembles stunning and zany costume jewels from *objets trouvés*, using old watch faces, old bits of jewellery, charms, chains, clasps, items from hardware shops, toy and novelty shops; he has even turned spun-sugar cake decorations into earrings.

In 1985 John Wind, together with Hilary Jay, set up a company called Maximal Art, creating jewellery that they describe as 'romantic surrealism'. They met as students at the University of Pennsylvania and John then won a scholarship to the Slade School of Art in London where Hilary spent a considerable amount of time. John began dabbling in costume jewellery-making in 1984 in London, buying bagloads of old, broken, dusty costume jewellery, beads and pearls in Brick Lane market. His experiments

eventually proved to be a commercial success and he sold them to London boutiques. He first collaborated with Hilary on a collection commissioned by the Thomson Twins, and when John moved back to the United States they decided to set up Maximal Art in Philadelphia. At first they continued making individual pieces, but soon realized the need for manufacturing their designs in somewhat larger numbers. In May 1986 they launched their multi-watch bracelet comprised of four linked antique wristwatches, setting the trend for *fausse-montre* jewellery. They have continued with their witty collages and watch bracelets, adding a range of reproduction 1930s and 1940s watches.

*Watch-face jewels created by John Wind and Hilary Jay for Maximal Art. American, 1987–8.*

*Painted resin and paste-set jewellery by Billy Boy, working in the surreal spirit of Schiaparelli; Vampire Ears earrings, with hand-moulded glass beads, 1986.*

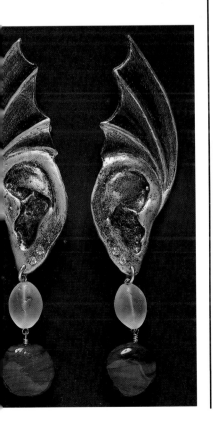

Ceri Evans sells jewellery in London's *avant-garde* fashion hypermarket, Hyper Hyper, and he also has a degree in jewellery from the Central School of Art but he chose to make fashion jewels from crumpled pewter or lacquered furniture mouldings, with scrolls and curls. Glad of his conventional training in putting the jewels together he turned to costume jewellery for its freedom to experiment without fear of making expensive mistakes. He too has worked closely with fashion designers and made enormous and flamboyant jewels for fashion shows.

The fashion shows of the mid to late 1980s that started many designers on the costume jewellery trail had more than a touch of the theatre about them and there are obvious links between fantasy jewels and the theatre, which has also yielded some talented jewellery designers. Barry Parmon used to make theatre props and fully understands the sheer fantasy, escapism and theatre in today's costume jewels. From painted vacuum-formed plastic and resin moulds, he makes brooches of huge cats' faces with dashing bow ties, exuberant marblized or sequinned bows, larger than life, decorated with old beads or jet. Like so many designers and makers, he is attracted by magic, myth and total illusion.

In Paris the magic and success of costume jewellery has always derived less from illusion and figurative fantasy and more from chic or shocking colour and form – altogether more seriously 'designed', less frivolous. In the late 1980s *avant-garde* specialist boutiques such as Utility B-B, Fabrice and Anémone, whose jewels were created by Lucien Pellat-Finet, showed compelling displays of sophisticated and daring fashion accessories intended to turn conventional ideas about precious jewels upside down. The zany jewels of Billy Boy, an American in Paris, were to be seen in Utility B-B and all over the city. Unlike the fiercely French abstract jewels, his work is funny, childlike, naïve.

Billy Boy is the great Schiaparelli expert. He has the world's largest private collection of *haute couture* accessories, jewellery and documents, and he designs his own range of costume jewellery in the spirit of Schiaparelli. Like Billy Boy himself it is colourful, eccentric, rebellious. It is anti-jewellery, hand-made from substances like plastic resin, or hand-assembled and decorated in unstructured, amorphous shapes, strangely pleasing, with soft and dimpled textures, painted in crude, strong colours. Exotic, primitive mixtures of pink and orange and purple are highlighted with splatterings of gold leaf. There are huge pulsating shocking pink hearts, and other Schiaparelli-inspired themes such as starfish, snails and dancing bows, as well as earrings like pointed devil's ears, strange monstrous faces, golden gingerbread men and jewels like

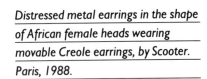

Distressed metal earrings in the shape of African female heads wearing movable Creole earrings, by Scooter. Paris, 1988.

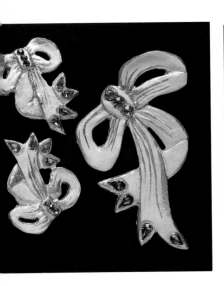

Dancing Bow brooch and earrings, Billy Boy, 1986.

cookies in home-made forked, swirly shapes. Other jewels seem to be mysteriously tribal. They are all irresistibly funny and light-hearted and Billy Boy's newest ideas have included ranges called 'Bubble Gum from Outer Space' and 'Reincarnation of a Sneeze'. Slightly less idiosyncratic is a line based on geometric forms, hand-made pyramid and square-shaped glass beads, reminiscent of ancient amulets and Arabian Nights hoards. Working with a small team of assistants in a Paris workshop, Billy Boy uses hand-made glass beads, and sometimes adds antique beads and paste to the jewellery made in homage to the zany creativity of Elsa Schiaparelli.

Scooter, the jewellery shop in the rue Turbigo, Paris, was conceived by Zaza van Hulle in 1979. She began by selling 1950s American clothes as well as records, motor scooters and some pieces of outrageous jewellery made out of old pieces bought at the Flea Market. The response to the jewels was enthusiastic and gradually Zaza and Scooter concentrated more and more on jewellery. Zaza designed the jewels, had them manufactured in quantity and then sold them all over France, in the United States, England, West Germany, Italy, Japan, Australia. Based on her earlier baubles, the jewels were large and dashing but with a baroque air of rich treasures, a pirates' hoard of long lost booty. From the early 1980s Scooter was famous for massive creole hoop earrings, for jewels of hammered, lacquered or distressed metals. Zaza went on to create brightly coloured paste-set jewels, rivière necklaces, huge cuff bracelets, absurdly glamorous paste pendants in the Hollywood tradition. Enormous steel curb link bracelets and necklets came next, Gothic crosses, earrings like spiders' webs embedded with a single diamanté stone, or like huge feathered wings, lacquered white. Scooter sold to bejewelled rock stars like Madonna, Annie Lennox, Boy George. Later in the 1980s Scooter switched to an African look with stridently barbaric jewels made of embossed copper or bronze, then exotic woods studded with metal, all capturing the potency of ritualistic ornament.

Italy's thriving jewellery industry, centred in the northern town of Valenza, extends to producing high-fashion costume jewellery from non-precious materials. The large paste-set metallic concoctions of ever-shifting chic design have a Continental character suggestive of 1940s design fashions and incorporating flounced reddish gilt metal and huge chunks of paste.

The firm of Pellini is probably best known for more individual jewels made of synthetics and resins adapted to graphic and futuristic themes. Donatella Pellini is the third in a family of female jewellery designers.

*Pellini's luminous and seductive resins and synthetics in warm colours of russet, amber and tortoiseshell. Italian, 1987.*

Her grandmother designed jewellery for Dior and Balenciaga, and her mother continued the tradition, achieving great popularity in New York in the 1950s with real-looking jewels. Now Donatella has taken over from her mother and continues to work with leading Italian fashion designers, Fendi, Basile and Romeo Gigli. She lives and works in the family 17th-century palazzo in Milan. On the ground floor is the shop and behind that the workshop in which a small team experiments with new materials. For Pellini, the mood-altering accessories of the 1980s were initially imperative to counteract the simplicity of the decade's clothes. She is fascinated by new materials and bases her designs around the substances she uses, preferring chunky, sculptural forms, strong lines and deep colours and a determined shameless showing off of frankly fake ornament: her beads and bracelets are designed to be worn several at a time. Classic Pellini models of the 1980s have been jewels of semi-translucent Perspex in all colours, a range of *craquelé* jewels reminiscent of the crazed or crackled ceramics of the 1930s, distressed bronze beads and an attention-grabbing range of mock amber jewellery, also made of resin, in glorious glowing colours from a golden butter-yellow through simmering sherry to tawny brown. Other synthetics have mimicked monumental shapes seemingly hewn from flecked granite, motifs moulded in a dense matt terracotta or shiny cochineal pink. One season she created for Fendi lumps of resinous coal, encrusted with diamanté like a diamond-bearing mineral.

Costume jewellery makers have also been culled from the worlds of sculpture and fashion, attracting ever more versatile and idiosyncratic talents. Andrew Logan is an artist and sculptor and English eccentric, famous for his bizarre cosmic structures of fragments of mirror and glass. He works in London, in a studio called the Glasshouse in the Sky, a dreamland jungle of giant flowers and plants nodding against the glass ceiling, eerie Egyptianesque bejewelled human statues, massive mirrored sculptures, a flashing blue Pegasus with magnificent wings, a gigantic golden sun, a chandelier like spun sugar. His jewels are miniature versions of his sculptures, misshapen, crackled and encrusted symbols of pure fun, sold mainly by Zandra Rhodes in her London boutique to complement her glittering and flamboyant clothes. Andrew started working with glass in 1969, and his jewellery venture began in 1972, when the designer Thea Porter asked him to make jewellery for her shows. In 1972 when the jewellery world was in the midst of the gold chain syndrome, Andrew Logan began setting shards of shattered mirror into resin encrusted with glitter, studded with glass stones, gold beading,

*Uninhibited jewels made of broken mirror, resin and jewel-like pastes by glass artist Andrew Logan. British, mid-1980s.*

bits of old embroidery or ephemera. It took ten years, he says, before the jewellery started selling in the new climate of the fantasy ornament. Andrew often paints the glass, and has recently found a technique for coating glass with copper, gold or titanium to produce a dark iridescence. He introduces any little objects he has picked up, shells, peacock feathers, old beads, an old crushed playing card found in the gutter. He uses mirror of varying thicknesses, often thin powder compact mirror or mirror balls used for Christmas decorations. He smashes everything himself with a hammer, works quickly and is immensely prolific. Speed is important as his work has to be unstudied, spontaneous. He likes to see his jewels as portable sculptures, also as magical ritualistic charms. Favourite shapes and themes recur; he is well known for his Paisley shapes, a questionmark, pyramid, eggs, hearts, fishes, eyes, stars, universal shapes that he feels will have meaning for everyone and many of which come from his travels: he made Buddhas after a trip to Burma and Thailand, Third Eye jewels after India and pyramid jewels after a visit to Egypt. Since 1980 he has been working with the fashion designer Zandra Rhodes, designing and stage-managing her shows and producing two collections a year.

The last word in inventive materials must go to Simon Costin. Another renegade from theatre design, Simon searches out dead insects and animals which he turns into beautiful but bizarre jewels. Exquisitely presented, they are clearly created with a special talent and dedication, and with a passion for theatrical if macabre ornament and symbolism. In some way the jewels seem to belong to the Victorian stuffed- animal mentality. They are compelling visions, and the use of colour, material and line is peculiarly seductive; it takes some time to realize that what you are looking at and touching is in fact a preserved fish head, a shed snake skin, a painted scorpion or bleached rabbit's skull. Simon has always been interested in natural history, and particularly in taxidermy and 'arresting decay'. He took a degree in theatre design and was involved in making jewels for theatre and cinema, including the period jewellery for Derek Jarman's *Caravaggio*.

At the same time he began to produce a collection of jewels made from animals, an idea which sprang from one jewel created quite spontaneously from a trout head, encrusted with fragments of copper which turned green and echoed the shimmering scales of the fish. He began to experiment with other fish and animals; 'Flash Harry', the fishmonger in Harrods, saved fish heads for him, and the London Zoo began to send him dead creatures. A friendly lady in the reptile house

*Compelling, other-worldly beauty of a brooch made from a tinted hare's skull, with glass eyes, copper wire, peacock feathers and pastes, in its own case, by Simon Costin. British, 1987.*

kindly saved him shed snakeskins, which Simon transformed into gossamer-light ruched necklaces, entwined with fake pearls and little bleached bones, all in harmonious natural shades of white and cream. Simon preserved the creatures using taxidermy techniques, then painted or lacquered them, adding beads, shells, feathers, gold dust and glass pastes, and fixing his fish heads and skulls with unnerving taxidermists' glass eyes. He made brooches, necklaces and dramatic masks and headdresses and presented each piece in a specially made box, marblized or covered with 1930s endpaper, lined with watered silk or taffeta and inscribed with a symbolist quote or poem. A black-painted condor's claw from which hangs a ruby red paste drop of blood is turned into a dramatic brooch; a small and perfect shiny golden crab dotted with stones is intended to sit calmly on a shoulder; another preserved claw brooch is hung with a shell pendant decorated with brass ivy leaves, rock crystal drops and peacock breast feathers, bearing the brass wire inscription 'Passion'. A sinister shiny black scorpion necklace was a special commission, while amongst Simon's early favourites is a fantastic silky peacock-feather fringe necklace, brooches made of skulls soaked in a copper solution to turn them an eerie green and jewels encrusted with shiny iridescent stag beetles and cockroaches (brought back by Simon from New York).

Costume jewels, gloriously artificial, have traditionally been conjured out of man-made substances to create their illusions of grandeur. As plastics, acrylics, synthetics became more sophisticated, it is interesting that Simon Costin upset traditions by turning the purely natural into the most unnatural visions to join the parade of extraordinary 20th-century personal ornaments.

From the 18th century, costume jewellery has been conceived as a wholly commercial product, to satisfy a basic need for self-adornment, a need to be noticed which in turn leads to the survival of the fittest. But now, looking at the heritage of today's inventive jewels, it seems that the finest of non-precious, fashion jewellery, wittily expressive of its age and wearers, will surely come to be regarded as an art form.

# BIBLIOGRAPHY

Yvonne Amic, *L'Opaline Française au XIX Siècle*, Librairie Gründ, Paris 1952

Victor Arwas, *Art Deco*, Academy Editions, 1980

Lillian Baker, *Fifty Years of Collectable Fashion Jewellery, 1925–1975*, Collector Books, 1986

Martin Battersby, *The Decorative Twenties*, Studio Vista, 1971

Martin Battersby, *The Decorative Thirties*, Studio Vista, 1969

Martin Battersby, *Art Deco Fashion*, Academy Editions, 1974

Vivienne Becker, *Art Nouveau Jewelry*, Thames & Hudson, 1985

Vivienne Becker, *Antique and Twentieth Century Jewellery* (second edition), NAG Press, 1987

Barbara Bernard, *Fashion in the Sixties*, Academy/St Martins, 1978

Charles Castle, *La Belle Otero, The Last Great Courtesan*, Michael Joseph, 1981

Andrée Chanlot, *Les Ouvrages en Cheveux*, Editions de l'Amateur, 1986

Edmonde Charles-Roux, *Chanel and her World*, Weidenfeld & Nicolson, 1981

Anne Clifford, *Cut Steel and Berlin Iron Jewellery*, Adams & Dart, 1971

Derek Clifford, *Anne Clifford's Antique Jewellery, the Story of a Collection*, Nottingham Court Press, 1985

Cunnington and Cunnington, *English Costume in the 18th Century*, Plays Inc., 1972

C. W. Cunnington, *The Perfect Lady*, Max Parrish & Co., 1948

H. R. D'Allemagne, *Les Accessoires du Costume et du Mobilier depuis le XIII jusqu'au milieu du XIX siècle*, Schmidt, Paris, 1928

Andrea DiNoto, 'Bakelite Envy, Jazz Age Plastic Jewelry', *Connoisseur*, July 1985

Barbara Ellman, *The World of Fashion Jewelry*, Aunt Louise Imports, 1986

Joan Evans, *A History of Jewellery 1100–1870*, Faber & Faber, 1953

Margaret Flower, *Victorian Jewellery*, Cassell, 1953

Melissa Gabardi, *Gioielli Anni '40*, Giorgio Mondadori, 1982

Charlotte Gere, *Victorian Jewellery Design*, William Kimber, 1972

Charlotte Gere, *European and American Jewellery*, Heinemann, 1975

Yvonne Hackenbroch, *Renaissance Jewellery*, Sotheby Parke Bernet, 1979

Hans Haug, 'Les Pierres de Stras et leur Inventeur', *Cahiers de la Céramique du Verre et des Arts du Feu*, No. 23, 1961,

Société des Amis du Musée National de Céramique, Sèvres

Graham Hughes, *Modern Jewelry*, Studio Vista, 1968

Peter Hinks, *Twentieth-Century British Jewellery*, Faber & Faber, 1983

Peter Hinks, *Nineteenth-Century Jewellery*, Faber & Faber, 1975

Thomas Hoving, 'Cellini, Fabergé and Me' (the Jewels of Schlumberger), *Connoisseur*, April 1982

Sylvia Katz, *Classic Plastics*, Thames & Hudson, 1984

James Laver, *Costume and Fashion*, Thames & Hudson (revised edition), 1986

Neil Letson, 'The Peerless Verdura', *Connoisseur*, March 1983

M. D. S. Lewis, *Antique Paste Jewellery*, Faber & Faber, 1970

Felice Mehlman, *Phaidon Guide to Glass*, Phaidon, 1982

Suzy Menkes, *The Windsor Style*, Grafton, 1987

Helen Muller, *Jet*, Butterworths, 1987

Hans Nadelhoffer, *Cartier, Jewellers Extraordinary*, Thames & Hudson, 1984

Jack Ogden, *Jewellery of the Ancient World*, Trefoil, 1982

Georgina O'Hara, *The Encyclopedia of Fashion*, Thames & Hudson, 1986

Sylvie Raulet, *Art Deco Jewellery*, Thames & Hudson, 1985

Julian Robinson, *Fashion in the Forties*, Academy/St Martins, 1980

Judy Rudoe, 'From Oroide to Platinageld: Imitation Jewellery in the Late 19th Century', Jewellery Studies 3, The Society of Jewellery Historians, 1988

Diana Scarisbrick, *Jewellery*, Batsford, 1984

Nancy Schiffer, *Plastic Jewellery*, Schiffer, 1987

Nancy Schiffer, *Costume Jewellery: The Great Pretenders*, Schiffer 1987

Brigitte Stamm, *Blicke auf Berliner Eisen*, Staatliche Schlösser & Gärten, Berlin, 1979

Jane Stancliffe, *Costume and Fashion Jewellery of the Twentieth Century*, The V & A Album, 1985

Hugh Tait (ed), *The Art of the Jeweller, A Catalogue of the Hull Grundy Gift to the British Museum*, British Museum Publications, 1984

Lou Taylor, *Mourning Dress, a Costume and Social History*, Allen & Unwin, 1983

Henri Vever, *La Bijouterie Française au XIXe Siècle*, Paris, 1904–08

Palmer White, *Schiaparelli, Empress of Paris Fashion*, Aurum Press, 1986

EXHIBITION CATALOGUES

*Homage à Schiaparelli*, Musée de la Mode et du Costume, Palais Galliéra, 1984

*The Jewellery of René Lalique*, Goldsmiths' Hall, 1987

*Eisen Gold und Bunte Steine*, Schmuckmuseum, Pforzheim, 1984

# PHOTO CREDITS

Chapter-opening photographs by Frank Herholdt

SYMBOLS OF POWER
La Goutte d'Eau by René Magritte *Courtesy of The Marlborough Gallery, London, ADAGP, Paris and DACS, London 1988*
Ancient Etruscan beads *Victoria and Albert Museum*
Portrait of a 17th-century lady *Roger-Viollet*
Portrait of a lady by Marc Gheeraerts *Bridgeman Art Library*

GEORGIAN SPLENDOUR
Toilette de la Duchesse des Plumes © *Museum of London*
Maria, Grand Duchess of Tuscany *British Museum*
Fashion plate showing Court dress
Paste rivière *Courtesy of Harvey & Gore*
Two paste cluster brooches *Harvey & Gore*
Pendant aquamarine paste earrings *Harvey & Gore*
Group of 18th- and 19th-century paste jewels *Harvey & Gore*
Two paste jewels with shell motifs *Victoria and Albert Museum*
Two pairs of chandelier earrings *Harvey & Gore*
Silver and marcasite buckle *Victoria and Albert Museum*
Set of red paste buttons *Harvey & Gore*
Paste flower ring *Harvey & Gore*
Crescent and feather hair ornament *Harvey & Gore*
Fashion plate showing two day dresses
Topaz paste watch key *Harvey & Gore*
Aquamarine paste suite *Harvey & Gore*
Two paste pansy brooches *Harvey & Gore*
Harlequin paste necklace and lyre brooch *Harvey & Gore*
White paste flower brooch *Harvey & Gore*
White amethyst paste diadem *Harvey & Gore*
Aquamarine paste necklace *Harvey & Gore*
Group of white paste jewels *Harvey & Gore*
Set of opaline jewellery *Victoria and Albert Museum*
Set of gold and rock crystal jewellery *Courtesy of Christie's*
Pinchbeck châtelaine *From the Hull Grundy Collection, Kenwood*
Three Pinchbeck tiaras
Harlequin paste and pearl necklace *Harvey & Gore*

NEO-CLASSIC TO ROMANTIC
Two pictures of Merveilleuses *Roger-Viollet*
Cut steel group with scissors *Courtesy of Diana Foley*
Group of 19th-century cut steel jewels *Diana Foley*
Cut steel chains *Diana Foley*
Two cut steel necklaces *Diana Foley*
Berlin Iron gauze bracelet *Courtesy of Sotheby's*
Two Berlin Iron necklaces *Diana Foley*
Berlin Iron bracelet *Diana Foley*
Berlin Iron bracelet by Geiss *Courtesy of Sotheby's*
Coloured Pinchbeck and amethyst paste bracelet *Harvey & Gore*
Pinchbeck châtelaine and telescope charm *Harvey & Gore*
Mme Marcotte de Sainte Marie *Louvre/Giraudon*
Pinchbeck textured chain *Harvey & Gore*
Pinchbeck snake earrings *Courtesy of Jesse and Laski Gallery, London*
Pinchbeck belt buckle
Group of Pinchbeck bracelet clasps *Courtesy of Brian and Lynn Holmes*
Bracelet and earrings in gilt metal *Brian and Lynn Holmes*
Portrait of Claire de Bearn by Winterhalter *Courtesy of Sotheby's*
Gilt metal vine-leaf hair ornament *Glasgow Art Gallery and Museum*
Gilt metal and pansy locket *Brian and Lynn Holmes*
Gilt metal knot 'REGARD' brooch *Glasgow Art Gallery and Museum*
Three jet snake bracelets *Courtesy of Allison Massey*
Plaited hair bracelet *Harvey & Gore*
Whitby jet necklace *Allison Massey*
Faceted jet necklace *Allison Massey*
Bogwood ring brooch *Brian and Lynn Holmes*
Gilt metal bracelet with heart design *Brian and Lynn Holmes*
Three gilt metal bangles *Brian and Lynn Holmes*
Bird and nest earrings *Jesse and Laski Gallery, London*
Vauxhall glass moth brooch and earrings *Author's Collection*
Vauxhall glass necklace, diadem and brooch *Diana Foley*
Group of piqué jewellery *Brian and Lynn Holmes*
Blue glass and marcasite suite *Courtesy of Madeline Popper*
The Hon. Elaine Guest by Bassano *National Portrait Gallery*
Group of aluminium jewellery *Courtesy of Hancocks & Co.*
Paste diamond floral spray *Victoria and Albert Museum*

EDWARDIAN ELEGANCE TO THE SHOCK OF CHANEL
Gilt metal and paste serpent arm ornament *Jesse and Laski Gallery, London*
Liane de Pougy photograph *Paul Nadar*
Owl-shaped paste shoe buckles *Jesse and Laski Gallery, London*
Edwardian love bird jewel *Brian and Lynn Holmes*
Edwardian paste shoe-buckles *Jesse and Laski Gallery, London*
Favourite Edwardian silver and diamond paste jewels *Brian and Lynn Holmes*
Advertisement for the Parisian Diamond Company *Illustrated London News*
Society ladies at Trouville *Roger-Viollet*
Paste drop earrings *Diana Foley*
Group of classically inspired Edwardian paste jewels *Brian and Lynn Holmes*
Carved wood cloak clasp *Jesse and Laski Gallery, London*
Lizard and centipede brooches *Jesse and Laski Gallery, London*
French jet sautoir *Allison Massey*
Paste lizard brooch *Author's Collection*
Silver gilt and paste Art Nouveau buckle *Brian and Lynn Holmes*
Matt enamel peacock feather buckle *Author's Collection*
Paste peacock feather buckle *Courtesy of Editions Graphiques*
Paste dragonfly brooch *Brian and Lynn Holmes*
Coco Chanel by Man Ray *Courtesy of Chanel © ADAGP, Paris and DACS, London 1988*
Duchess of Marlborough *From 'The Book of the Pearl' pub. 1908*
Chanel bangle *Courtesy of Sotheby's*
Chanel flower brooch *Billy Boy Collection*
African-influenced Chanel jewel *Billy Boy Collection*
Group of Chanel chains *Courtesy of Cobra & Bellamy*
Chanel pearl and paste ruby necklace *Cobra & Bellamy*
Schiaparelli pea pod necklace *Jesse and Laski Gallery, London*
Elsa Schiaparelli at Jacques Fath's party *Photograph André Ostier*
Schiaparelli fish bangle *Billy Boy Collection*
Schiaparelli necklace by Clément *Billy Boy Collection*
Schiaparelli gilt metal brooch *Billy Boy Collection*
Schiaparelli leaf jewels *Billy Boy Collection*
Schlumberger feather brooch *Billy Boy Collection*
Dali-inspired gilt brooch *Billy Boy Collection*
Schiaparelli seaweed necklace *Billy Boy Collection*
Schlumberger dangling hearts brooch *Billy Boy Collection*
Schlumberger bow brooch *Billy Boy Collection*
Schiaparelli bug necklace *The Brooklyn Museum, Gift of Paul and Arturo Peralta-Ramos from the Estate of Millicent Rogers*
Schiaparelli pink jewellery *Billy Boy Collection*
Schiaparelli leaf-shaped brooch *Billy Boy Collection*
Schiaparelli drop earrings *Billy Boy Collection*

SOPHISTICATED BARBARISM: THE ART DECO YEARS
Advertisement for 'Indra' pearls *Courtesy of Academy Editions*
Group of paste jewels *Jesse and Laski Gallery, London*
Emerald paste and diamanté bracelet and clips *Cobra & Bellamy*
Gertrude Lawrence photographed by Paul Tanqueray *National Portrait Gallery*
Black and white diamanté necklace *Cobra & Bellamy/Joel Degen*
Design for paste necklace *Antique Collector Magazine*
Black and white paste clip and necklace *Cobra & Bellamy/Joel Degen*
Bell-hop brooch *Jesse and Laski Gallery, London*
Group of silver and paste jewellery *Cobra & Bellamy/Joel Degen*
Nancy Cunard photographed by Cecil Beaton *Courtesy of Sotheby's*
Napier Company advertisement *Courtesy Napier, NY*
Claudette Colbert as Cleopatra *Kobal Collection*
Design for Egyptian revival bracelet *Antique Collector Magazine*
Cutting from *Women's Wear Daily* *Courtesy Napier, NY*
Diamanté and turquoise bead necklace *Cobra & Bellamy/Joel Degen*
Plastic bangle and necklace *Jesse and Laski Gallery, London*
Red plastic and chrome jewellery *Jesse and Laski Gallery, London*
Multi-coloured plastic bangles *Jesse and Laski Gallery, London*
Galalith and chrome jewellery by Henkel & Grosse *Courtesy of Henkel & Grosse*
Plastic jewellery by Bonaz *Jesse and Laski Gallery, London*
Plastic dog brooches *Jesse and Laski Gallery, London*
Black plastic and chrome necklace *Jesse and Laski Gallery, London*
Three plastic, paste and marcasite brooches *Courtesy of the Fior Collection/Joel Degen*
Two silver and paste brooches *Fior Collection/Joel Degen*
Novelty brooches *Brian and Lynn Holmes*
Silver openwork bracelet by Napier *Courtesy Napier, NY*
Group of paste bracelets *Cobra & Bellamy/Joel Degen*
Group of Eisenberg jewels *Collection of Sir Kenneth MacMillan/Joel Degen*
Advertisement for Schiaparelli bracelet *Courtesy of Napier, NY*

Photograph from *Life* article *Courtesy of Napier, NY*
Lalique pendant *Courtesy of the Worshipful Company of Goldsmiths*

THE COCKTAIL STYLE
Diamanté and sapphire double clip *Cobra & Bellamy*
Lana Turner *Kobal Collection*
Marlene Dietrich *Kobal Collection*
Group of Napier gilt brooches *Courtesy of Napier, NY*
Four cocktail bracelets *Fior Collection/Joel Degen*
Trifari wasp brooch *Cobra & Bellamy*
Joan Crawford *Kobal Collection*
Starfish brooch *Jesse and Laski Gallery, London*
Group of Pennino brooches *Sir Kenneth MacMillan/Joel Degen*
Two bow brooches *Cobra & Bellamy/Joel Degen*
Gilt collar necklace *Fior Collection/Joel Degen*
Buckle brooch and bracelet *Cobra & Bellamy*
Trifari flower brooch *Courtesy of Trifari*
Trifari tree brooch *Cobra & Bellamy*
Butterfly brooch and earrings *Cobra & Bellamy*
Trifari advertisement *Courtesy of Trifari*
Group of three brooches *Cobra & Bellamy/Joel Degen*
Frog brooch *Cobra & Bellamy*
Diamanté double clip *Courtesy of Marianne Taylor/Joel Degen*
Trifari advertisement *Courtesy of Trifari*
Mitchel Maer jewels *Fior Collection/Joel Degen*
Diamanté fringed necklace *Cobra & Bellamy*
Henkel & Grosse bracelet *Courtesy of Henkel & Grosse*
Diamanté loop necklace and flower brooch *Fior Collection/Joel Degen*
Group of Dior jewellery *Jesse and Laski Gallery, London*
Group of Miriam Haskell jewellery *Cobra & Bellamy/Joel Degen*
Group of Hobé jewels *Sir Kenneth MacMillan/Joel Degen*
Diamanté necklace set *Cobra & Bellamy/Joel Degen*
Spiral brooch *Cobra & Bellamy*
Pearl and diamanté bangle *Fior Collection/Joel Degen*
Carriage and posy brooches *Fior Collection/Joel Degen*
Mamie Eisenhower's jewels *Courtesy of Trifari*
Duke of Windsor from *Society* cover *Courtesy of Napier, NY*
Trifari Coronation jewels advertisement *Courtesy of Trifari*

GLAM ROCK: THE 1960S ONWARDS
Model wearing Butler & Wilson pearls and bow *Photograph Neil Kirk/Butler & Wilson Collection*
Diamanté and pearl Dior brooch *Cobra & Bellamy*
Models wearing Paco Rabanne jewellery *Rex Features*
Model wearing Op-Art jewellery *Rex Features*
Pierre Cardin bracelet *Jesse and Laski Gallery, London*
Model wearing Napier earring *Courtesy of Napier, NY*
Paulene Stone wearing Ken Lane jewels *Weidenfeld & Nicolson Archives*
Group of Ken Lane jewels *Sir Kenneth MacMillan/Joel Degen*
Monet bracelet and earrings *Cobra & Bellamy/Joel Degen*
Autumn leaves necklace and bangle *Fior Collection/Joel Degen*
Dior pendant and chain *Jesse and Laski Gallery, London*
Serpent necklace *Cobra & Bellamy/Joel Degen*
Bulgari-style jewels *Fior Collection*
Yves Saint Laurent jewels *Courtesy of Sotheby's*
Attwood & Sawyer designs *Courtesy of Attwood & Sawyer*
Pearl and Big Cat choker *Courtesy of Ken Lane*
Group of modern Chanel jewels *Courtesy of Chanel*
Model wearing Butler & Wilson diamanté collar and bracelets *Photograph John Swannell/Butler & Wilson Collection*
Faye Dunaway wearing Butler & Wilson jewels *Photograph Terry O'Neill/Butler & Wilson Collection*
Model wearing Butler & Wilson Red Indian bangles and brooch *Photograph Terry O'Neill/Butler & Wilson Collection*
Model wearing heavy metal look jewellery *Photograph Jamie Morgan/Butler & Wilson Collection*
Model wearing Butler & Wilson snake brooches *Photograph Neil Kirk/Butler & Wilson Collection*
Group of Monty Don jewels *Courtesy of Monty Don*
Carolyn Stephenson jewels *Courtesy of Carolyn Stephenson/Joel Degen*
Model wearing Louise Sant jewels *Courtesy of Louise Sant/photography Jonathan Root*
Michael DeNardo earrings *Courtesy of Michael DeNardo/Joel Degen*
Watch-face jewels *Courtesy of Maximal Art, Philadelphia*
Ear-shaped earrings *Billy Boy*
African-inspired earrings *Courtesy of Scooter, Paris/Joel Degen*
Dancing Bow brooch and earrings *Billy Boy*
Group of Pellini jewels *Courtesy of Pellini, Milan*
Model wearing Andrew Logan jewels *Courtesy of Andrew Logan/Robyn Beeche*
Brooch by Simon Costin *Courtesy of Simon Costin/Crafts Magazine*

# INDEX